Point/Counterpoint

Opposing Perspectives on Issues of Drug Policy

Charles F. Levinthal

Hofstra University

Boston   New York   San Francisco
Mexico City   Montreal   Toronto   London   Madrid   Munich   Paris
Hong Kong   Singapore   Tokyo · Cape Town   Sydney

For Beth

Executive Editor: *Carolyn Merrill*
Editorial Assistant: *Kate Edwards*
Marketing Manager: *Wendy Gordon*
Editorial-Production Administrator: *Beth Houston*
Editorial-Production Service: *Walsh & Associates, Inc.*
Composition Buyer: *Linda Cox*
Manufacturing Buyer: *JoAnne Sweeney*
Cover Administrator: *Kristina Mose-Libon*

Between the time Website information is gathered and published, it is not unusual for some sites to have closed. Also, the transcription of URLs can result in typographical errors. The publisher would appreciate notification where these errors occur so that they may be corrected in subsequent editions. Thank you.

Library of Congress Cataloging-in-Publication Data

Levinthal, Charles F., 1945–
  Point / counterpoint : opposing perspectives on issues of drug policy / Charles F. Levinthal.
    p.   cm.
  Includes index.
  ISBN 0-205-33607-8
  1. Narcotics, Control of—United States.   2. Drug abuse—Government policy—United States.   3. Substance abuse—Government policy—United States.   4. Drug legalization—United States.   I. Title.

HV5825 .L455 2002
34.1'77'0973—dc21

2002069208

BRIEF CONTENTS

Preface   ix

Introduction: The Wisdom in Debating Drug Policy   xi

1   Question: Should We Legalize Drugs?   1

2   Question: Should Drug Interdiction Be Our Primary Goal in the War on Drugs?   26

3   Question: Should We Encourage Needle Exchange Programs for Intravenous Drug Abusers?   50

4   Question: Should Harm Reduction Be Our Overall Goal in Fighting Drug Abuse?   70

5   Question: Should Drug and Alcohol Dependence Be Considered a Brain Disease?   90

6   Question: Is Alcoholics Anonymous the Best Strategy for the Treatment of Alcoholism?   115

7   Question: Should Stimulant Drugs Be Used to Treat Attention Deficit Disorder (ADD) in Children?   139

8   Question: Should Marijuana Be Legally Available as a Medicine?   162

9   Question: Should the Government Act More Aggressively in Regulating Drugs and Drug Prices?   185

C O N T E N T S

Preface   ix

Introduction: The Wisdom in Debating Drug Policy   xi

1 Question: Should We Legalize Drugs?   1

Selection 1   4
Marshall, Donnie (1999, June 16). Congressional testimony on drug legalization, decriminalization, and harm reduction, U.S. House of Representatives, Washington, DC.

Selection 2   12
Sullum, Jacob (2001). Mind alteration: Drug-policy scholar Ethan Nadelmann on turning people against drug prohibition. *Reason Online, Reason Magazine.*

Selection 3   21
The case for legalisation: Time for a puff of sanity (2001, July 28–August 3). *The Economist.*

Looking at Both Sides—The Debate Continues   23

2 Question: Should Drug Interdiction Be Our Primary Goal in the War on Drugs?   26

Selection 4   28
Brown, Robert E., Jr. (2001, May 1). Congressional testimony on U.S. air interdiction efforts in South America. U.S. House of Representatives, Washington, DC.

Selection 5   33
DeWine, Mike, Senator from Ohio (2000, June 30). Senate floor debate: Statement in favor of authorizing appropriations for Plan Colombia operations. U.S. Senate, Washington, DC.

Selection 6   35
Wellstone, Paul, Senator from Minnesota (2000, June 30). Senate floor debate: Statement in opposition to authorizing appropriations for Plan Colombia operations. U.S. Senate, Washington, DC.

Selection 7   36
LeoGrande, William M. and Sharpe, Kenneth E. (2000, Fall). Two wars or one? Drugs, guerrillas, and Colombia's new *Violencia. World Policy Journal.*

Looking at Both Sides—The Debate Continues   48

3   Question: Should We Encourage Needle Exchange Programs for Intravenous Drug Abusers?   50

Selection 8   52
Vlahov, David and Junge, Benjamin (1998, June). The role of needle exchange programs in HIV prevention. *Public Health Reports.*

Selection 9   58
Center for AIDS Prevention Studies (2001). Does IV needle exchange work?

Selection 10   61
Loconte, Joe (1998, July–August). Killing them softly. *Policy Review.*

Looking at Both Sides—The Debate Continues   68

4   Question: Should Harm Reduction Be Our Overall Goal in Fighting Drug Abuse?   70

Selection 11   74
Glasscock, Bruce D. (1999, July 13). Congressional testimony in opposition to drug legalization. U.S. House of Representatives, Washington, DC.

Selection 12   77
MacCoun, Robert J. and Reuter, Peter (1999, July 13). Congressional testimony in favor of a harm-reduction policy. U.S. House of Representatives, Washington, DC.

Selection 13   81
Goldstein, Avram (2001). New strategies for rational drug policy. *Addiction: From biology to drug policy* (2nd ed.).

Looking at Both Sides—The Debate Continues   88

5   Question: Should Drug and Alcohol Dependence Be Considered a Brain Disease?   90

Selection 14   92
Leshner, Alan I. (1997, June). Addiction is a brain disease: An interview with Alan Leshner, director of the National Institute on Drug Abuse. *USIA Electronic Journal,* United States Information Agency.

Selection 15   98

Satel, Sally L. (1999, Fall). The fallacies of no-fault addiction. *The Public Interest.*

Selection 16   105

Lambert, Craig (2000, March–April). Deep cravings: New research on the brain and behavior clarifies the mystery of addiction. *Harvard Magazine.*

Looking at Both Sides—The Debate Continues   113

6   Question: Is Alcoholics Anonymous the Best Strategy for the Treatment of Alcoholism?   115

Selection 17   117

Alcoholics Anonymous World Services. The twelve steps of Alcoholics Anonymous. A.A. traditions. A.A. World Services, New York.

Selection 18   119

Hopson, Ronald E. and Beaird-Spiller, Bethany (1995). Why AA works: A psychological analysis of the addictive experience and the efficacy of Alcoholics Anonymous. *Alcoholism Treatment Quarterly.*

Selection 19   130

Peele, Stanton (1998, March/April). All wet: The gospel of abstinence and twelve-step, studies show, is leading American alcoholics astray. *The Sciences.*

Looking at Both Sides—The Debate Continues   136

7   Question: Should Stimulant Drugs Be Used to Treat Attention Deficit Disorder (ADD) in Children?   139

Selection 20   141

Eberstadt, Mary (1999, April/May). Why Ritalin rules. *Policy Review.*

Selection 21   149

Accardo, Pasquale and Blondis, Thomas A. (2001, January). What's all the fuss about Ritalin? *Journal of Pediatrics.*

Selection 22   154

Taylor, Eric (1999, December). Commentary: Development of clinical services for attention-deficit/hyperactivity disorder. *Archives of General Psychiatry.*

Looking at Both Sides—The Debate Continues   160

8   Question: Should Marijuana Be Legally Available as a Medicine?   162

Selection 23   164
Drug Enforcement Administration, U.S. Department of Justice (1995, June 20). Say it straight: The medical myths of marijuana.

Selection 24   167
McDonough, James R. (2000, April–May). Marijuana on the ballot. *Policy Review.*

Selection 25   176
Grinspoon, Lester (2000, Spring). Whither medical marijuana? *Contemporary Drug Problems.*

Looking at Both Sides—The Debate Continues   183

9   Question: Should the Government Act More Aggressively in Regulating Drugs and Drug Prices?   185

Selection 26   186
Calfee, John E. (2000, May). Drugs, drug prices and your health. *Consumers' Research.*

Selection 27   193
Koller, Christopher F. (2001, June 15). Prescription for trouble: Why drug prices keep exploding. *Commonweal Magazine.*

Selection 28   199
Miller, Henry I. and Longtin, David (2000, October). Time to assure safe dietary supplements: Innovative protection needed. *Consumers' Research.*

Looking at Both Sides—The Debate Continues   207

PREFACE

As the American historian Christopher Lasch has expressed it, "Information, usually seen as the precondition of debate, is better understood as its by-product." In other words, when we engage in debate, we benefit by being better informed as a result. The more controversial the issues, the more strenuous the debates, the better off we are. The goal of this book is to present the basis for a series of strenuous and serious-minded debates on nine important issues of drug policy. Unfortunately, drug policy issues have too often been debated through emotional appeals. Drug use has been viewed as a matter of good versus evil, and the result has been a moral debate in which no amount of data can effectively shed light upon the question. *Point/Counterpoint: Opposing Perspectives on Issues of Drug Policy* is intended to provide an opportunity to debate drug policy on the basis of facts and logic.

The twenty-eight selections in this book of readings are contemporary in nature, provocative, and highly readable. They consist of statements and analyses by respected individuals and representatives of influential institutions concerned with drug policy. They are taken from Congressional testimony, debates in the U.S. Senate, book chapters, position papers, and diverse articles that have appeared in the electronic and print media. A common thread that runs through them all is that they are contending with the difficult problems and issues of drug use. Read these selections carefully and with an open mind. Don't think you have come up with the final answer, nor should you necessarily agree with the last argument you read.

In each chapter, instead of having a representative opinion "for" or "against" a particular policy, there are three or more selections representing a more nuanced approach to a particular drug policy issue. Opening each chapter is a survey of the historical roots of the controversy, and ending the chapter is a section that includes a series of thought-provoking questions as an opportunity for critical thinking and a listing of informative Internet websites and further readings. In this way, each of the nine chapters becomes a total package, giving you a sense of the past, an understanding of the present, and a foundation for future inquiry. That is ultimately what *Point/Counterpoint* is all about. Drug policy, whether it pertains to illegal drug use or legal drug use, affects everyone in our society. Everyone needs to be informed about the process through which drug policy decisions have been made in the past, as well as the ongoing process of policy debate that will continue in the years ahead. On a personal note, I welcome your reactions and ideas as you read the book. I can be reached at the following address: Dr. Charles F. Levinthal, Department of Psychology, Hofstra University, Hempstead, NY 11549. You can also fax comments and questions to (516) 463-6052 or e-mail them to me at PSYCFL@hofstra.edu. I look forward to hearing from you.

In the course of preparing *Point/Counterpoint: Opposing Perspectives on Issues of Drug Policy,* I have been very fortunate to have worked with a superb team at Allyn and Bacon. I am especially indebted to my editor, Carolyn Merrill, and my production editor, Beth Houston. I also want to acknowledge the contributions of those individuals who provided production services for this book, particularly Kathy Whittier of Walsh & Associates, Inc. Finally, I appreciate the abiding love and support of my wonderful family—my wife Beth and my sons David and Brian.

INTRODUCTION

The Wisdom in Debating Drug Policy

The question of a coherent, rational, and effective drug policy in the United States remains one of the pivotal issues of our day. How do we handle the immense problems that drugs have created in our communities, our nation, and society in general? It is with a sense of great urgency that we address these problems and seek some kind of solution. The facts are, unfortunately, all too clear:

- An estimated 120,000 lives are lost in the United States each year, as a direct result of alcohol or illicit drug use. In addition, more than 400,000 die from medical conditions associated with tobacco use. These numbers constitute fully one-half of all U.S. deaths annually.
- The estimated costs due to the loss in productivity among workers who abuse alcohol and other drugs amount to $60–$100 billion each year.
- In 2001, national surveys indicated that, by the end of high school, about 64 percent of young people have been drunk at least once and 49 percent have smoked marijuana. Experimentation with new forms of psychoactive substances during adolescence constitutes a major problem.
- An annual federal drug-control budget of more than $18 billion is spent on stemming the tide of drugs flooding the United States from other countries and on drug abuse treatment and prevention programs. Each year, a highly expensive "war on drugs" is waged. The extent to which drug use has been reduced by such efforts is a matter of continuing controversy.
- Despite strenuous efforts on the part of the Food and Drug Administration to restrict and regulate access to pharmaceutical drugs, there are increasing problems with the misuse of medications such as OxyContin (a long-lasting form of synthetic opiate used for pain relief) and Ritalin (a stimulant used in the treatment of Attention Deficit Disorder) among individuals taking these drugs for purely recreational purposes.

Unfortunately, we live in a social environment filled with mixed messages with regard to drug use and abuse. While restrictions on the marketing of tobacco products have been in effect since 1998, we still have memories of Joe Camel, the Marlboro Man, and the Virginia Slims woman, images in print advertisements that have made cigarettes attractive to millions of people. At the same time, we read the warning labels on cigarette packs or hear the public service announcements that tell us, often in graphic terms, the serious health consequences of smoking. Prominent political figures, including a former U.S. president (Bill Clinton) and a former U.S. vice president (Al Gore), have admitted their experiences with marijuana earlier in their lives. Yet, in the United States, marijuana remains an illegal substance, officially classified since 1970 in the same category as heroin. While antidrug campaigns in the media discourage young people from being involved with drugs, we see a continual stream of sport figures, entertainers, and other high-profile individuals engaging in drug-taking behavior. Even though careers are frequently jeopardized and, in some cases, lives are lost as a result, powerful media messages promoting drug use continue to influence our lives.

We must recognize that we are all in this together. Drug abuse is not just a "young person's problem" but one that encompasses every segment of our society. The availability of drugs and the potential for drug abuse present a challenge for people of all ages, from the young to the elderly. The personal and social problems associated with drugs extend in one way or another to both men and women and to people of all ethnic groups and socioeconomic levels. No one should feel exempt. Whether we like it or not, the decision to use drugs of all types and forms has become one of life's choices in American society and in communities around the world.

All of us recognize the personal damage and social havoc wrought by the sale, distribution, and consumption of illicit drugs. All of us are appalled by the magnitude of preventable death associated with licit (legal) drugs such as alcohol and nicotine. We are continually reminded that we have to "do something" about it. Yet, the issues are complex, and none of the answers come easily. We can be guided to a thoughtful and rational discussion of the possible options, however, by keeping three overall principles in mind.

First and foremost, we need to remember that drug problems in our society arise from a wide range of psychoactive substances. Not all drugs are equivalent; each one has its own biological, psychological, sociological, and historical profile. Drug abuse and drug dependence can involve legally available sources such as alcohol and tobacco, as well as illicit (illegal) sources such as heroin, cocaine, and marijuana. Sources might be as accessible as lighter fluid or cleaning solvents. They might be the medicinal drugs that we use to treat legitimate medical disorders. In order to achieve a comprehensive plan of action, all these possibilities need to be considered. The debate on drug policy, therefore, should be considered actually as a series of debates, each with a particular issue at stake.

Second, as you will see in the selections of this book, perspectives on the issues of drug policy need not be black or white; there are often intermediate shades of gray. Policies should not be necessarily equated with all-or-nothing solutions. Moreover, the decision to implement a given drug policy should be based as much upon its feasibility as its desirability. We need to look closely at the practicality of a given approach and the possibility of unanticipated consequences. In other words, things might not work out the way we thought they would.

Third, we cannot ignore the symbolic effects that drug policies have on the American public. What kind of drug policy we have in America, in the eyes of many people, is a statement of what kind of country we wish to live in. As sociologist Erich Goode has expressed it,

> Regardless of whether it reduces crime or not, does endorsing methadone maintenance clinics for all addicts who wish to enroll tell you the society is too "soft" on drugs? Do needle exchange programs seem to encourage use? Regardless of whether it reduces drug abuse or not, does permitting the police to break down doors and roust residents on mere suspicion strike you as unjust? Does it strike you as too much like a military dictatorship? Does the term "legalization" sound like an endorsement of drug use to you? The balancing act between ideology and fact will continue to dog us throughout any exploration of the issue of drug policy.

In the final analysis, there is great wisdom in airing the perspectives of differing minds on drug policy issues, to experience the clash of ideas, and to understand that no one has all the answers. We are far better off, it has been said, to hear debates without necessarily settling the question than to settle the question without debates. We certainly cannot afford to stand aloof from the decisions that are made with regard to drugs in America.

In this book of readings, nine prominent issues regarding drug policy have been highlighted and arguments have been presented. Fittingly, they encompass the wide spectrum of drugs, both legal and illegal, that present problems in our society. We will be considering the issues related to foreign relations between the United States and those countries producing and trafficking in illicit drugs (Chapter 2), specific approaches in the use of needles among intravenous drug abusers (Chapter 3), and whether we should seek to eliminate alcohol and other drug use entirely or simply reduce the harm that arises from it (Chapters 4 and 6). We will be considering issues related to the biological basis for drug dependence (Chapter 5) and the use of stimulant drugs in children diagnosed with Attention Deficit Disorder (ADD) (Chapter 7). Other issues include whether marijuana should be exempted from its illegal status when used as a medical treatment (Chapter 8) and whether the federal government should be more aggressive in regulating medicinal drugs and spiraling drug costs (Chapter 9). All these issues touch upon important problems facing us today.

We begin with the drug-policy issue that has attained the greatest prominence in the public mind in the last several years: the arguments for or against drug legalization.

REFERENCES

Goode, Erich (1997). *Between politics and reason: The drug legalization debate.* New York: St. Martin's Press. Quotation on page 3.

Johnston, Lloyd D., O'Malley, Patrick M., & Bachman, Jerald G. (2001). *Monitoring the future national results on adolescent drug use: Overview of key findings, 2001.* (NIH Publication No. 02-5105) Bethesda, MD: National Institute on Drug Abuse.

Levinthal, Charles F. (2002). *Drugs, behavior, and modern society* (3rd edition). Boston: Allyn and Bacon.

1 Question: Should We Legalize Drugs?

If you viewed the drug legalization debate in a historical context, the real question would not be whether we should legalize drugs but rather whether we should *relegalize* them. We are so accustomed to the present-day reality of illicit drugs in our society that we fail to recognize that, prior to the early part of the twentieth century, drugs such as opiates (including opium, morphine, and heroin) and cocaine were completely legal, unregulated, and openly available to the American public. Of course, we are all too aware of the significant changes in our society since the nineteenth century. Nonetheless, it is important to look at that earlier time in our history, as a guide toward understanding the sociological and psychological aspects of the drug legalization controversy today.

During the nineteenth century, many of the drugs that we associate today with a dark, dangerous, and illicit world were openly consumed without any official interference. For centuries, supplies of opium, for example, had been unlimited. Medical opinion was divided on the question of any potential harm. There was no negative public opinion about opium use and seldom was there any trouble with the police. Infants and young children were given opium, often from the day they were born. Patent medicines, based upon a liquid form of opium called laudanum, were widely available at the nearest general store. They were marketed with appealing and benign-sounding names like Godfrey's Cordial and Mrs. Winslow's Soothing Syrup.

When the hypodermic syringe was introduced in America during the 1880s, injections of morphine (the active ingredient in opium) became standard medical practice in the treatment of disease. One distinguished physician at the time referred to these injections as "G.O.M.—God's Own Medicine," and a popular medical textbook of that time listed fifty-four diseases that could be treated with morphine injections.

By the late nineteenth century, however, doctors and health professionals were beginning to be concerned that their patients were developing a dependence on the treatments they were administering. It was against a background of increased worry about opium and morphine addiction that the Bayer Company of Germany proudly introduced in 1898 an opium derivative called heroin that was several times stronger than morphine itself. Initially, heroin was promoted as a significant scientific breakthrough in medical care and considered, strangely enough, to be completely free of any potential for dependence. It took almost a decade for health professionals to recognize that heroin was about twice as addictive as morphine.

In a way similar to opium and morphine, cocaine was also a staple of patent medicines and beverages in the nineteenth century, widely consumed by people of all ages. One particular mixture of coca (the source of cocaine) and alcohol, invented in 1863 by Angelo

Mariani, became known as "Vin Mariani" and was enormously popular at that time as a wine beverage. Until 1903, the nonalcoholic version of Mariani's formulation, Coca-Cola, contained coca as well. Early adverstisements for Coca-Cola emphasized the drink as a brain tonic that made you feel more productive and as a remedy for such assorted nervous ailments as sick headaches and melancholia (a word used at the time for depression). After 1903, however, cocaine was removed from the Coca-Cola formula and henceforth the "pause that refreshed" America would now be due only to the presence of sugar and caffeine. In Austria, Sigmund Freud, prior to his development of concepts that would later be known as psychoanalysis, promoted the use of cocaine as a cure for mental depression. His advocacy of the drug caused a surge of cocaine use both in Europe and America. While Freud later personally recanted his endorsement, after discovering cocaine dependence in a close friend, cocaine remained popular well into the beginning of the twentieth century.

By the early 1900s, there was a general notion in the United States that heroin and cocaine created problems of dependence, but the government as well as society in general operated under a policy often referred to as *laissez-faire* (roughly translated as "allow people to do as they please"), which meant little or no encouragement for regulation or control. Addiction was considered as simply an unfortunate development in life. No one pressed for governmental intervention. One historian writes:

> Employees were not fired for addiction. Wives did not divorce their addicted husbands, or husbands their addicted wives. Children were not taken from their homes and lodged in foster homes or institutions because one or both parents were addicted. Addicts continued to participate fully in the life of the community. Addicted children and young people continued to go to school, Sunday school, and college.

All of this changed rather quickly. In 1906, the Pure Food and Drug Act required for the first time a listing of the ingredients in patent medicines, specifically those that might be "habitforming." The Harrison Act of 1914 went further, making the sale of opiates and cocaine (later marijuana) illegal for the first time in the United States. In less than twenty years, the American attitude toward drug use was completely reversed, from legality to illegality.

The Harrison Act changed the face of drug use in America. As one historian has put it, a user of heroin and cocaine in particular was:

> . . . no longer seen as a victim of drugs, an unfortunate with no place to turn and deserving of society's sympathy and help. He became instead a base, vile degenerate who was weak and self-indulgent, who contaminated all he came in contact with and who deserved nothing short of condemnation and society's moral outrage and legal sanction.

In the decades that followed, restrictions on cocaine, opiates, and marijuana steadily tightened and penalties became harsher. The widening of the drug use population during the 1960s, particularly among middle-class, suburban young people, was met with increasing public alarm by governmental officials and the media. In addition, new hallucinogenic drugs, such as LSD and mescaline, previously unfamiliar to the general public, suddenly appeared on the scene, encouraging lawmakers at federal and state levels to enlarge the range of drugs classified as illegal to sell and illegal to use.

Since 1970, drugs in the United States have been classified in five "schedules" of controlled substances, defining in effect the extent of their availability and access to the American public (see Table 1.1). Schedule I and II drugs refer to those substances with the highest

TABLE 1.1   The Five Schedules of Controlled Substances in the Comprehensive Drug Abuse Prevention and Control Act of 1970 (updated)

Schedule	Abuse Potential	Examples	Medical Use
I	Highest	heroin, LSD, marijuana, mescaline, hashish	No accepted medical use
II	High	morphine, cocaine, short-acting barbiturates, methadone, codeine, amphetamines	Some accepted medical use, though use may lead to severe physical or psychological dependence
III	Medium	long-acting barbiturates, tincture of opium in alcohol	Accepted medical use, though use may lead to low to moderate physical dependence or severe psychological dependence
IV	Low	antianxiety drugs and sedative-hypnotics	Accepted medical use
V	Lowest	prescription cough medicines not containing codeine, laxatives	Accepted medical use; minimal restrictions

Source: Drug Enforcement Administation, U.S. Department of Justice, Washington, DC.

potential for abuse and carry the highest penalties on the drug user and for drug trafficking. Schedule I drugs are those with no accepted medical use: heroin, LSD, mescaline, and marijuana. (Note that the possibility of marijuana as a medical treatment is a highly controversial issue that will be taken up individually in Chapter 8 in this volume.) Schedule II drugs are those with some accepted medical use, though the use of these drugs may lead to severe physical or psychological dependence: codeine, morphine, cocaine, methadone, amphetamines, and short-acting barbiturates. On the other hand, Schedule V drugs have minimal abuse potential, widespread medical use, and minimal controls or restrictions for selling and dispensing: prescription cough medicines not containing codeine, laxatives. While an imperfect system to be sure, the five categories of controlled substances are the present law of the land and the basic framework for distinguishing illicit from licit drugs in America.

It is in this context that we consider the question of drug legalization. We begin with a presentation of the official position of the Drug Enforcement Administration (DEA) that drugs should not be legalized. Opposing the DEA position is Ethan Nadelmann, a spokesman for those who have criticized drug prohibition and have encouraged a consideration of legalizing drugs. Supporting Nadelmann's position is a recent 2001 editorial in *The Economist*.

REFERENCES

Brecher, Edward M., and the editors of *Consumer Reports*. (1972). *Licit and illicit drugs*. Mount Vernon, NY: Consumers Union. First quotation from pages 6–7.

Levinthal, Charles F. (1988). *Messengers of paradise: Opiates and the brain*. New York: Anchor Press/Doubleday.

———. (2002). *Drugs, behavior, and modern society* (3rd ed.). Boston: Allyn and Bacon.

Smith, Roger (1966). Status politics and the image of the addict. *Issues in Criminology*, 2(2), 159–175. Second quotation from pages 172–73.

SELECTION 1

The following selection is the congressional testimony of Donnie Marshall, Deputy Administrator for the Drug Enforcement Administration, U.S. Department of Justice, before the House Committee on Government Reform, Subcommittee on Criminal Justice, Drug Policy, and Human Resources, on June 16, 1999. His testimony expresses the views of the Drug Enforcement Administration (DEA) on the question of drug legalization as well as related issues of decriminalization and harm reduction.

■ *Congressional Testimony on Drug Legalization, Decriminalization, and Harm Reduction*

DONNIE MARSHALL

Mr. Chairman and Members of the Subcommittee, I appreciate the opportunity to appear before you today on the issue of drug legalization, decriminalization and harm reduction.

I am not a scientist, a doctor, a lawyer, or an economist. So I'll do my best to leave the scientific, the medical, the legal and the economic issues to others. At the Drug Enforcement Administration, our mission is not to enact laws, but to enforce them. Based on our experience in enforcing drug laws, I can provide you with information and with our best judgment about policy outcomes that may help put into context the various arguments in this debate.

I would like to discuss what I believe would happen if drugs were legalized. I realize that much of the current debate has been over the legalization of so-called medical marijuana. But I suspect that medical marijuana is merely the first tactical maneuver in an overall strategy that will lead to the eventual legalization of all drugs.

Whether all drugs are eventually legalized or not, the practical outcome of legalizing even one, like marijuana, is to increase the amount of usage among all drugs. It's been said that you can't put the genie back in the bottle or the toothpaste back in the tube. I think those are apt metaphors for what will happen if America goes down the path of legalization. Once America gives into a drug culture, and all the social decay that comes with such a culture, it would be very hard to restore a decent civic culture without a cost to America's civil liberties that would be prohibitively high.

There is a huge amount of research about drugs and their effect on society, here and abroad. I'll let others better acquainted with all of the scholarly literature discuss that research. What I will do is suggest four probable outcomes of legalization and then make a case why a policy of drug enforcement works.

Legalization Would Boost Drug Use
The first outcome of legalization would be to have a lot more drugs around, and, in turn, a lot more drug abuse. I can't imagine anyone arguing that legalizing drugs would reduce the

Testimony by Donnie Marshall, Deputy Administrator, Drug Enforcement Administration, United States Department of Justice, before the House Committee on Government Reform, Subcommittee on Criminal Justice, Drug Policy, and Human Resources, Washington, DC, June 16, 1999.

amount of drug abuse we already have. Although drug use is down from its high mark in the late 1970s, America still has entirely too many people who are on drugs.

In 1962, for example, only four million Americans had ever tried a drug in their entire lifetime. In 1997, the latest year for which we have figures, 77 million Americans had tried drugs. Roughly half of all high school seniors have tried drugs by the time they graduate.

The result of having a lot of drugs around is more and more consumption. To put it another way, supply drives demand. That is an outcome that has been apparent from the early days of drug enforcement.

What legalization could mean for drug consumption in the United States can be seen in the drug liberalization experiment in Holland. In 1976, Holland decided to liberalize its laws regarding marijuana. Since then, Holland has acquired a reputation as the drug capital of Europe. For example, a majority of the synthetic drugs, such as Ecstasy (MDMA) and methamphetamine, now used in the United Kingdom are produced in Holland.

The effect of supply on demand can also be seen even in countries that take a tougher line on drug abuse. An example is the recent surge in heroin use in the United States. In the early 1990s, cocaine traffickers from Colombia discovered that there was a lot more profit with a lot less work in selling heroin. Several years ago, they began to send heroin from South America to the United States.

To make as much money as possible, they realized they needed not only to respond to a market, but to create a market. They devised an aggressive marketing campaign which included the use of brand names and the distribution of free samples of heroin to users who bought their cocaine. In many cases, they induced distributors to move quantities of heroin to stimulate market growth. The traffickers greatly increased purity levels, allowing many potential addicts who might be squeamish about using needles to snort the heroin rather than injecting it. The result has been a huge increase in the number of people trying heroin for the first time, five times as many in 1997 as just four years before.

I don't mean to imply that demand is not a critical factor in the equation. But any informed drug policy should take into consideration that supply has a great influence on demand. In 1997, American companies spent $73 billion advertising their products and services. These advertisers certainly must have a well-documented reason to believe that consumers are susceptible to the power of suggestion, or they wouldn't be spending all that money. The market for drugs is no different. International drug traffickers are spending enormous amounts of money to make sure that drugs are available to every American kid in a school yard.

Dr. Herbert Kleber, a professor of psychiatry at Columbia University College of Physicians and Surgeons, and one of the nation's leading authorities on addiction, stated in a 1994 article in the *New England Journal of Medicine* that clinical data support the premise that drug use would increase with legalization. He said:

> There are over 50 million nicotine addicts, 18 million alcoholics or problem drinkers, and fewer than 2 million cocaine addicts in the United States. Cocaine is a much more addictive drug than alcohol. If cocaine were legally available, as alcohol and nicotine are now, the number of cocaine abusers would probably rise to a point somewhere between the number of users of the other two agents, perhaps 20 to 25 million . . . the number of compulsive users might be nine times higher than the current number. When drugs have been widely available—as . . . cocaine was at the turn of the century—both use and addiction have risen.

I can't imagine the impact on this society if that many people were abusers of cocaine. From what we know about the connection between drugs and crime, America would certainly have to devote an enormous amount of its financial resources to law enforcement.

Legalization Would Contribute to a Rise in Crime

The second outcome of legalization would be more crime, especially more violent crime. There's a close relationship between drugs and crime. This relationship is borne out by the statistics. Every year, the Justice Department compiles a survey of people arrested in a number of American cities to determine how many of them tested positive for drugs at the time of their arrest. In 1998, the survey found, for example, that 74 percent of those arrested in Atlanta for a violent crime tested positive for drugs. In Miami, 49 percent; in Oklahoma City, 60 percent.

There's a misconception that most drug-related crimes involve people who are looking for money to buy drugs. The fact is that the most drug-related crimes are committed by people whose brains have been messed up with mood-altering drugs. A 1994 study by the Bureau of Justice Statistics compared Federal and State prison inmates in 1991. It found, for example, that 18 percent of the Federal inmates had committed homicide under the influence of drugs, whereas 2.7 percent committed homicide to get the money to buy drugs. The same disparities showed up for State inmates: almost 28 percent committed homicide under the influence versus 5.3 percent to get money to buy drugs.

Those who propose legalization argue that it would cut down on the number of drug-related crimes because addicts would no longer need to rob people to buy their drugs from illicit sources. But even supposing that argument is true, which I don't think that it is, the fact is that so many more people would be abusing drugs, and committing crimes under the influence of drugs, that the crime rate would surely go up rather than down.

It's clear that drugs often cause people to do things they wouldn't do if they were drug-free. Too many drug users lose the kind of self-control and common sense that keeps them in bounds. In 1998, in the small community of Albion, Illinois, two young men went on a widely reported, one-week, nonstop binge on methamphetamine. At the end of it, they started a killing rampage that left five people dead. One was a Mennonite farmer. They shot him as he was working in his fields. Another was a mother of four. They hijacked her car and killed her.

The crime resulting from drug abuse has had an intolerable effect on American society. To me, the situation is well illustrated by what has happened in Baltimore during the last 50 years. In 1950, Baltimore had just under a million residents. Yet there were only 300 heroin addicts in the entire city. That's fewer than one out of every 3,000 residents. For those 300 people and their families, heroin was a big problem. But it had little effect on the day-to-day pattern of life for the vast majority of the residents of Baltimore.

Today, Baltimore has 675,000 residents, roughly 70 percent of the population it had in 1950. But it has 130 times the number of heroin addicts. One out of every 17 people in Baltimore is a heroin addict. Almost 39,000 people. For the rest of the city's residents, it's virtually impossible to avoid being affected in some way by the misery, the crime and the violence that drug abuse has brought to Baltimore.

People who once might have sat out on their front stoops on a hot summer night are now reluctant to venture outdoors for fear of drug-related violence. Drug abuse has made it a matter of considerable risk to walk down the block to the corner grocery store, to attend evening services at church, or to gather in the school playground.

New York City offers a dramatic example of what effective law enforcement can do to stem violent crime. City leaders increased the police department by 30 percent, adding 8,000 officers. Arrests for all crimes, including drug dealing, drug gang activity and quality of life violations which had been tolerated for many years, increased by 50 percent. The capacity of New York prisons was also increased.

The results of these actions were dramatic. In 1990, there were 2,262 homicides in New York City. By 1998, the number of homicides had dropped to 663. That's a 70 percent reduction in just eight years. Had the murder rate stayed the same in 1998 as it was in 1990, 1,629 more people would have been killed in New York City. I believe it is fair to say that those 1,629 people owe their lives to this effective response by law enforcement.

Legalization Would Have Consequences for Society
The third outcome of legalization would be a far different social environment. The social cost of drug abuse is not found solely in the amount of crime it causes. Drugs cause an enormous amount of accidents, domestic violence, illness, and lost opportunities for many who might have led happy, productive lives.

Drug abuse takes a terrible toll on the health and welfare of a lot of American families. In 1996, for example, there were almost 15,000 drug-induced deaths in the United States, and a half-million emergency room episodes related to drugs. The Centers for Disease Control and Prevention has estimated that 36 percent of new HIV cases are directly or indirectly linked to injecting drug users.

Increasing drug use has had a major impact on the workplace. According to estimates in the 1997 National Household Survey, a study conducted by the Substance Abuse and Mental Health Services Administration (SAMHSA), 6.7 million full-time workers and 1.6 million part-time workers are current users of illegal drugs.

Employees who test positive for drug use consume almost twice the medical benefits as nonusers, are absent from work 50 percent more often, and make more than twice as many workers' compensation claims. Drug use also presents an enormous safety problem in the workplace.

This is particularly true in the transportation sector. Marijuana, for example, impairs the ability of drivers to maintain concentration and show good judgment on the road. A study released by the National Institute on Drug Abuse surveyed 6,000 teenage drivers. It studied those who drove more than six times a month after using marijuana. The study found that they were about two-and-a-half times more likely to be involved in a traffic accident than those who didn't smoke before driving.

The problem is compounded when drivers have the additional responsibility for the safety of many lives. In Illinois, for example, drug tests were administered to current and prospective school bus drivers between 1995 and 1996. Two hundred tested positive for marijuana, cocaine and other drugs. In January 1987, a Conrail engineer drove his locomotive in front of an Amtrak passenger train, killing 16 people and injuring 170. It was later determined that just 18 minutes before the crash, both he and his brakeman had been smoking marijuana.

In addition to these public safety risks and the human misery costs to drug users and their families associated with drug abuse, the Office of National Drug Control Policy has put a financial price tag on this social ill. According to the 1999 National Drug Control Strategy, illegal drugs cost society about $110 billion every year.

Proponents of legalization point to several liberalization experiments in Europe—for example, the one in Holland that I have already mentioned. The experiment in Holland is now 23 years old, so it provides a good illustration of what liberalizing our drug laws portends.

The head of Holland's best known drug abuse rehabilitation center has described what the new drug culture has created. The strong form of marijuana that most of the young people smoke, he says, produces "a chronically passive individual—someone who is lazy, who doesn't want to take initiatives, doesn't want to be active—the kid who'd prefer to lie in bed with a joint in the morning rather than getting up and doing something."

England's experience with widely available heroin shows that use and addiction increase. In a policy far more liberal than America's, Great Britain allowed doctors to prescribe heroin to addicts. There was an explosion of heroin use, and by the mid-1980s known addiction rates were increasing by about 30 percent a year. According to James Q. Wilson, in 1960, there were 68 heroin addicts registered with the British Government. Today, there are roughly 31,000.

Liberalization in Switzerland has had much the same results. This small nation became a magnet for drug users the world over. In 1987, Zurich permitted drug use and sales in a part of the city called Platzspitz, dubbed "Needle Park." By 1992, the number of regular drug users at the park had reportedly swelled from a few hundred in 1982 to 20,000 by 1992. The experiment has since been terminated.

In April, 1994, a number of European cities signed a resolution titled "European Cities Against Drugs," commonly known as the Stockholm resolution. The signatories include some of the major European cities, like Berlin, Stockholm, Paris, Madrid, London, Warsaw and Moscow. As the resolution stated: "the answer does not lie in making harmful drugs more accessible, cheaper and socially acceptable. Attempts to do this have not proved successful. We believe that legalizing drugs will, in the long term, increase our problems. By making them legal, society will signal that it has resigned to the acceptance of drug abuse." I couldn't say it any better than that. After seeing the results of liberalization up close, these European cities clearly believe that liberalization is a bad idea.

You do not have to visit Amsterdam or Zurich or London to witness the effects of drug abuse. If you really want to discover what legalization might mean for society, talk to a local clergyman or an eighth-grade teacher, or a high school coach, or a scout leader or a parent. How many teachers do you know who come and visit your offices and say, Congressman, the thing that our kids need more than anything else is greater availability to drugs. How many parents have you ever known to say, "I sure wish my child could find illegal drugs more easily than he can now."

Or talk to a local cop on the beat. Night after night, they deal with drug-induced domestic violence situations. They roll up to a house and there is a fight, and the people are high on pot or speed, or their husband or father is a heroin addict, and you can't wake him up or he's overdosed in the family bedroom. That's where you see the real effects of drugs.

Anyone who has ever worked undercover in drug enforcement has witnessed young children, 12- and 14-year-old girls, putting needles into their arms, shooting up heroin or speed. To feed their habit, the kids start stealing from their parents and their brothers and sisters, stealing and pawning the watch that's been handed down from their grandmother to buy a bag of dope. Drug addiction is a family affair. It's a tragedy for everyone involved. And it wouldn't matter a bit to these families if the drugs were legal. The human misery would be the same. There would just be more of it.

Legalization Would Present a Law Enforcement Nightmare

The fourth outcome of legalization would be a law enforcement nightmare. I suspect few people would want to make drugs available to 12-year-old children. That reluctance points to a major flaw in the legalization proposal. Drugs will always be denied to some sector of the population, so there will always be some form of black market and a need for drug enforcement.

Consider some of the questions that legalization raises? What drugs will be legalized? Will it be limited to marijuana? If the principle is advanced that drug abuse is a victimless crime, why limit drug use to marijuana?

I know that there are those who will make the case that drug addiction hurts no one but the user. If that becomes part of the conventional wisdom, there will certainly be pressure to legalize all drug use. Only when people come to realize how profoundly all of us are affected by widespread drug abuse will there be pressure to put the genie back in the bottle. By then, it may be too late.

But deciding what drugs to legalize will only be part of the problem. Who will be able to buy drugs legally? Only those over 18 or 21? If so, you can bet that many young people who have reached the legal age will divert their supplies to younger friends. Of course, these young pushers will be in competition with many of the same people who are now pushing drugs in school yards and neighborhood streets.

Any attempt to limit drug use to any age group at all will create a black market, with all of the attendant crime and violence, thereby defeating one of the goals of legalization. That's also true if legalization is limited to marijuana. Cocaine, heroin and methamphetamine will be far more profitable products for the drug lords. Legalization of marijuana alone would do little to stem illegal trafficking.

Will airline pilots be able to use drugs? Heart surgeons? People in law enforcement or the military? Teachers? Truck drivers? Workers in potentially dangerous jobs like construction?

Drug use has been demonstrated to result in lower workplace productivity, and often ends in serious, life-threatening accidents. Many drug users are so debilitated by their habit that they can't hold jobs. Which raises the question, if drug users can't hold a job, where will they get the money to buy drugs? Will the right to use drugs imply a right to the access to drugs? If so, who will distribute free drugs? Government employees? The local supermarket? The college bookstore? If they can't hold a job, who will provide their food, clothing and shelter?

Virtually any form of legalization will create a patchwork quilt of drug laws and drug enforcement. The confusion would swamp our precinct houses and courtrooms. I don't think it would be possible to effectively enforce the remaining drug laws in that kind of environment.

Drug Enforcement Works

This is no time to undermine America's effort to stem drug abuse. America's drug policies work. From 1979 to 1994, the number of drug users in America dropped by almost half.

Two things significantly contributed to that outcome. First, a strong program of public education; second, a strict program of law enforcement.

If you look over the last four decades, you can see a pattern develop. An independent researcher, R. E. Peterson, has analyzed this period, using statistics from a wide variety of sources, including the Justice Department and the White House Office of National Drug Control Strategy. He broke these four decades down into two periods: the first, from 1960 to 1980, an era of permissive drug laws; the second, from 1980 to 1995, an era of tough drug laws.

During the permissive period, drug incarceration rates fell almost 80 percent. During the era of tough drug laws, drug incarceration rates rose almost 450 percent. Just as you might expect, these two policies regarding drug abuse had far different consequences. During the permissive period, drug use among teens climbed by more than 500 percent. During the tough era, drug use by high school students dropped by more than a third.

Is there an absolute one-to-one correlation between tougher drug enforcement and a declining rate of drug use? I wouldn't suggest that. But the contrasts of drug abuse rates between the two eras of drug enforcement are striking.

One historian of the drug movement has written about America's experience with the veterans of Vietnam. As you may recall from the early 1970s, there was a profound concern in the American government over the rates of heroin use by our military personnel in Vietnam. At the time, U.S. Army medical officers estimated that about 10–15 percent of the lower ranking enlisted men in Vietnam were heroin users.

Military authorities decided to take a tough stand on the problem. They mandated a drug test for every departing soldier. Those who failed were required to undergo drug treatment for 30 days. The theory was that many of the soldiers who were using heroin would give it up to avoid the added 30 days in Vietnam. It clearly worked. Six months after the tests began, the percentage of soldiers testing positive dropped from 10 percent to 2 percent.

There may be a whole host of reasons for this outcome. But it demonstrates that there is nothing inevitable about drug abuse. In fact, the history of America's experience with drugs has shown us that it was strong drug enforcement that effectively ended America's first drug epidemic, which lasted from the mid-1880s to the mid-1920s.

By 1923, about half of all prisoners at the Federal penitentiary in Leavenworth, Kansas, were violators of America's first drug legislation, the Harrison Act. If you are concerned by the high drug incarceration rates of the late 1990s, consider the parallels to the tough drug enforcement policies of the 1920s. It was those tough policies that did much to create America's virtually drug-free environment of the mid-20th century.

Drug laws can work, if we have the national resolve to enforce them. As a father, as someone who's had a lot of involvement with the Boy Scouts and Little Leaguers, and as a 30-year civil servant in drug enforcement, I can tell you that there are a lot of young people out there looking for help. Sometimes helping them means saying "no," and having the courage to back it up.

Let me tell you a story about one of them. He was a young man who lived near Austin, Texas. He had a wife who was pregnant. To protect their identities, I'll call them John and Michelle. John was involved in drugs, and one night we arrested him and some of his friends on drug charges. He went on to serve a six-month sentence before being turned loose.

Sometime after he got out, he and his wife came to our office looking for me. They rang the doorbell out at the reception area, and my secretary came back and said they were here to see me. I had no idea what they wanted. I was kind of leery, thinking they might be looking for revenge. But I went out to the reception area anyway.

John and Michelle were standing there with a little toddler. They said they just wanted to come in so we could see their new baby. And then Michelle said there was a second reason they came by. When he got arrested, she said, that's the best thing that ever happened to them.

We had been very wholesome people, she said. John was involved in sports in high school. He was an all-American guy. Then he started smoking pot. His parents couldn't reach him. His teachers couldn't reach him. He got into other drugs. He dropped out of high school. The only thing that ever got his attention, she said, was when he got arrested.

Meanwhile, John was listening to all this and shaking his head in agreement. He said that his high school coach had tried to counsel him, but he wouldn't listen to him. He said his big mistake was dropping out of sports. He thought that if he had stayed in sports he wouldn't have taken the route he did.

When I arrested those kids that night I had no idea of the extent to which I would ultimately help them out of their problems and influence their lives in a positive way. In 30 years of dealing with young Americans, I believe that John is more typical than not.

America spends millions of dollars every year on researching the issue of drugs. We have crime statistics and opinion surveys and biochemical research. And all of that is important. But what it all comes down to is whether we can help young people like John—whether we can keep them from taking that first step into the world of drugs that will ruin their careers, destroy their marriages and leave them in a cycle of dependency on chemicals.

Whether in rural areas, in the suburbs, or in the inner cities, there are a lot of kids who could use a little help. Sometimes that help can take the form of education and counseling. Often it takes a stronger approach. And there are plenty of young people, and older people as well, who could use it.

If we as a society are unwilling to have the courage to say no to drug abuse, we will find that drugs will not only destroy the society we have built up over 200 years, but ruin millions of young people like John.

Drug abuse, and the crime and personal dissolution and social decay that go with it, are not inevitable. Too many people in America seem resigned to the growing rates of drug use. But America's experience with drugs shows that strong law enforcement policies can and do work.

At DEA, our mission is to fight drug trafficking in order to make drug abuse the most expensive, unpleasant, risky, and disreputable form of recreation a person could have. If drug users aren't worried about their health, or the health and welfare of those who depend on them, they should at least worry about the likelihood of getting caught. Not only do tough drug enforcement policies work, but I might add that having no government policy, as many are suggesting today, is in fact a policy, one that will reap a whirlwind of crime and social decay.

Thank you, Mr. Chairman and members of the Committee, for the opportunity to testify before you.

SELECTION 2

The following selection is an interview with drug-policy scholar Ethan Nadelmann by John Sullum, Managing Editor of *Reason Magazine.* In 1994, Ethan Nadelmann founded The Lindesmith Center, a leading drug policy and research institute established to investigate alternative strategies to current drug regulations. He now serves as the Executive Director of the Drug Policy Alliance (formerly The Lindesmith Center–Drug Policy Foundation, a merger of the two organizations in 2000). Nadelmann is author of *Cops across Borders: The Internationalization of U.S. Criminal Law Enforcement* (1993) and coeditor of *Psychoactive Drugs and Harm Reduction: From Faith to Science* (1993).

■ *Mind Alteration*

Drug-Policy Scholar Ethan Nadelmann on Turning People against Drug Prohibition

INTERVIEWED BY JACOB SULLUM

In 1988 the conventional wisdom about U.S. drug policy could be summed up in two dogmatic phrases: "zero tolerance" and "Just Say No." Republicans and Democrats were competing to see who could be tougher on drugs. Doubts about the wisdom of prohibition—let alone proposals for legalization—were beyond the pale of acceptable discussion.

That climate started to change in the spring, after two respectable people publicly criticized the war on drugs and said it was time to examine alternatives. One of them was Baltimore Mayor Kurt Schmoke, who told a group of mayors and police chiefs in April that the drug war was a failure and said drug use should be decriminalized. The other was a young Princeton professor named Ethan Nadelmann, who attacked prohibition and made the case for legalization in the March issue of *Foreign Policy.* Nadelmann argued that drug-control efforts had skewed U.S. foreign policy while accomplishing remarkably little, and he noted that most of the harms associated with the drug trade—including violence, corruption, disease, and crime—were caused or exacerbated by prohibition.

The juxtaposition of the Schmoke and Nadelmann critiques, coming amid growing antidrug hysteria, attracted intense interest from the mainstream news media. In late April, Nadelmann came back from a meeting in Mexico to find 20 messages on his answering machine, including calls from *The New Republic,* local radio and television stations, and ABC's "Nightline." The first TV appearance of my life was on "Nightline" with Kurt Schmoke and [Rep.] Charlie Rangel (D-N.Y.)," Nadelmann recalls. "The next day I came to my office, and the phone list was 40 calls long, including the *New York Times,* the *Washington Post, Time, Newsweek.* There was this incredible media onslaught."

During the next few months, Nadelmann debated drug warriors on "Donahue," "Larry King Live," and various other talk shows. He began receiving invitations to speak. At last count, he had given speeches on drug legalization in 31 states and 13 countries. In addition to the piece in *Foreign Policy,* he has written articles on legalization for *The Public Interest, Science, Daedalus, The New Republic, American Heritage,* and *Rolling Stone,* among other publications. (He also contributed to a forum on "America After Prohibition" in the October 1988 issue of *Reason.*)

In Nadelmann the drug legalization cause has found a spokesman who is thoughtful, personable, and quick on his feet. As a centrist, an expert on international law enforcement (he is the author of *Cops Across Borders: The Internationalization of U.S. Criminal Law Enforcement*), and an assistant professor at Princeton's Woodrow Wilson School of Public and International Affairs, he has helped bring credibility to a viewpoint long associated with hippies and wild-eyed libertarians. His relaxed, reasonable manner contrasts with the bombastic rhetoric of many drug warriors and helps him communicate with the disparate factions of the reform movement.

In 1990 with funding from the Smart Family Foundation, Nadelmann assembled a panel of 18 drug-policy scholars into the Princeton Working Group on the Future of Drug Use and Alternatives to Drug Prohibition. The working group, which meets periodically, plans to produce two reports, one on short-term "harm reduction" measures, such as needle-exchange programs and marijuana decriminalization, the other on long-term strategies, including a variety of legalization schemes. Nadelmann also serves on the boards of the Drug Policy Foundation and the International Anti-Prohibitionist League.

This summer Nadelmann will leave Princeton to direct the Center on Markets and Morals, a new think tank funded by billionaire investor George Soros. The center will study a range of vice issues, including gambling and prostitution, but its main focus will be drug policy. Soros's goal, Nadelmann says, is to invigorate and support a broader debate on drug policy and to encourage a shift from drug war to "drug peace."

Reason Managing Editor Jacob Sullum interviewed Nadelmann in mid-April. In conversation Nadelmann is focused and calm, careful to make distinctions and allow for nuances. He is quick to admit when he has not thought an issue through or does not know enough to form an opinion. He is comfortable with the cost-benefit language of policy analysts yet firm in his support for individual autonomy, the value that animates his attack on drug prohibition.

REASON: How did you first become interested in drug policy?

NADELMANN: In 1983 I was working on a law degree and a Ph.D. in political science at Harvard. Until that point, I had focused on international relations, U.S. foreign policy, and Middle East politics. I was finding the subject depressing. The field was increasingly crowded, and I was finding it hard to relate to my law degree and legal studies. I was also at the point where I was going to have to learn the languages to be really serious about it. I was looking for something that would combine law and foreign policy, something that was interesting and had research potential, that was not a crowded field. I had always had an interest in the drug issue and crime, a sort of fascination with it. Part of it was having been one of a generation that smoked pot and experimented with other drugs. My dad was a rabbi, and I grew up with a very ethical background in many respects, seeing myself as a law-abiding person. And you go to college and you smoke pot, and you're struck by the fact that you could lose your freedom for engaging in an activity which seems entirely innocuous. Reading John Stuart Mill in my sophomore year clicked with that in certain ways.

REASON: Was there a point in your research when you became convinced that the illicit drugs should be legalized, or did the research confirm your initial views?

NADELMANN: I was inclined toward the legalization of marijuana and inclined toward the notion that possession and use of drugs should be legal in environments that were not harmful to other people. I was inclined that way, but I hadn't thought it through. I didn't know much about heroin or cocaine. In '83, '84, I started doing research on U.S. international drug-control policies and on the broader range of issues that lie at the intersection of U.S. foreign policy and criminal justice. I published my first article in '85 in the *Washington Quarterly.* I really pulled my punches, but I basically said that U.S. international drug policy didn't seem to be working very well.

At that point, I was a consultant to the Bureau of International Narcotics Matters in the State Department, working on a classified report on international efforts against drug-related money laundering. Between that job and my research as a graduate student, I traveled to Europe and South America, interviewing drug enforcement officials. Then I would go back to Cambridge, and I would do historical work on these issues. I began to get more of a historical perspective, to understand the racist origins of drug laws, learn more about the late 19th century and what drug use was like then. I began coming up with more of an analysis that sorted out the limits, costs, and consequences of prohibition.

In 1985 I wrote my first legalization paper, which was subtitled "The Radical Sound of Common Sense." I sent it to *Commentary,* and I got a very nice note from Norman Podhoretz, saying, "Thank you for your interesting article, but we remain firmly on the other side." In retrospect, I was very lucky that they didn't publish it, because it was a sort of sophomoric first take. But I circulated it among friends, and that was the first time I put those ideas down on paper.

The first talk I gave where I explicitly attacked prohibition and suggested that legalization might be the answer was in June 1987, just before I left Harvard, at Ft. Bolling Air Force Base in Washington. It was a conference sponsored by the Defense Intelligence College, where the audience consisted mostly of intelligence analysts and military people. I was on a panel with the number-two guy in the State Department narcotics bureau, the number-two guy in the DEA, the head of drug enforcement at the FBI, the head of the Marine Corps's antidrug program, and Mark Moore, my dissertation adviser. I said, "Look, let's face it. The problem here is drug prohibition. You're essentially no different from the Prohibition agents of the 1920s." People started hissing at me, saying, "What's he doing here? Get him out of here." It was quite a time.

REASON: How do you explain the response to your 1988 article in *Foreign Policy?*

NADELMANN: My article would not have done it without Schmoke. His speech was really the key thing. Part of it was that there was this war-on-drugs hysteria going on, and journalists kept looking for stories, any story with a new angle. Plus, there was this silent view, held fairly widely, that there was something screwy with the war on drugs. There were enough people around who realized that it struck a chord.

REASON: In what ways has the drug-policy debate changed since 1988? What did the reaction to Surgeon General Joycelyn Elders's remarks about legalization show?

NADELMANN: Now the legalization issue is being played less for entertainment value and more as a serious thing. Whereas before we were piggybacking this war-on-drugs craze, now that's died away, and there's a much more substantive interest in drug-policy alternatives. When Schmoke said it, the reaction was, "Oh my God, did you hear what he said?" There were a lot of jokes about him being a one-term mayor. With Elders, you had the talking heads on the Sunday morning programs and mayors, from Frank Jordan in San Francisco to Sharon Pratt Kelly in Washington, all saying, "Look, what's wrong with talking about this stuff?"

What did she say? She said legalization would reduce crime, which seems pretty clear. She said the Europeans are doing some interesting things. Well, that's certainly the case; we should learn more about their "harm reduction" approach. And she said we should study it. So she put it out there in a way that was quite acceptable to people. If you look at the editorial pages, I bet you'd find much more support for what Elders said than for what Schmoke said six years ago.

More and more people are coming up to me and other people who speak on this issue and saying, "You know, four or five years ago, when I first heard it, I thought it was crazy. Now I think I agree with you." So a lot of people are changing their minds, as opposed to four or five years ago, when people would come up to me or Schmoke and say, "You know, I agreed with this all along."

REASON: How would you describe your politics? What aspects of libertarianism appeal to you, and what aspects trouble you?

NADELMANN: I vote for the Democratic Party pretty consistently, with an occasional protest vote for a Libertarian. My politics are fairly eclectic. They're probably more conventionally liberal than they are conventionally conservative. I'm sympathetic to a lot of what the ACLU does, but I don't agree with the whole social agenda. I identify more with the Democratic Party than the Republican Party, but I'm definitely not comfortable, given a lot of the bullshit that they've put forward, especially on issues I care about.

On drugs, and crime generally, there's an overemphasis on criminal justice approaches. The general trend toward the federalization of crime has been a big mistake. The Democrats are not more wrong than the Republicans in this area. The damage has been that they've followed the Republicans on a lot of these issues. They've essentially sold out their own principles. People like Charlie Rangel, [Sen.] Joe Biden, and [Rep.] Charlie Schumer use the drug issue as their way to be tough on crime.

The most important aspect of libertarianism to me is the focus on individual autonomy in areas that to me are the logical extension of First and Fourth Amendment rights—the ones that have to do with privacy especially. When you get into drugs and other vices, I like the notion of treating adults as fully responsible: on the one hand, giving them the freedom to make their own mistakes and pursue their own virtues and vices; on the other hand, holding people responsible for their behavior. There should not be an abundance of excuses for that type of stuff.

What's especially appealing is that the libertarians seem to have a coherent understanding of what individual autonomy means in the context of a complex society. That's what most motivates me. What I most care about is advancing this notion of individual autonomy. When women talk about having control over their own bodies vis-à-vis abortion, they should realize that's one and the same as talking about control over one's own consciousness vis-à-vis drugs. If people want the power to sell their bodies—the same thing. When gays and others talk about sexual privacy, once again it's the same thing. And all these freedoms are not fundamentally different from the freedoms of speech, press, and religion that most Americans now take for granted—but that were once as contentious as the right to control one's body and one's consciousness is now. Drugs are an integral dimension of that.

The emphasis of libertarians on property rights is something that I've never cared as much about. Yes, the privacy of one's home and one's property is very important. But the notion that we reach optimal solutions, whether based on some sort of cost-benefit analysis or on purely ideological grounds, by having the government uninvolved in economic transactions, is something I'm not persuaded about, although I haven't studied it in any great depth.

REASON: What is the main obstacle to getting people to think seriously about legalization? What is the most important thing that someone who is skeptical about legalization should know?

NADELMANN: The most important objective now—rhetorically, intellectually, and conceptually—is getting people to focus on prohibition as the problem, in the way that people saw alcohol prohibition as the problem. The fact of the matter is, it's a prohibition system, but most Americans don't think of it that way, because we've all grown up under it. We don't envision the alternative. The most important thing is to get people, when they hear about shootings in the street, to say, "Damn that prohibition" not "Damn those drugs." Or when they hear about the courts being overflooded and the prisons being overflooded and violent prisoners being let out, they should say, not "Damn drugs," but "Damn prohibition." Or when they hear about a rash of overdose deaths on the street, or the drug-AIDS connection, same thing. It s getting people to talk about it and think about it in those terms, to understand the analogy to alcohol prohibition.

The most important obstacle is this deep-seated fear of drugs that's very much analogous to the fear of communism. The roles that communism and drugs have played in American politics are quite similar. In the case of communism, there was an external threat, but the communists were not knocking on our doors. Drugs do come from abroad, but it's not as if we're being overwhelmed by these things. And yes, there were communist spies in this country, but there wasn't a commie under every bed. Yes, there is a drug problem in this country, but there isn't a drug addict in every corner. "Invasion of the Body Snatchers" symbolized communist brainwashing in the '50s; it symbolizes drug brainwashing and the capture of our children today. One of the core truths in Thomas Szasz's *Ceremo-*

nial Chemistry is about the role that drugs play as a bogeyman in our society, in the same way that witches and Jews and others have in the past.

This deep-seated fear of drugs is totally inconsistent with the scientific evidence, and it's inconsistent to a large extent with people's personal experience. There's an analogy here with homosexuals. Thirty years ago, almost everyone in the country knew someone who was gay. They just didn't know they knew somebody who was gay. Now they do. Well, 60 to 70 million Americans have violated the drug laws; everybody knows somebody who has used illegal drugs. But not everyone knows that they know them.

Of the huge part of our generation who have used drugs, how many have told their parents, to this day, even though they are now successful professionals and parents and what have you? There's a need to come out of the closet and talk openly about drug use. As things stand, the only kind of use that is visible is either the dysfunctional drug use or the media portraits of it. So there's this incredibly skewed view of what drugs are about.

I think that may be changing. I've noticed a real loosening in the past year in terms of people talking about their drug use, an opening up about that. And you can't get away from the fact that we now have a president who smoked but didn't inhale and a vice president who smoked and did inhale. It's probably the case that half the administration has used illicit drugs. You can only sustain the hypocrisy so long.

REASON: What sort of mistakes have you seen advocates of reform make when they're addressing a general audience? Are there mistakes that libertarians in particular tend to make?

NADELMANN: A lot of people are looking for a way out of the current morass but don't know what to do with the radical alternative. They just don't see how to get from here to there. And the libertarians have maybe not thought enough about how you move people down that spectrum, because a lot of those intermediate steps involve compromise measures that are inherently distasteful to libertarians.

On the positive side, the libertarians are articulating a pretty clear set of principles which resonate with a certain sector of the country and which are important. So I'm glad the libertarians are out there, even though occasionally I have to deal with the people who say, "Well, you want to sell crack in candy stores," because that's what Milton Friedman or Thomas Szasz would do. I have to say, "No, that's not the only approach; there are a whole range of other things, and I don't even know if that's the ideal." It may in fact be the ultimate goal. Their assumption that no one is going to buy those products, more or less, because other products are around may in fact be true.

Probably the most serious mistake I've seen is the tendency of so many academics and others to write for a very limited audience. I've always been conscious of the need to write for a wider audience. Even when I wrote for *Science* or *Foreign Policy,* I tried to write in a way that was accessible. I'll spend the time to write something for *Rolling Stone* rather than a more narrow, academic journal.

REASON: Should advocates of reform tie the issue of illegal drugs to the issue of prescription drugs?

NADELMANN: I took a poll of the Princeton Working Group, asking how many people believe that we should eliminate the doctor's role as a gatekeeper. This is the
fundamental element of the prescription drug system, which really lies at the heart
of drug control, as Thomas Szasz and others have recognized. The group was
almost evenly split.

On a broad rhetorical level, the relationship between prohibition and the prescription drug system is beyond the understanding or imagination of a lot of the
people who casually think about this issue. They just haven't seen the connection.
I'm not tempted to use it in my own speeches, except for the most sophisticated
audiences. People are so accustomed to the idea that doctors have control over
this. But one of the things that we're going to do at the Center [on Markets and
Morals] is a seminar series that raises the issue of whether we need a prescription
drug system.

REASON: In an article you wrote for the Summer 1992 issue of *Daedalus,* you note
that the "public health" approach to drugs has totalitarian implications if you follow it to its logical conclusion. Yet you support this approach to some extent. How
do you decide which public-health measures are acceptable and which go too far?

NADELMANN: It's a matter of how far it infringes on individual autonomy. I see the
slippery slope. It's a matter of drawing the line somewhere. I'm inclined to say we
should look for restrictions which infringe less on individual autonomy.

I look on the notion of a totally free market in, say, cigarettes, without the
government playing any sort of inhibitory role, as not a desirable thing. I actually
think the government should play some role in shaping society—especially the
external environment, but even in encouraging people to act in their own interests—
but that it should do so with a much softer hand than it's using in a whole range of
areas. I'm willing to use the tax system to discourage consumption among kids, and
even among adults to some extent. But I'd be wary of using more invasive measures. I'm sympathetic to the idea of banning vending machines for cigarettes. But
then [ACLU Executive Director] Ira Glasser says, "First you ban cigarette
machines. The next thing you'll be banning is condom machines." So he sees that
slippery slope, and I see where he's coming from. I'm undecided. Same thing with
advertising. One of the biggest problems for libertarians, it seems to me, is how you
devise methods to limit access by kids that don't infringe too much on adults.

I think it's legitimate for government to play a role in trying to discourage
people from using cigarettes. If they want to put the information out there, that
sounds fine to me. But I find incredibly distasteful the way that they're demoniz-
ing cigarette users now. What's happening now, with [FDA Commissioner David]
Kessler, is they're heading in a prohibitionist direction, which is something I
would regard as very bad on both policy grounds and ethical grounds.

REASON: You've written that drug policy should minimize the harm caused both
by drugs and by government intervention. What are the weaknesses of this cost-
benefit approach?

NADELMANN: The main weakness is how you define costs and benefits. The econ-
omists don't identify issues like privacy, freedom, tolerance. They give these
things zero value. And to me, those are very significant.

REASON: In the *Daedalus* article, you propose a mail-order system for drugs that the Princeton Working Group has discussed. How would that work, and what advantages do you think it has over a more free market approach?

NADELMANN: We're trying to balance three competing sets of interests. You want to minimize the negative consequences of prohibition. But on the other hand, I'm persuaded by evidence from the public health field that restrictions on the availability of drugs like alcohol and tobacco are effective in reducing the negative consequences to the users themselves and to others. There's also a tension between the individual's right to consume drugs and a community's right to control its external environment. And then there's the fact that we live in a federal system; ideally, we want local approaches to local problems. You don't necessarily want the same drug policy everywhere, but state policies can't vary so much that we generate enormous interstate smuggling problems.

Then the question becomes, "What's the minimum way to accommodate these concerns?" You need an individual adult right of consumption, anywhere in the country, and you need a legally protected right to obtain drugs of known purity, potency, and quality—also anywhere in the country. The minimum way to accommodate these two rights is a system where you can call up and order drugs by mail. Anyone would have the right to obtain this stuff and to possess it anywhere in the country, even though you might not be able to sell it or market it out in the open, and you might not be able to use it out in the open.

This is a minimal system. It guts the criminal side of things. And it gets past concerns about advertising, about drugs in every corner store, and so on. The individual right to obtain and possess this stuff, and even transfer it in small amounts, is essentially sacrosanct. It also eliminates the role of the doctor; you can obtain any drugs through the system. On the other hand, it allows communities to control their external environment.

REASON: Might some municipalities allow an open retail trade, including taverns?

NADELMANN: You might have modern-day opium dens or drug cooperatives. But the state of Mississippi might remain totally dry for external purposes. It might prohibit advertising, prohibit public consumption, prohibit sale in taverns. Yet every adult would have the right to possess and consume in private.

REASON: Would the mail-order source be the government, or would there be competing private suppliers?

NADELMANN: I haven't thought about it. But to me, it's not fundamental whether it's governmental or nongovernmental.

REASON: You've noted that competition encourages innovation and movement toward better, less harmful drugs. With a government monopoly, there wouldn't be much room for that.

NADELMANN: Right. I want to find ways to promote less dangerous products. It might very well be private producers, and there could be multiple distributors.

REASON: In his book *Against Excess,* Mark Kleiman proposes a phased-in ban on tobacco, coupled with a system of "grudging toleration" for alcohol and marijuana, including drug licenses and rationing. What do you think of that approach?

NADELMANN: I think prohibiting access to tobacco products by adults is a mistake, both on policy grounds and on ethical grounds. I think it will generate a black market; it will create a lot of the same problems we've had with other prohibitions. And I think it's immoral to punish, and especially incarcerate people for making that sort of decision.

Licensing is an intriguing idea. Suppose that each time you buy a drug, you have to pass a little 10-question test on drug safety, which every junkie in town would be able to pass in two minutes, once they knew the basic answers. Or you could avoid the test by getting a license that shows you've already passed a test. Mark [Kleiman] would have the government revoking people's licenses for misbehavior. I'm not sure that's the way to go. I'd prefer to have something that resembles a license test that people could easily pass but that at least would ensure they were aware of basic precautions and other information.

REASON: What are the prospects for drug reform during the next decade?

NADELMANN: The AIDS issue has been a blessing in disguise—a horrible blessing, but nonetheless it gives real momentum to a whole range of initiatives. We've got to put abstinence from drugs on the back burner, because AIDS is more important. Although the U.S. has been painfully slow to accept this, harm reduction is getting a serious push. You see it abroad—in Europe and Australia—and it's made some inroads here. Fifty cities in the country have needle-exchange programs, compared with one or two five years ago.

The replacement of the Bush administration with the Clinton administration was generally a good thing. It brought in a lot of new blood, new thinking. Lee Brown is not what I would call a desirable drug czar, but he's no William Bennett, either. There's more room for consideration of alternatives.

Progress in the rights of homosexuals, and increasing concerns about maintaining privacy in a technologically sophisticated environment, may redound to the benefit of the drug issue. I think also that the war on cigarette users—if you want to call it that—is raising the issue of individual autonomy vis-à-vis drug use in a context to which tens of millions of Americans still relate. And the more that cigarettes get tarred as a drug, the more that connection is going to become prominent. You're going to have tens of millions of Americans beginning to identify more and more with the heroin and cocaine and marijuana users. At the same time, you're going to have these arguments about individual rights and the freedom to use drugs in your own home.

If amphetamine really starts to come on big in this country, that's a drug that's pretty hard to control. It doesn't come from abroad; it's domestically produced; it's easily produced; pretty dumb people can make it. The government's capacity to control it may turn out to be remarkably limited. So are we then going to go to widespread drug testing, or are we going to be forced to look at some alternatives?

There's a sense that the drug war has proven its failure. Five or six years ago, people would say, "Well, we haven't really tried it." It's hard to say that with credibility any more. People tend to get bored with old ideas, and the war on drugs is becoming an old idea. There's a kind of natural pendulum or circularity, where people begin to think that change is inevitable. And that's going to happen in the drug area.

SELECTION 3

A major series of articles entitled "High Time" appeared in *The Economist* on July 28, 2001, presenting the case for drug legalization in the United States. The following selection is the editorial expressing this position.

■ *The Case for Legalisation*

Time for a Puff of Sanity

It is every parent's nightmare. A youngster slithers inexorably from a few puffs on a joint, to a snort of cocaine, to the needle and addiction. It was the flesh-creeping heart of "Traffic," a film about the descent into heroin hell of a pretty young middle-class girl, and it is the terror that keeps drug laws in place. It explains why even those politicians who puffed at a joint or two in their youth hesitate to put the case for legalising drugs.

The terror is not irrational. For the first thing that must be said about legalising drugs, a cause *The Economist* long advocated and returns to this week (see our survey in this issue), is that it would lead to a rise in their use, and therefore to a rise in the number of people dependent on them. Some argue that drug laws have no impact, because drugs are widely available. Untrue: drugs are expensive—a kilo of heroin sells in America for as much as a new Rolls-Royce—partly because their price reflects the dangers involved in distributing and buying them. It is much harder and riskier to pick up a dose of cocaine than it is to buy a bottle of whisky. Remove such constraints, make drugs accessible and very much cheaper, and more people will experiment with them.

A rise in drug-taking will inevitably mean that more people will become dependent—inevitably, because drugs offer a pleasurable experience that people seek to repeat. In the case of most drugs, that dependency may be no more than a psychological craving and affect fewer than one in five users; in the case of heroin, it is physical and affects maybe one in three. Even a psychological craving can be debilitating. Addicted gamblers and drinkers bring misery to themselves and their families. In addition, drugs have lasting physical effects and some, taken incompetently, can kill. This is true both for some "hard" drugs and for some that people think of as "soft": too much heroin can trigger a strong adverse reaction, but so can ecstasy. The same goes for gin or aspirin, of course: but many voters reasonably wonder whether it would be right to add to the list of harmful substances that are legally available.

Of Mill and Morality

The case for doing so rests on two arguments: one of principle, one practical. The principles were set out, a century and a half ago, by John Stuart Mill, a British liberal philosopher, who urged that the state had no right to intervene to prevent individuals from doing something that harmed them, if no harm was thereby done to the rest of society. "Over himself, over his own body and mind, the individual is sovereign," Mill famously proclaimed. This is a view that *The Economist* has always espoused, and one to which most democratic governments adhere, up to a point. They allow the individual to undertake all manner of dangerous activities unchallenged, from mountaineering to smoking to riding bicycles through city streets. Such pursuits alarm insurance companies and mothers, but are rightly tolerated by the state.

True, Mill argued that some social groups, especially children, required extra protection. And some argue that drug-takers are also a special class: once addicted, they can no longer make rational choices about whether to continue to harm themselves. Yet not only are dependent users a minority of all users; in addition, society has rejected this argument in the case of alcohol—and of nicotine (whose addictive power is greater than that of heroin). The important thing here is for governments to spend adequately on health education.

The practical case for a liberal approach rests on the harms that spring from drug bans, and the benefits that would accompany legalisation. At present, the harms fall disproportionately on poor countries and on poor people in rich countries. In producer and entrepot countries, the drugs trade finances powerful gangs who threaten the state and corrupt political institutions. Colombia is the most egregious example, but Mexico too wrestles with the threat to the police and political honesty. The attempt to kill illicit crops poisons land and people. Drug money helps to prop up vile regimes in Myanmar and Afghanistan. And drug production encourages local drug-taking, which (in the case of heroin) gives a helping hand to the spread of HIV/AIDS.

In the rich world, it is the poor who are most likely to become involved in the drugs trade (the risks may be high, but drug-dealers tend to be equal-opportunity employers), and therefore end up in jail. Nowhere is this more shamefully true than in the United States, where roughly one in four prisoners is locked up for a (mainly non-violent) drugs offence. America's imprisonment rate for drugs offences now exceeds that for all crimes in most West European countries. Moreover, although whites take drugs almost as freely as blacks and Hispanics, a vastly disproportionate number of those arrested, sentenced and imprisoned are non-white. Drugs policy in the United States is thus breeding a generation of men and women from disadvantaged backgrounds whose main training for life has been in the violence of prison.

Legalise to Regulate

Removing these harms would bring with it another benefit. Precisely because the drugs market is illegal, it cannot be regulated. Laws cannot discriminate between availability to children and adults. Governments cannot insist on minimum quality standards for cocaine; or warn asthma sufferers to avoid ecstasy; or demand that distributors take responsibility for the way their products are sold. With alcohol and tobacco, such restrictions are possible; with drugs, not. This increases the dangers to users, and especially to young or incompetent

users. Illegality also puts a premium on selling strength: if each purchase is risky, then it makes sense to buy drugs in concentrated form. In the same way, Prohibition in the United States in the 1920s led to a fall in beer consumption but a rise in the drinking of hard liquor.

How, if governments accepted the case for legalisation, to get from here to there? When, in the 18th century, a powerful new intoxicant became available, the impact was disastrous: it took years of education for gin to cease to be a social threat. That is a strong reason to proceed gradually: it will take time for conventions governing sensible drug-taking to develop. Meanwhile, a century of illegality has deprived governments of much information that good policy requires. Impartial academic research is difficult. As a result, nobody knows how demand may respond to lower prices, and understanding of the physical effects of most drugs is hazy.

And how, if drugs were legal, might they be distributed? The thought of heroin on supermarket shelves understandably adds to the terror of the prospect. Just as legal drugs are available through different channels—caffeine from any café, alcohol only with proof of age, Prozac only on prescription—so the drugs that are now illegal might one day be distributed in different ways, based on knowledge about their potential for harm. Moreover, different countries should experiment with different solutions: at present, many are bound by a United Nations convention that hampers even the most modest moves towards liberalisation, and that clearly needs amendment.

To legalise will not be easy. Drug-taking entails risks, and societies are increasingly risk-averse. But the role of government should be to prevent the most chaotic drug-users from harming others—by robbing or by driving while drugged, for instance—and to regulate drug markets to ensure minimum quality and safe distribution. The first task is hard if law enforcers are preoccupied with stopping all drug use; the second, impossible as long as drugs are illegal. A legal market is the best guarantee that drug-taking will be no more dangerous than drinking alcohol or smoking tobacco. And, just as countries rightly tolerate those two vices, so they should tolerate those who sell and take drugs.

Looking at Both Sides—The Debate Continues

The core arguments with regard to the possibility of legalizing drugs are aptly represented by the following two excerpts from selections in this chapter:

It's been said that you can't put the genie back in the bottle or the toothpaste back in the tube. . . . Once America gives into a drug culture, and all the social decay that comes with such a culture, it would be very hard to restore a decent civic culture without a cost to America's civil liberties that would be prohibitively high. . . . At DEA, our mission is to fight drug trafficking in order to make drug abuse the most expensive, unpleasant, risky, and disreputable form of recreation a person could have. If drug users aren't worried about their health, or the health and welfare of those who depend on them, they should at least worry about the likelihood of getting caught. Not only do tough drug enforcement policies work, but I might add that having no government policy, as many are suggesting today, is in fact a policy, one that will reap a whirlwind of crime and social decay. (from Marshall's congressional testimony, selection 1)

To legalise will not be easy. Drug-taking entails risks, and societies are increasingly risk-averse. But the role of government should be to prevent the most chaotic drug-users from harming others—by robbing or by driving while drugged, for instance—and to regulate drug markets to ensure minimum quality and safe distribution. The first task is hard if law enforcers are preoccupied with stopping all drug use; the second, impossible as long as drugs are illegal. A legal market is the best guarantee that drug-taking will be no more dangerous than drinking alcohol or smoking tobacco. And, just as countries rightly tolerate those two vices, so they should tolerate those who sell and take drugs. (from the *Economist* editorial, selection 3)

Matters to Ponder

■ Do you think that drug legalization would substantially increase the prevalence of drug use? Would certain segments of the general population be more greatly affected than others?

■ Do you think that any of your friends and acquaintances who presently abstain from drug use would change their behavior if penalties on drug use were removed?

■ Do you view the demographic features of American cities as sufficiently different from European cities so as to make it difficult to apply European drug control policies to the United States?

■ It has been stated in this chapter that "Precisely because the drugs market is illegal, it cannot be regulated. . . . With alcohol and tobacco, such restrictions are possible; with drugs, not." What regulatory controls, if any, do you think would be adequate in preventing an increased level of drug abuse, if presently illegal drugs were legalized?

Further Sources to Seek Out

Goode, Erich (1997). *Between politics and reason: The drug legalization debate.* New York: St. Martin's Press. A well-written and balanced analysis of the arguments in favor of and against drug legalization, from a sociological perspective.

Gray, James P. (2001). *Why our drug laws have failed and what we can do about it: A judicial indictment on the war on drugs.* Philadelphia: Temple University Press. The writing of this author, a California Superior Court Judge, has been reviewed as "mercifully short on legalese" and having "the structural clarity of an accessible legal text."

Kleiman, Mark A. R. (2001, May/June). Science and drug abuse control policy. *Society,* pp. 7–12. An essay on the positive impact the scientific community can make on rational policy decisions regarding drug abuse, as well as the inherent limitations of the role of science in that process.

U.S. Department of Justice, Drug Enforcement Administration. Speaking out against drug legalization. Internet address—*http://www.usj.gov.* This web site has been issued to assist "members of law enforcement, educational, prevention, and social service communities (who) are frequently faced with the need to address many of the positions which are advocated by those calling for the legalization of drugs."

Web Sites to Explore

www.dea.gov
The web site for the Drug Enforcement Administration, where publications expressing its antilegalization stance can be found.

www.druglibrary.org/schaffer
The web site for the Schaffer library of drug policy, oriented toward a prolegalization position.

www.reason.com
The web site for *Reason Magazine,* where the libertarian point of view is expressed on topics of politics, culture, and ideas.

Question: Should Drug Interdiction Be Our Primary Goal in the War on Drugs?

Reducing the availability of drugs to the general public would seem to be a perfectly reasonable approach in waging a war on drugs. Keep them out of people's hands, and your problem would be solved. This approach is often called the "supply side" strategy in drug control, since it refers to a reduction or elimination in the supply of drugs. This strategy is often contrasted with the "demand side" strategy, in which the goal is to reduce the dependence of individuals on abusable drugs through treatment and prevention. Drug interdiction, the interruption of the flow of drugs into the United States from their sources in foreign countries, is at the heart of the "supply side" strategy. Successful drug interdiction can be accomplished by either stopping the flow of drugs when they arrive at our borders or stopping the production and export of drugs where they are originally produced.

Clearly, drug interdiction represents a high-priority mission of the United States government. As stated in the 2001 annual report of U.S. Office of National Drug Control Policy,

> Borders delineate the sovereign territories of nation-states. Guarding our country's 9,600 miles of land and sea borders is one of the federal government's most fundamental responsibilities—especially in light of the historically open, lengthy borders with our northern and southern neighbors. The American government maintains the hundred ports-of-entry, including airports where officials inspect inbound and outbound individuals, cargo, and conveyances. All are vulnerable to the drug threat. By curtailing the flow of drugs across our borders, we reduce drug availability throughout the United States and decrease the negative consequences of drug abuse and trafficking in our communities.

In this chapter, we consider the issues surrounding our current policy regarding drug interdiction.

While efforts to reduce the problems of drug use in America steadily mounted through various presidential administrations in the twentieth century, an official "declaration of war" was not made until the Nixon administration in 1971. A great deal of resources were initially put into programs involving treatment and prevention (the "demand side"), but since the Reagan administration in the 1980s, the focus has become directed primarily to the "supply side," with the major emphasis being placed upon drug interdiction. The Drug Enforcement Administration (DEA), the lead agency in the drug interdiction program, presently has agents in more than forty foreign countries, working with the Departments of Defense and State, Central Intelligence Agency (CIA), U.S. Coast Guard and other branches of the military, and Immigration and Naturalization Service (INS). Yet, despite the tens of billions of dollars spent on drug interdiction, successes have been few. Our attempts have been complicated by a number of economic and political factors on a global scale.

In the 1960s, the major source of white powder heroin smuggled into the United States was Turkey, where the opium was grown, and the center of heroin manufacture and distribution was Marseilles in southern France (the infamous French Connection, as popularized in the 1970 movie of the same name). International control, led by the United States, over the growing of Turkish opium in 1973 brought this route of heroin distribution to an end, but it succeeded only in encouraging other parts of the world to fill the vacuum. The "Golden Triangle" region of Laos, Myanmar (formerly Burma), and Thailand became the principal players in providing the United States with heroin. Joining southeast Asian heroin suppliers were southwest Asian nations such as Afghanistan, Pakistan, and Iran, as well as the central Asian nations of Kazakhstan, Kyrgystan, Tajikistan, and Uzbekistan that had been, until 1991, regions of the Soviet Union. Some forms of heroin appeared from suppliers in Mexico. In the mid-1990s, the pattern of heroin trafficking and distribution changed once more, with the greatest proportion of imported heroin now coming to the United States no longer from Asian sources but rather from South America, specifically Colombia.

In contrast, the location for sources of cocaine over the years has remained more constant. Traditionally, coca is grown in the high-altitude rain forests and fields that run along the slopes of the Peruvian and Bolivian Andes in South America. Cocaine is processed and distributed primarily by Colombian drug cartels, some of whom have been intercepted by local and international authorities and some of whom have not.

It is fair to say that there has been as much frustration in our attempts at the interdiction of cocaine as there has been with heroin. Despite recent American pressure to spray herbicides on more than 135,000 acres of coca fields in Colombia, for example, cocaine production in 1998 set an all-time record. Colombia now is the largest grower and processor of coca in the world, establishing itself as the supplier of 80 percent of the world's cocaine. Despite its status as a principal trading partner with the United States, Mexico, immediately to our south, remains a major drug trafficking route not only for cocaine and heroin but for marijuana, methamphetamine, and illegal prescription medications as well. In the wake of the September 11, 2001, terrorist attacks in the United States, truck and car inspections at the U.S.–Mexico border have been tightened and increased scrutiny for terrorist-related material has increased. As a result, there has been increased interception of illegal drugs as well, but whether there will be long-term effects on the success rate for drug interdiction through this route remains to be seen.

It was in the context of increased concern about illegal drugs entering from Latin America that the United States conceived and initiated Plan Colombia in 2001, a comprehensive partnership of the U.S. with the civilian and military elements in Colombia to reduce the production and export of cocaine and other illicit drugs. In April of that year, however, a serious and saddening international incident threatened to undermine this policy. A Peruvian jet shot down an unarmed plane, killing missionary Roni Bowers, 35, and her 7-month-old daughter. Peruvian authorities, under orders to intercept suspicious flights in the region, had mistakenly identified the plane as involved in drug trafficking. This chapter's first selection Congressional testimony by Robert E. Brown, Jr., acting deputy director for the Supply Reduction Office of the National Drug Control Policy, refers to this tragic event and proceeds to express the official position on the necessity for Plan Colombia. The congressional debate in 2000 over the proposed funding for Plan Colombia is represented by statements by Senator Mike DeWine of Ohio (in favor) and Senator Paul Wellstone of Minnesota (against). In the last selection, an essay by William M. LeoGrande and Kenneth E. Sharpe provides an in-depth critique of recent U.S. drug policy initiatives among Andean nations in South America and an analysis of the effects these initiatives have had on the ongoing internal struggles of people living in these nations.

REFERENCES

Levinthal, Charles F. (2002). *Drugs, behavior, and modern society* (3rd ed.). Boston: Allyn and Bacon.
Office of National Drug Control Policy (2001). *The national drug control strategy: 2001 annual report.* Washington, DC: Office of National Drug Control Policy, Executive Office of the President. Quotation on page 92.

SELECTION 4

The following is the Congressional testimony of Robert E. Brown, Jr., Acting Deputy Director for Supply Reduction, Office of National Drug Control Policy, before the House Committee on Government Reform, Subcommittee on Criminal Justice, Drug Policy, and Human Resources, on May 1, 2001. His topic concerns the U.S. air interdiction efforts in South America and a defense of these efforts. He opens his remarks with a reference to the tragic loss of two Americans, a 35-year-old missionary and her 7-month old daughter, whose unarmed plane was mistakenly shot down over Peru.

■ *Congressional Testimony on U.S. Air Interdiction Efforts in South America*

ROBERT E. BROWN, JR.

Good afternoon. Chairman Souder, Ranking Member Cummings, and distinguished members of the Subcommittee. All of us at the Office of National Drug Control Policy (ONDCP) appreciate your longstanding support and interest in all aspects of drug control policy, as well as the guidance and leadership of the House Committee on Government Reform. A terrible tragedy has occurred, and we extend our condolences to James Bowers and all of the family

Testimony by Robert E. Brown, Jr., Acting Deputy Director for Supply Reduction Office of National Drug Control Policy, before the House Committee on Government Reform, Subcommittee on Criminal Justice, Drug Policy, and Human Resources, Washington, DC, May 1, 2001.

and friends of Roni and Charity Bowers. We also express our concern for the health of Kevin Donaldson, who piloted the plane and saved the lives of the other passengers on board.

This tragedy occurred within the context of what has been a remarkably successful U.S.-supported international drug control program. Clearly, when implemented, all parties believed that the established procedures would protect against loss of innocent life both in the air and on the ground. Now, after this tragedy, we need to take a close look to see whether the policies or their implementation need to be adjusted. The Administration has suspended U.S. participation in air interdiction programs in Colombia and Peru until it determines what went tragically awry in this incident. We should withhold discussion on the particular facts surrounding this tragic accident until ongoing investigations and program reviews are complete. With this in mind, I would like to focus my testimony today on the strategic purposes that have led three Administrations to provide support to Colombian and Andean air interdiction programs and to briefly outline the accomplishments of these programs to date.

The Strategic Context for Drug Control

Illegal drugs exact a staggering cost on American society, accounting for about 50,000 drug-related deaths a year and an estimated $110 billion annually in social costs. Cocaine inflicts most drug-related damage to American society, enslaving over 3 million hard-core addicts and sending more than 160,000 Americans to hospital emergency rooms annually. In producer countries such as Colombia and Peru, illegal drug production puts money and power into the hands of criminal elements and illegal armed groups. Drug trafficking exacerbates corruption, generates violence against civil society, causes environmental degradation, and promotes political and economic instability. It constitutes a threat to the national security of the United States and other involved countries.

Our *National Drug Control Strategy* is a balanced plan to reduce the demand for illegal drugs through prevention and treatment, reduce drug-related crime and violence through law enforcement, and reduce the supply of illegal drugs domestically and abroad. Within the Office of National Drug Control Policy, I lead the Office of Supply Reduction. My office is responsible for developing U.S. international drug control strategy and coordinating the efforts of U.S. departments and agencies involved in international drug control.

International Supply Reduction and
the National Drug Control Strategy

Although reducing the demand for illegal drugs is the centerpiece of the *National Drug Control Strategy,* supply reduction is an essential component of a well-balanced strategic approach to drug control. Cheap and readily available drugs undercut the effectiveness of demand reduction programs because they draw in new users and increase the population of potential addicts. Restricted availability and higher prices hold down the number of first-time users, prevent aggressive marketing of illegal drugs to the most at-risk population by criminal drug organizations, and reduce the human, social, and economic costs of drug abuse. Supply reduction enforcement programs also provide a strong prevention message that controlled drugs are harmful.

Internationally, supply reduction includes coordinated investigations, interdiction, drug crop eradication, control of precursors, anti-money-laundering initiatives, alternative development linked to eradication, strengthening of public institutions, foreign assistance, and reinforcement of political will. These programs are implemented through bilateral, regional, and global accords. They not only reduce the volume of illegal drugs that reach the U.S., they also attack the power and pocketbook of international criminal organizations that threaten our national security, strengthen democratic institutions in allied nations under attack from illegal drug trafficking and consumption, and honor our international commitments to cooperate against illegal drugs.

The Andean Regional Initiative—
The Vital Role of Interdiction

The illicit industry that cultivates coca and produces, transports, and markets cocaine is vulnerable to effective law enforcement action. Coca, the raw material for cocaine, is produced exclusively in the Andean region of South America. U.S. intelligence knows precisely the geographic coordinates of the growing areas. Trafficking routes must link to these growing areas to move precursor chemicals into cocaine labs and cocaine products out towards the market. Coca cultivation and production is labor intensive and requires sufficient infrastructure to feed and house the labor force and provide sufficient transportation to support the production process and move product to market. The industry can only thrive in geographic areas devoid of effective law enforcement control.

Air interdiction can play a vital role in the establishment of effective law enforcement control over coca cultivation and production regions. Source country interdiction supports our international drug control strategy in two ways. Directly, interdiction ensures that the illegal drugs captured or destroyed will do no further harm. Indirectly, and more powerfully, interdiction fundamentally disrupts illegal drug production when it eliminates a link in the production chain.

The recent history of drug control in Peru shows the potential of the program. In 1995, more than 60 percent of the world's coca was grown in Peru. Local Peruvian farmers converted the coca leaf into cocaine base, an intermediate product much less bulky than coca leaf. The cocaine base was then transported by light aircraft to Colombia, where it was further processed into cocaine hydrochloride and transported on to the world market. Prior to 1995, an average of 600 drug trafficking flights transited along the Peru-to-Colombia air bridge each year. This air transport link from Peru to Colombia was vulnerable to disruption.

U.S. support to Peruvian air interdiction dates back to the early 1990s. Although there were some early successes in the program, it failed to achieve major disruptions in the illicit cocaine industry. The program was suspended in 1994 when it became known that U.S. government officials could be prosecuted under U.S. law if they provided intelligence information used to force down civilian aircraft in flight.

Later that year, Congress passed a new law that permitted U.S. officials to assist other nations in the interdiction of drug trafficking aircraft. In the National Defense Authorization Act for FY 1995, Congress provided a procedure for allowing U.S. government employees to assist foreign nations in the interdiction of aircraft when there is "reasonable suspicion" that the aircraft is primarily engaged in illicit drug trafficking. This law provided for this activity in cases where (1) the aircraft is reasonably suspected to be primarily engaged in illicit drug trafficking, and (2) the President of the United States has determined that (a) interdiction is necessary because of the extraordinary threat posed by illicit drug trafficking to the national security of that foreign country, and (b) the country has appropriate procedures in place to protect against innocent loss of life in the air or on the ground in connection with such interdiction, which at a minimum shall include effective means to identify and warn an aircraft before the use of force is directed against the aircraft.

The United States began providing assistance to Peruvian air interdiction programs again in March 1995. The results were immediate and dramatic. Between March 1995 and the end of 1996, the Government of Peru had forced down or seized on the ground many aircraft. Drug trafficking pilots were no longer willing to fly into the central growing regions. Coca farmers could no longer move their coca products to market. The price for coca leaf and cocaine base in Peru collapsed. Coca farmers could not feed their families. By the summer of 1996, the U.S. embassy in Lima was reporting widespread hunger in the coca growing regions. Coca farmers began abandoning their illicit crops, clamored for U.S. alternative development assistance, and welcomed the presence of the Peruvian governmental institutions necessary to deliver aid. USAID rapidly established a $25 million alternative development program for the region that provided the coca farmers immediate relief and speeded their transition to licit sources of income. At the same time, the power and reach of Peruvian law enforcement institutions expanded into these growing areas and began eradicating illicit coca from public lands. By the end of 1997, the coca crop had been reduced in Peru by 40 percent. Dramatic reductions have continued; by the end of 2000, coca cultivation was less than one-third of its 1995 totals.

The cocaine industry in Peru has suffered long-term disruption due to the successful implementation of a synchronized, coordinated, multifaceted U.S.-supported Peruvian drug control campaign that included vital interdiction, alternative development, eradication, and expanded law enforcement programs. The air interdiction program achieved the first vital disruption of the industry, depressed prices received by coca farmers, and established conditions for successful alternative development and law enforcement programs. By first destroying the profitability of coca, long-term drug control successes were achieved in Peru without risk of violent confrontation with the coca labor force.

It is noteworthy as well that law enforcement and interdiction programs are mutually reinforcing. Intelligence developed by monitoring routes and supporting interdiction programs is useful for the sort of investigations undertaken by the DEA. Route information can also be obtained or amplified through law enforcement cases.

Source Country Interdiction Programs Today
The Andean region nations face considerable challenges today. Democracy is under pressure there, in large measure because of funds derived from narcotics production and trafficking available to well-armed antidemocratic groups. Illegal armed groups at both ends of the political spectrum control almost all Colombian coca growing and production areas and derive a significant proportion of their total income from supporting this outlaw industry. U.S. support to Plan Colombia envisions establishing a Colombian version of the multifaceted drug control campaign that has proven so effective in Peru and Bolivia. In Colombia, as in Peru, the goal of U.S. support to interdiction is to assist the host government in isolating the coca-growing region, to keep precursor chemicals out, and to prevent the coca farmers from moving their crops to market. As the government of Colombia, with substantial U.S. assistance, begins to make inroads against the massive increase in coca production in

areas under illegal armed group control, drug traffickers will look for new sources of coca supply.

Since mid-1998 coca leaf prices in Peru and Bolivia have nearly quadrupled, although the governments in those two nations have done an excellent job of keeping the amount of coca production low. In Peru, rebounding prices indicate that some traffickers have successfully adapted to the airbridge interdiction program and have found new ways to move reduced amounts of product to market. Traffickers are now substituting land and river transportation for air routes. Drug trafficking aircraft avoid long flight times over Peruvian territory and usually limit their flights to short cross border flights to pick up drugs from Peruvian staging areas near the border. In addition, there is evidence that smugglers have recently attempted illegal flights south over Bolivia and Brazil to bring cocaine to market through more indirect routes.

With the price incentive as it is, it will be necessary to support Peru and Bolivia, as well as Ecuador and other regional countries, to assure that coca production does not migrate as a result of pressure being exerted in Colombia. The Administration has requested $882 million in non-DOD funds in the FY 2002 budget for the Andean Regional Initiative to be applied in Bolivia, Brazil, Colombia, Ecuador, Panama, Peru, and Venezuela. About half of the assistance is for Colombia's neighbors, while the remainder is for sustaining ongoing programs in Colombia. The assistance is nearly evenly split between promotion of democracy and law enforcement and security assistance.

Reviewing Processes and Procedures

Clearly, something went tragically awry to cause the incident on April 20, 2001. The United States has suspended its support for air interdiction programs in Peru and Colombia pending the outcome of program reviews in both countries and a joint investigation begun April 30, 2001, in Peru. The United States is well-represented by an experienced interagency team led by the Assistant Secretary of State for International Narcotics and Law Enforcement, Rand Beers. After all of the facts have been gathered, we will be in a better position to make determinations about what issues need to be addressed and how to proceed. We will keep Congress informed as we move ahead in this process. For now, our thoughts remain with the family and friends of Roni and Charity Bowers, and we hope for the speedy recovery of Kevin Donaldson.

Conclusion

On April 21, 2001, at the Summit of the Americas, President Bush said: "Too many people in our hemisphere grow, sell, and use illegal drugs. The United States is responsible to fight its own demand for drugs. And we will expand our efforts to work with producer and transit countries to fortify their democratic institutions, promote sustainable development, and fight the supply of drugs at the source."

The U.S. counter-drug strategy is multi-faceted and long term in response to a problem that has similar characteristics. A crucial element in the strategy is reduction of the supply of drugs, and a key part of supply reduction has been disruption of the illegal drug production and marketing process. By breaking the link between coca fields and cocaine laboratories, U.S.-supported Andean programs caused a collapse of the coca market in Peru and Bolivia that has had major long-term consequences. U.S.-supported international drug control programs have reduced the global potential supply of cocaine by 17 percent since 1995. As the government of Colombia moves against coca production in its territory, it will be increasingly important to assure that drug traffickers are not easily able to find new growing areas in Peru and Bolivia.

As we seek the most appropriate and effective way to reduce drug supply, it is most important to thoroughly examine our programs and their implementation. We must assure ourselves that whatever action we take is effective, that risks are appropriately balanced against rewards, and that every precaution is taken to ensure that programs are implemented to make them as safe as they can be in an often dangerous environment.

SELECTION 5

The following selection is the commentary by the Honorable Mike DeWine, U.S. Senator from Ohio, during the Senate floor debate on the Military Construction Appropriations Act for Fiscal Year 2001 on June 30, 2000. His remarks express his support for Plan Colombia, the 2001 U.S.–Colombia partnership to reduce drug smuggling.

■ *Senate Floor Debate: Statement in Favor of Authorizing Appropriations for Plan Colombia Operations*

HONORABLE MIKE DEWINE
U.S. Senator, Ohio, Republican

Today, the U.S. Congress took a very important and necessary step toward bringing stability to countries in our hemisphere, and communities in our own country, that are caught in the death grip of drug trafficking.

Today, we are sending to the President more than just an assistance package to Colombia—we are sending a blueprint of a partnership with Colombia and other countries in the hemisphere to reduce illegal drug production and distribution. This is a partnership among democracies in our hemisphere.

No one denies that an emergency exists in Colombia. The country is embroiled in a destabilizing and brutal civil war—a civil war that has gone on for decades with a death toll estimated at 35,000. The once-promising democracy is now a war zone. Human rights abuses abound and rule of law is practically nonexistent.

The situation in Colombia today bears little resemblance to a nation once considered to be a democratic success story. But today, the drug trade has threatened the sovereignty of the Colombian democracy and the continued prosperity and security of our entire hemisphere. And, tragically, America's drug habit is what's fueling this threat in our hemisphere.

Honorable Mike DeWine, U.S. Senator, Ohio, from Senate floor debate on the Military Construction Appropriations Act for Fiscal Year 2001, June 30, 2000.

It is our own country's drug use that is causing the instability and violence in Colombia and in the Andean region. When drug deals are made on the streets of our country, they represent a contribution to continued violence in Colombia and in the Andean region.

The sad fact is that the cultivation of coca in Colombia has doubled from over 126,000 acres in 1995 to 300,000 in 1999. Not surprisingly, as drug availability has increased in the United States, drug use among adolescents also has increased. To make matters worse, the Colombian insurgents see the drug traffickers as a financial partner who will sustain their illicit cause, which only makes the FARC and the ELN grow stronger.

A synergistic relationship has evolved between the drug dealers and the guerrillas— a relationship bonded by the money made selling drugs here in the United States. Each one benefits from the other. Each one takes care of the other. This is not a crisis internal to Colombia. It is a crisis driven by those who consume drugs in our country, and a crisis that directly impacts all of us right here in the United States.

It is a crisis that has flourished in part because the [Clinton] Administration made a significant and unwise policy change in its drug control strategy in 1993. When President George Bush left the White House, we were spending approximately one-quarter of our total Federal antidrug budget on international drug interdiction—spending it either on law enforcement in other countries, on Customs, on the DEA [Drug Enforcement Administration], on crop eradication—basically on stopping drugs from ever reaching our shores.

After six years of the Clinton presidency, that one-quarter was reduced to approximately 13 to 14 percent, a dramatic reduction in the percentage of money we were spending on international drug interdiction.

Fortunately, in the last few years, Congress has had the foresight to recognize the escalating threats in Colombia, and has worked to restore our drug-fighting capability outside our borders. In 1998, Congress passed the Western Hemisphere Drug Elimination Act (WHDEA), which not only has begun to restore our international eradication, interdiction, and crop alternative development capabilities, it contained the first substantial investment in Colombia for counter-narcotics activities in almost a decade.

Today, we are building on that effort with a more focused plan to eliminate drugs at the source and to reduce the financial influence of drug trafficking organizations on the paramilitaries and insurgents within Columbia. In short, we are reversing the direction of our drug policy for the better. Congress saw what the Administration was doing. We said the policy has to change; we need to put more money into interdiction and source country programs; and that's exactly what we did.

We must not lose sight of why we are providing this assistance. The bottom line is this: The assistance package we put together because Columbia is our neighbor—and what affects our neighbors affects us too. We have a very real interest in stabilizing Colombia, keeping it democratic and keeping it as a trading partner, and keeping its drugs off our streets.

As we consider the great human tragedy that Colombia is today, we must not lose sight of the fact that the resources we are providing to Colombia now are an effort to stop drugs from ever coming into our country in the future. And ultimately, the emergency aid package is in the best interest of the Colombia-Andean region. It is in the best interest of the United States. And, it is clearly something we had to do.

SELECTION 6

The following selection is the commentary of the Honorable Paul Wellstone, U.S. Senator from Minnesota, during the Senate floor debate on the Military Construction Appropriations Act for fiscal year 2001 on June 30, 2000. In contrast to the previous statement of Senator DeWine of Ohio, Senator Wellstone's remarks express his opposition to Plan Colombia, the 2001 U.S.–Colombia partnership to reduce drug smuggling.

■ *Senate Floor Debate: Statement in Opposition to Authorizing Appropriations for Plan Colombia Operations*

HONORABLE PAUL WELLSTONE
United States Senator, Minnesota, Democrat

I rise in strong opposition to the changes that were made to Plan Colombia in the military construction conference report. As if this body did not originally give enough to the military push into southern Colombia with $250 million, this conference report increases that amount by $140 million, to fund a $390 million, first-time offensive military action in southern Colombia.

Plan Colombia has been added to this conference report as an emergency supplemental. We are moving it through this Congress quickly under the guise of a "drug emergency." But, if there is truly a drug emergency in this country, and I believe there is, why are there no resources in this plan targeted to where they will do the most good: providing funding for drug treatment programs at home? And, honestly, if the purpose of this military aid is to stop the supply of drugs, shouldn't some of that aid target the North as well?

During our debate over Plan Colombia, I heard over and over again not only how much the Colombian government needed this assistance, but also how urgently it had to have it. I heard over and over again how if Colombia did not get this money now, all hope for democracy would be lost, not only in Colombia but also for many other Latin and South American countries as well. This is a far cry from stopping the flow of drugs into the United States. This is choosing sides in a civil war that has raged for more than 30 years. And I think the American people deserve to know this.

This massive increase in counter-narcotics aid for Colombia this year puts the United States at a crossroads: Do we back a major escalation in military aid to Colombia that may worsen a civil war that has already raged for decades, or do we pursue a more effective policy of stabilizing Colombia by promoting sustainable development, strengthening civilian democratic institutions, and attacking the drug market by investing in prevention and treatment at home? I see today that we have chosen the former.

Honorable Paul Wellstone, U.S. Senator, Minnesota, from Senate floor debate on the Military Construction Appropriations Act for Fiscal Year 2001, June 30, 2000.

We are choosing to align ourselves with a military that is known to have close contacts with paramilitary organizations. Paramilitary groups operating with acquiescence or open support of the military account for most of the political violence in Colombia today. In its annual report for 1999, Human Rights Watch reports: "In 1999 paramilitary were considered responsible for 78 percent of the total number of human rights and international humanitarian law violations" in Colombia. Our own 1999 State Department Country Report on Human Rights notes that "at times the security forces collaborated with paramilitary groups that committed abuses."

We should support Colombia during this crisis. Being tough on drugs is important, but we need to be smart about the tactics we employ. This conference report decreases by $29 million the aid this chamber gave to support alternative development programs in Colombia. It cuts by $21 million support for human rights and judicial reform. It also cuts support for interdiction by $3.1 million. Yet, it increases by $140 million funding for the military push into southern Colombia. What are we doing here? Guns never have and never will solve Colombia's ills, nor will they address our drug problem here in the United States.

I reiterate how unbalanced Plan Colombia is in this conference report. It cuts the good and increases the bad. A more sensible approach would have been to permit extensive assistance to Colombia in the form of promoting sustainable development and strengthening civilian democratic institutions. This would have safeguarded U.S. interests in avoiding entanglement in a decades-old civil conflict and partnership with an army implicated in severe human rights abuses. Instead, we are funding a military offensive and denying resources where they would be the most effective: drug treatment programs at home.

SELECTION 7

The following selection is an essay written by William M. LeoGrande and Kenneth E. Sharpe, published in *World Policy Journal* (Fall, 2000). They discuss the expanded involvement of American interdiction efforts in Colombia in the context of political instability in the Andean region of South America. LeoGrande is Professor of Political Science at the School of Public Affairs, American University, and author of *Our Own Backyard: The United States in Central America, 1927–1992* (1998). Sharpe is Professor of Political Science at Swarthmore College and coauthor of *Drug War Policies: The Price of Denial* (1996).

■ *Two Wars or One?*

Drugs, Guerrillas, and Colombia's New Violencia

WILLIAM M. LEOGRANDE AND KENNETH E. SHARPE

The recently approved $1.3 billion aid package for the war on drugs in Colombia and the Andean region marks a major shift in U.S. policy, reminiscent of the shift in 1980–81 that

LeoGrande, William, and Sharpe, Kenneth (2000, Fall). Two wars or one: Drugs, guerillas, and Colombia's new *Violencia. World Policy Journal,* pp. 1–11. Reprinted with permission.

deepened U.S. involvement in El Salvador's civil war. By focusing on military aid and options in the name of fighting the traffic in illegal drugs, the United States is preparing to join the Colombian armed forces in a counterinsurgency war against Marxist guerrillas—a war that has been raging inconclusively for more than 40 years. Until recently, Washington has been wise enough to minimize its role in this protracted conflict, both because of the Colombian military's abysmal human rights record and because the war can only end through negotiations.

The rationale for abandoning this restraint is what U.S. drug czar Gen. Barry McCaffrey has called a "drug emergency" in Colombia—a dramatic increase in coca leaf cultivation in the southern provinces of Putumayo and Caqueta, strongholds of the Revolutionary Armed Forces of Colombia (FARC), the largest of three leftist guerrilla movements. McCaffrey and other Clinton administration officials argue that Colombia is losing the drug war because it cannot eradicate coca in the areas under guerrilla control, and it is losing the guerrilla war because the Colombian armed forces are outgunned by insurgents flush with the "taxes" they collect from coca growers.

By outfitting the Colombian army to wage a counterinsurgency war, Washington hopes to enable elite "eradication battalions" to "push into southern Colombia" where small peasants grow coca under the FARC's protection. Thus, in the vain hope that joining two losing ventures will somehow produce success, Colombia's two wars—against drugs and guerrillas—will become one war. In fact, whether pursued separately or together, neither of these wars is winnable. The military escalation contemplated by the United States will only intensify the violence in Colombia, make a negotiated settlement of the insurgency more difficult, and have no impact whatsoever on the supply of drugs entering the United States.

The Drug War

For Washington, the drug war in Colombia is just one front in a global struggle. In response to drug abuse and addiction at home, the government tries to restrict the supply available from abroad, thereby raising street prices enough to reduce domestic demand. Since the late 1970s, the United States has attacked marijuana, heroin, and cocaine production and trafficking in such "source" countries as Colombia, Peru, and Bolivia by eradicating crops, attacking refining labs, seizing shipments, and arresting traffickers.

Despite tactical successes in each of these areas, source country operations have consistently been a strategic failure, never significantly raising the price of cocaine or heroin in the United States for more than a few months. In fact, while spending on eradication and interdiction programs has grown from a few million dollars in the early 1970s to billions annually today, the street price of a pure gram of cocaine has dropped from $1,400 to under $200 during that time, and the price of heroin has dropped from about $4,000 to a few hundred dollars. This strategic failure is not due to a lack of will or resources, but rather to the structure of the market for illegal drugs, which invariably thwarts Washington's best efforts to suppress supply.

Drugs are so cheap to produce, the barriers to entry in the market are so low, and the potential profits are so enormous that market forces invariably attract willing growers, producers, and traffickers. Official measures of success—tons of cocaine seized, numbers of traffickers arrested, acres of coca leaf eradicated—are as misleading as the "body counts" during the Vietnam War because high profits generate a limitless supply of new growers and traffickers even as the war on drugs drives some out of business. Analysts of the drug market refer to this as the balloon effect: squeeze the trade in one place and it pops up somewhere else.

Even if the United States could significantly cut coca acreage, the market structure for cocaine would undermine the drug war in another way. Most of the markup on drugs occurs after they enter the United States; the actual costs of growing and processing illegal drugs abroad are a tiny fraction of their street price. In 1997, the price of the coca leaf needed to make a pure kilo of cocaine was $300. Refined and ready for export from Colombia, it was worth $1,050. The cost of smuggling that kilo into the United States raised its price in Miami to $20,000, and black market distribution costs raised its retail price in Chicago to $188,000. This means that even an incredibly successful crop eradication program that tripled the price of coca leaf to $900 would raise retail prices in the United States imperceptibly.

Nevertheless, the United States has expended billions of dollars trying to reduce source country drug supplies. The main thrust of U.S. strategy in Colombia in the 1980s and early 1990s was to target major drug trafficking organizations, which imported most of their coca leaf from Peru and Bolivia. Breaking the big cartels, it was thought, would disrupt distribution networks in the United States and raise prices. Under U.S. pressure, the Colombian government went after the drug lords, either to prosecute them or extradite them to the United States. By the mid-1990s, the principal leaders of the Medellín and Cali cartels had been killed or captured. But smashing the cartels did not reduce the flow of drugs. It simply changed the structure of the industry, creating space in the market for many new small and intermediate producers whose business plan, as described by a Colombian weekly, was to "export a little, earn a lot, and make little noise." Some of the business was displaced to Mexico, whose growing criminal enterprises replaced the Cali cartel as the major distributor of cocaine to the western United States.

For Colombia, the cost of attacking the cartels was severe. The drug lords, who had been living in relative peace with the government, retaliated by killing hundreds of government officials, judges, police officers, and journalists, including Justice Minister Rodrigo Lara Bonilla, Attorney General Mauro Hoyos Jiménez, and Liberal Party presidential candidate Luís Carlos Galán. Corruption infected every institution of government involved with the drug war, including the executive branch, the judiciary, and the security forces.

As Colombian coca leaf production expanded in the mid-1990s, the emphasis of U.S. policy shifted from a war against traffickers to a war against growers. Coca leaf acreage increased from 37,500 hectares (about 94,000 acres) in 1991 to 122,500 hectares (306,000 acres) in 1999, despite an aggressive aerial fumigation program that began in 1994. The increase followed U.S. eradication and interdiction efforts in Bolivia and Peru, which reduced coca production in those countries but led the Colombian traffickers to seek new sources of coca leaf closer to home. Since no legal crop in Colombia's coca growing regions is nearly as profitable as coca, the traffickers found no shortage of growers, especially in areas outside the government's control.

This pattern of displacement is typical. During the past decade, despite Washington's best efforts, there has been little change in the total amount of land planted in coca in the

Andean region—about 200,000 hectares. Faced with eradication campaigns, peasants simply plant elsewhere. Reliance on aerial fumigation in Colombia over the past several years has led peasants to retreat deeper into the Amazonian rain forest and has recently called forth a revival of production in Bolivia and Peru.

In short, the new eradication campaign that Washington envisions in southern Colombia will have little effect on regional cocaine production and supply, and no impact on the retail price of drugs in the United States. Moreover, it will entail significant collateral damage. Reinvolving the Colombian military in counternarcotics operations risks further corruption—a common pattern whenever Latin American militaries have touched the tar baby of the drug war. Before his death in 1989, Colombian trafficker José Gonzalo Rodríguez Gacha provided multimillion-dollar payoffs to entire brigades of the Colombian army, according to bank records. Throughout the 1990s, traffickers have paid the police and military to overlook processing labs and smuggling. The low salaries paid to soldiers and police make such corruption inescapable. Militarization of the drug war will inevitably deepen the narco-military connection.

More serious, however, is the violence that this policy will inflict on the civilian population. The coca growers who will be displaced from their lands by crop spraying and the deployment of elite army battalions are mostly poor peasants who fled to this frontier region in the 1960s and 1970s because they were previously displaced by violence, often at the hands of large landowners. They are civilians, not organized criminals or guerrilla combatants. They grow coca because it is one of the only crops that can provide them a livelihood. The "push into southern Colombia" will add tens of thousands of these farmers and their families to the 1.5 million Colombians already displaced by the war, and it will surely produce more recruits for the guerrillas. In this way, Washington's escalation of the drug war will inevitably escalate the guerrilla war as well.

The Guerrilla War

Colombia's two major guerrilla movements, the aforementioned FARC and the National Liberation Army (ELN), were founded in the 1960s, but their roots lie further back, in *la Violencia*. From 1948 to 1958, partisans of the Liberal and Conservative parties fought a civil war that cost the lives of some 200,000 people. The ghastly violence of the period was only nominally about party politics. Primarily rural, *la Violencia* was an explosive expression of peasant grievances and local conflicts. Weak governmental authority in many areas gave rise to armed self-defense groups of various ideological stripes. These same factors, along with the added fuel provided by revenue from the drug trade, remain central to understanding Colombia's contemporary violence.

La Violencia ended with the creation of the National Front in 1958, a pact between Liberal and Conservative leaders to form a consociational system in which the two parties alternated in power and shared control of the government. The corollary to this elite arrangement was that other political parties and movements were effectively excluded from politics, an exclusion enforced by repression when necessary. The armed forces remained formally subordinate to civilian rule but exercised near autonomy on issues of national security and enjoyed impunity despite persistent and serious human rights violations. The National Front formally ended in 1974, but the two traditional parties continued to divide government offices between them into the mid-1980s.

Colombia's guerrilla movements arose in resistance to the National Front. Founded in 1966, the FARC grew out of rural self-defense groups organized by the Colombian Communist Party during *la Violencia*. Its leader, Manuel "Tirofijo" ("Sureshot") Marulanda, took up arms in 1949 at the age of 19. The ELN was organized by students inspired by the example of the Cuban Revolution, and has focused its attention on the oil industry, blowing up pipelines and kidnapping oil executives for ransom. In the 1970s, several new guerrilla groups developed, the most important of which was the Movimiento 19 de Abril (April 19th Movement, M-19), founded in reaction to alleged fraud in the 1970 presidential election.

Throughout the 1960s and 1970s, Colombia's guerrilla wars were low-intensity affairs. None of the half-dozen guerrilla groups (which operated independently) could seriously challenge the armed forces for control of the state, but neither could the armed forces defeat the guerrillas, especially those with a well-established rural base. For three decades, a stalemate prevailed.

Every Colombian president since Belisario Betancur (1982–86) has recognized the need to find a political solution to the insurgency. In 1984, Betancur signed a cease-fire with the FARC and M-19, which lasted for about a year, despite efforts by the armed forces to subvert it. The cease-fire with the M-19 ended when guerrilla commandos seized the Palace of Justice and the military assaulted the building without presidential authorization, leading to the death of 11 Supreme Court justices.

The FARC used the cease-fire to test the openness of Colombian politics. In 1985, it organized the Unión Patriótica (Patriotic Union, UP), which achieved some modest electoral success in 1986, winning about a dozen seats in the national legislature and several dozen municipal posts. A wave of repression ensued, in which some 3,000 UP activists, candidates, and elected officials were murdered by rightist paramilitary groups, thereby eliminating the Patriotic Union as a viable party. The FARC had no incentive to lay down its arms, and the war went on.

Presidents Virgilio Barco, César Gaviria, and Ernesto Samper all conducted negotiations with various guerrilla groups, leading to the demobilization of the M-19 and several smaller organizations in 1991. But talks with the FARC and the ELN made no headway, as these larger groups refused to settle for amnesty alone, demanding negotiations on a fuller agenda of social and economic reforms.

During the 1980s and 1990s, Colombia's violence became more intense and more complex. Intensification of the war was fueled by revenue from the drug trade. Estimates of how much money the FARC raises from taxing drug production and commerce in its zones of control vary enormously, from a low of about $100 million a year to a high of $500 million. Regardless of the amount, there is no doubt drug revenue has enabled the FARC to significantly expand its ranks, increase its firepower, and extend its area of operations. In 1986, the FARC had about 9,000 combatants operating on 27 "fronts" (local self-supporting and semi-autonomous units). By 1999, it had 15,000 combatants on some 60 fronts, and was active in 40 percent of Colombia's municipalities. In the past few years, the FARC has taken the initiative, inflicting a series of embarrassing defeats on the army, and the conflict has begun to spill over into neighboring countries.

The war became more complex with the rise of the paramilitary right, or "self-defense" groups, many of which made their appearance in the 1980s. The paramilitaries sprang from multiple roots. Some were organized and financed directly by drug traffickers in retaliation for guerrilla kidnappings of their relatives. Others were organized by local landowners and mid-level military officers intent on eliminating grass-roots activists and leftist politicians. Still others were organized by the armed forces as part of a national counterinsurgency strategy (that U.S. military advisers helped design) in which local self-defense militias would confront the guerrillas in areas where the military's presence was weak.

The paramilitaries have flourished as a result of two enabling conditions: financing from the drug trade and tolerance (and sometimes active assistance) on the part of the Colombian armed forces. Most paramilitary groups are financed by drug money; they are either paid directly by traffickers, engage in trafficking themselves, or tax drug commerce in areas they control. The paramilitaries, with about 6,000 members in all, have coalesced around the leadership of Carlos Castaño and his United Self-Defense Forces of Colombia (AUC), an alliance formed to give the paramilitaries a national political voice.

Civilian governments in Colombia have regarded the paramilitaries as criminal but have never been able to bring them under control because of the close ties these groups have enjoyed with the armed forces. The military has a long, well-documented history of condoning and cooperating with paramilitary operations. In recent years, as the military has come under pressure from national and international human rights groups, abuses by the armed forces have fallen dramatically, but abuses by the paramilitaries have risen, leading some analysts to conclude that state-sponsored violence is being privatized.

By the late 1990s, Colombia's agony appeared to be reaching a point of crisis. The guerrilla war was expanding and intensifying. Paramilitary violence against suspected leftist sympathizers and other "social delinquents" was growing apace. Kidnappings by guerrillas and paramilitaries alike had become epidemic. From 1987 to 1997, a rising tide of criminal as well as political violence took the lives of more people than were killed in *la Violencia*. The government seemed unable to provide even a modicum of personal safety for its citizens.

Pastrana's Quest for Peace

The United States welcomed the election of Andrés Pastrana to Colombia's presidency in June 1998. Having disengaged from Colombia politically and diplomatically (though not militarily) during the Samper administration because of its ties to drug traffickers, Washington was eager to resume active cooperation with the new government to fight the drug war. On balance, the Clinton administration also supported Pastrana's pledge to negotiate peace with Colombia's guerrilla movements, although some U.S. officials were skeptical about whether the guerrillas were really interested. During an October 1998 state visit to Washington, however, Pastrana convinced the administration to back his strategy of "peace first." By negotiating an end to the guerrilla war, he argued, the government would regain control over Colombia's territory, thus facilitating drug eradication and interdiction programs in areas controlled by the FARC.

Pastrana had run for president on a peace platform, harnessing a deep popular desire for an end to Colombia's decades of violence—a desire that gave rise to a powerful civic peace movement in 1997. Before his inauguration, Pastrana met with the FARC's legendary

commander, Manuel Marulanda, to initiate new peace talks. Immediately after his inauguration, he replaced the entire high command of the armed forces, signaling his intention to
crack down on the military's human rights abuses and its silent partnership with rightist
paramilitary groups.

But the decision that sowed the seeds of Pastrana's subsequent political problems
both at home and abroad was his agreement to temporarily withdraw Colombian troops
from a 16,200-square-mile zone in southern Colombia to create a safe venue for peace talks
with the FARC. This concession was bitterly opposed by the armed forces (which had subverted a similar plan during the Samper administration) and by conservative Republicans in
the U.S. Congress. Within the Clinton administration, the creation of the demilitarized zone
fed the suspicions of some officials—especially in the Pentagon and the office of the drug
czar—that Pastrana was naive and soft on the guerrillas. The zone also impeded the drug
war, since antidrug operations there had to be suspended.

The peace talks got off to an inauspicious start when Marulanda failed to appear for
the opening ceremony with Pastrana on January 7, 1999. Later that month, the talks faltered
over a FARC demand that the government take decisive action against the paramilitary right
before negotiations could begin. Pastrana's subsequent firing of two generals with links to
the paramilitaries was seen in the armed forces as craven surrender to the FARC's demands.

Tensions between Colombia's president and the military precipitated a crisis in May
when Pastrana's minister of defense, Rodrigo Lloreda, and two dozen generals resigned,
publicly condemning Pastrana's conduct of the peace process. By some accounts, only
quick endorsement of the president by armed forces chief Gen. Fernando Tapias prevented
a coup d'état. Pastrana accepted Lloreda's resignation but refused to accept the others. In a
four-hour meeting with the high command, the president reaffirmed his commitment to the
peace process but agreed to take greater heed of the military's views about how to conduct
it. In practice, that meant putting more military pressure on the guerrillas.

Washington's "Drug Emergency"
The May crisis, followed by a major FARC offensive in early July 1999, set off alarm bells
in Washington, prompting a major policy review. General McCaffrey stole a march on other
administration officials by announcing his own proposal for $1 billion in new counterdrug
assistance—a move that annoyed his colleagues but put them on the spot politically. For
months, House Republicans had been blasting the Clinton administration for not doing
enough to stem the tide of drugs and guerrillas in Colombia; McCaffrey's plea confirmed
their critique. In the administration's internal debate, the need to appear tough on drugs
trumped concerns about human rights and the fragility of the peace process.

In August, Undersecretary of State Thomas Pickering traveled to Colombia to warn
Pastrana that he risked losing U.S. support if he made any further concessions to the guerrillas. On the other hand, if Colombia would craft a comprehensive national plan to take the
offensive against both the guerrillas and the drug traffickers, Pickering promised a significant increase in U.S. aid. Pressure from Washington, combined with pressure from his own
armed forces, pushed Pastrana toward a strategy of escalating the counterinsurgency war.

Over the next several months, U.S. and Colombian officials cooperated closely on
the design of "Plan Colombia"—a $7.5 billion program for fighting Colombia's two wars
and restoring its economy. The strategic thrust of the plan is a "push into southern Colom-

bia" by the armed forces in order to destroy coca cultivation in areas controlled by the FARC. To help fund the plan, the Clinton administration requested a total of $1.6 billion in aid for Colombia for FY 2000 and FY 2001, and Congress approved $1.3 billion, of which about $862 million is destined for Colombia (the rest will go to antidrug efforts elsewhere in Andean region). Seventy-five percent of the total is earmarked for military or security assistance.

Though couched within a counterdrug framework, the elements of Washington's military aid program for Colombia are taken straight from the Pentagon's counterinsurgency handbook for El Salvador. The Colombian army, like its Salvadoran counterpart in the 1980s, is mainly a static defense force; rank-and-file soldiers are poorly trained, weakly motivated, and ineffective at searching out and destroying guerrillas. To remedy such deficiencies, the United States will send hundreds of military advisers to train several rapid-deployment battalions, provide helicopters to make these elite forces more mobile, and intensify intelligence gathering so they know where to deploy. Once trained, the new battalions will push into FARC territory to secure the area for coca eradication. Some U.S. officials insist with a straight face that the purpose of this program is solely to combat drug trafficking, not counterinsurgency. No one in Colombia believes that, and no one in Washington ought to either.

Other U.S. officials acknowledge that this new policy targets the guerrillas, arguing its aim is to force them to the bargaining table. By strengthening the Colombian army and cutting into the FARC's coca revenues, they say, Plan Colombia will create a military stalemate. Realizing it has no chance of victory, the FARC will then settle for negotiated peace. This argument has several flaws. First, the war in Colombia has been a stalemate for over 30 years. The problem has not been getting the guerrillas to the bargaining table—they have been negotiating on and off with the government for almost two decades. Historically, the problem has been the Colombian armed forces, which have resisted and subverted the peace process at every turn—ignoring Betancur's 1984 cease-fire, cooperating with the paramilitary right to murder activists of the Patriotic Union party, and opposing both Samper's and Pastrana's proposed demilitarized zones.

The military in El Salvador represented an analogous obstacle to peace. A billion dollars of U.S. aid turned that army into a large, well-equipped, politically powerful force that murdered noncombatant civilians with impunity for over a decade—more than 60,000 of them in all. The war in El Salvador did not end because of a change in the guerrillas' attitude toward the government (the 1992 peace accord they signed was very similar to one they proposed in 1980). The war ended when the army finally recognized that it was unwinnable—a conclusion it reached when the United States cut military assistance by 50 percent, threatened to end it entirely, and threw its full diplomatic weight behind the peace process.

Thus, the message that nearly a billion dollars in U.S. military aid sends to the Colombian armed forces is precisely the wrong one. Some Colombian officers will conclude (probably mistakenly) that Washington is prepared to invest whatever resources are necessary to secure their victory over the guerrillas. None will take it as a signal that Washington has faith in the peace process or that the army should stop opposing it.

Nor is this aid package likely to have any material effect on the military balance. If the new U.S.-trained battalions do in fact target coca fields rather than guerrilla columns, the guerrillas will be able to avoid them, just as the Salvadoran guerrillas avoided U.S.-trained battalions. Late in that war, the Salvadoran guerrillas countered the military's helicopters with shoulder-launched surface-to-air missiles, which had such devastating effect that helicopter pilots refused to fly in daylight. The FARC has threatened to buy such weapons on the international arms market. Finally, if crop eradication operations succeed, they will deprive tens of thousands of peasants of their livelihood, creating a whole new pool of potential guerrilla recruits.

The most disturbing aspect of the U.S. aid package is its silence on the problem of the paramilitary right. The paramilitaries are mentioned only in passing, although they are at least as deeply implicated in drug trafficking as the guerrillas. Up to now, both the Clinton and Pastrana administrations have worked hard to control the paramilitaries and sever their links to the armed forces. But with the United States on the verge of joining the Colombian military's war against the guerrillas, will Washington now turn a blind eye to depredations by the army's other partner in this dirty war? In the early 1980s, the Reagan administration tolerated the death squads in El Salvador because they were inextricably linked to the military, on which Washington's counterinsurgency strategy depended.

The paramilitary right is a critical obstacle to a negotiated settlement of the Colombian conflict. Pastrana cannot guarantee the personal security of the guerrillas if they lay down their arms—just as the Christian Democrats could not guarantee the security of the Salvadoran guerrillas in the early 1980s. As long as the Colombian government is unwilling or unable to control the violent right, the guerrillas dare not agree to peace. In El Salvador, the army had no interest in reining in the death squads because they were an essential weapon in its war against the left. The Colombian situation is similar; by leaving the dirtiest work in this dirty war to the paramilitaries, the regular army can claim a clean human rights record as it seeks more military aid from Washington. The story of the paramilitary massacre of dozens of peasants labeled as guerrillas or guerrilla supporters in the village of El Salado this past summer reads like a page from Salvadoran history. Hundreds of heavily armed men occupied the village and, over the course of two days, held a kangaroo court and executed whomever they pleased, while the Colombian armed forces not only refused to intervene but blocked access to the village by outsiders.

Disentangling the Two Wars

Despite fits and starts, the peace process in Colombia is not nearly as moribund as some U.S. officials imply. Talks are under way, and there are new factors, both domestic and international, that give them impetus. Within Colombia, the rise of a powerful peace movement rooted in civil society is proof of the public's war weariness. In 1997, 10 million Colombians, half of the country's registered voters, voted for a peace referendum, and in October 1999, several million took to the streets to demonstrate their desire for an end to the violence. Running on a peace platform, Pastrana won the presidency with more votes than any Colombian candidate before him. Neither the guerrillas nor the traditional political parties can afford to ignore this popular demand for peace. The peace process, once in gear, will likely develop its own momentum, as neither side will want to shoulder the blame for its collapse. A similar public yearning for peace impelled the Salvadoran negotiations forward in the 1990s.

The international community has begun actively to assist the Colombian process, a development that Colombians resisted until recently. International interlocutors can play a pivotal role in overcoming the decades of distrust between the warring parties—as the United Nations did in Central America in the 1990s. U.N. secretary general Kofi Annan has appointed Norwegian diplomat Jan Egeland as his special adviser on the Colombian conflict, and in February Egeland organized a tour of Spain, Norway, Switzerland, and France for a joint delegation of FARC commanders and Colombian government officials, a trip intended to educate the insular guerrillas about post–Cold War realities. In June, more than 20 diplomats from Europe, Canada, Japan, and the United Nations met in Colombia with officials and guerrilla leaders to talk about economic alternatives to drug production. In July, representatives of Norway, Spain, France, Switzerland, and Cuba agreed to assist in the peace process and attended talks held in Switzerland between the government and ELN guerrilla commanders.

Do the guerrillas want a peace agreement? Or are they content to remain in their zones of control, making money from extortion and drug trafficking? The FARC's initial response to Pastrana's peace initiative was a not a good omen; it offered nothing in return for his concessions, instead exploiting the peace process for tactical advantage. They stepped up attacks on the army, thereby undercutting political support for the peace process, both in Colombia and in Washington. Still, most observers who have followed the FARC closely believe it remains fundamentally a political movement committed to an agenda of political and social reform. No doubt there are hard-line guerrilla commanders who are skeptical of peace, just as there are hard-line military officers. But negotiations have now moved farther ahead than at any time in the past decade and a half. The FARC could regain considerable credibility if it were quickly to agree to measures meant, in the language of human rights groups and negotiators, to "humanize the war," first and foremost by putting an end to kidnapping.

President Pastrana's commitment to peace and human rights is not in question. As the democratically elected president, he deserves the support of the United States. The issue is not whether to help, but how. Some Clinton administration officials argue that the United States should boost military aid because Pastrana asked for it and should not be second-guessed. These same officials had not the slightest reluctance to lambast Pastrana publicly and privately when they thought his pursuit of peace was too vigorous.

The parentage of Plan Colombia is mixed at best. It focuses on military solutions because U.S. policymakers decided last summer that they had to expand the war against the FARC if they were to have any hope of stemming the growth of coca production in Colombia. That decision was clearly communicated to the Colombians, and it shaped the aid package they requested. Pastrana complains that the United States is unwilling to make an adequate commitment to the social and economic reconstruction of his country. He comes to Washington for military aid, but he must go to Europe for economic assistance.

The United States has the ability to improve the prospects for peace in Colombia, but only if it disentangles its drug policy from the guerrilla war and acknowledges that neither problem is amenable to military solution. Washington should abandon plans to "push into southern Colombia" and instead focus its counterdrug resources on intercepting drugs in transit or on money laundering, actions that will not escalate the guerrilla war or displace tens of thousands of small peasants. Such programs may help Colombian drug enforcement, but we should not fool ourselves into thinking this will significantly reduce the supply of drugs entering the United States.

In approving Clinton's aid package, Congress added a requirement that the secretary of state must certify that the Colombian armed forces are acting affirmatively to punish human rights violators in their ranks and to sever their ties to the paramilitaries. Similar conditions were imposed on military aid to El Salvador in 1981, but President Ronald Reagan routinely ignored them, certifying human rights progress even when there was none. This time around, Congress gave President Clinton the option to waive the human rights conditions on "national security" grounds, and on August 22, a week before his scheduled trip to Colombia to show support for Pastrana, Clinton exercised the waiver. Thus the president did not flout the letter of the law, but in exercising the waiver he was forced to concede that Colombia's military does not meet even the most basic human rights requirements—requirements that must be met if there is to be a negotiated settlement of the war.

If the United States is truly interested in reducing human rights violations and taming the paramilitaries, the human rights provisions in the law provide a potent policy instrument. If, on the other hand, Washington treats the conditions as merely an obstacle to be circumvented, the Colombian military, like its Salvadoran brethren, will quickly recognize that Washington's concern for human rights is nothing but window dressing to sell the policy domestically. Now that a waiver has been granted, it is all the more important for Washington to demand that Colombia take effective steps to control military and paramilitary violence.

In his speech broadcast to the Colombian people on the eve of his August 30 visit, President Clinton insisted that his commitment to human rights was undiminished. "There is no such thing as democracy without respect for human rights," he declared. In six months, the secretary of state must report to Congress on what progress Colombia has made toward meeting the human rights conditions in the aid legislation. That will be a good opportunity for Congress and the American people to assess whether or not the White House's professed commitment to human rights is real. If Colombia's progress is no better than it has been so far, the president should rescind the waiver and halt the distribution of military aid.

Not only should the United States hold the Colombian armed forces accountable for human rights abuses, it should also put its full diplomatic weight behind the peace process, as it did eventually in El Salvador. This means encouraging the efforts of the United Nations and the European Union, urging the Colombians to remain open to international involvement, and using U.S. influence with the Colombian military to prevent it from obstructing peace.

The United States should devote the lion's share of new aid to economic assistance in order to help Colombia pull its faltering economy out of recession, and it should offer a "peace bonus"—aid earmarked for the conflict zones once a settlement has been reached. Postwar reconstruction programs might include a crop substitution plan to help small farmers kick the coca-growing habit.

For now, however, Washington is going down a different road. In pursuit of the ephemeral goal of coca eradication, the United States is about to put Colombia's fragile democracy at greater risk by escalating the new *Violencia*. The powerful talisman of "fighting drugs" has led sensible policymakers to endorse a futile and bloody war they would otherwise never countenance. Pouring military aid into Colombia will not reduce the availability of drugs in the United States, and it will not enable the army to win its war against the guerrillas. Instead, it will expand the war, leading to more casualties and the displacement of more civilians, harden animosities on all sides, and prolong a conflict that must ultimately be settled at the bargaining table.

The way out of Colombia's agony is a policy focused on encouraging negotiations, which alone hold the promise of finally resolving this decades-long social and political conflict. Despite being complicated by the cocaine trade, the civil conflict in Colombia is amenable to a negotiated peace. The war on drugs is not. If Washington makes these two wars one war, it will condemn Colombia to a future of endless violence and suffering. And it will do so in vain. America's war on drugs cannot be won in the Colombian rain forest. Even if the United States defoliates every acre given over to growing coca, burns every laboratory, and destroys every last gram of Colombian cocaine, it will have won a hollow victory. The drug business will simply move elsewhere, as it always does. But it is the people of Colombia who will pay the price for the inability of the United States to face the fact that its "war" on drugs can only be won at home.

NOTE

This article was made possible by a grant from the Rockefeller Foundation.

FOR FURTHER READING

Bruce M. Bagley and William O. Walker III, eds., *Drug Trafficking in the Americas* (Boulder, CO: Lynne Rienner, 1996).

David Bushnell, *The Making of Modern Colombia* (Berkeley: University of California Press, 1993).

Marc Chernick, "Negotiating Peace Amid Multiple Forms of Violence: The Protracted Search for a Settlement to the Armed Conflicts in Colombia," in *Comparative Peace Processes in Latin America,* Cynthia Arnson, ed. (Washington, DC: Woodrow Wilson Center Press, 1999).

Council on Foreign Relations and Inter-American Dialogue Interim Task Force on Colombia, *First Steps Toward a Constructive U.S. Policy in Colombia* (New York: Council on Foreign Relations, 2000).

Alma Guillermoprieto, "Our New War in Colombia"; "Colombia: Violence Without End?"; and "Colombia: The Children's War," *New York Review of Books,* vol. 42, nos. 6, 7, and 8 (2000).

Human Rights Watch, *The Ties that Bind: Colombia and Military-Paramilitary Links* (New York: Human Rights Watch, 2000).

Rafael Pardo, "Colombia's Two-Front War," *Foreign Affairs,* vol. 79 (July/August 2000).

Linda Robinson, "Where Angels Fear to Tread: Colombia and Latin America's Tier of Turmoil," *World Policy Journal,* vol. 16 (winter 1999/2000).

www.ciponline.org (an excellent source for documents, newsclips, and updated reports on Colombia).

In late December 2001, Congress attached a set of conditions to future U.S. aid to Colombia. Under new stipulations, the commander of Colombian armed forces must suspend troops who violate human rights and allow them to be prosecuted in civilian courts. The Colombian military must also disavow all paramilitary groups that have been involved, often with government-sponsored military intelligence and support, in increasingly brutal confrontations with leftist guerillas.—Levinthal

Look at Both Sides—The Debate Continues

The core arguments with regard to U.S. drug interdiction policy are aptly represented in the following two excerpts from selections in this chapter:

> We must not lose sight of why we are providing this assistance. . . . We have a very real interest in stabilizing Colombia, keeping it democratic and keeping it as a trading partner, and keeping its drugs off our streets. As we consider the great human tragedy that Colombia is today, we must not lose sight of the fact that the resources we are providing to Colombia now are an effort to stop drugs from ever coming into our country in the future. And ultimately, the emergency aid package is in the best interest of the Colombia-Andean region. It is in the best interest of the United States. And, it is clearly something we had to do. (from Senator DeWine's Senate floor debate statement, selection 5)

> The powerful talisman of 'fighting drugs' has led sensible policymakers to endorse a futile and bloody war they would otherwise never countenance. Pouring military aid into Colombia will not reduce the availability of drugs in the United States, and it will not enable the army to win its war against the guerrillas. Instead, it will expand the war, leading to more casualties and the displacement of more civilians, harden animosities on all sides, and prolong a conflict that must ultimately be settled at the bargaining table. (from LeoGrande and Sharpe's article, selection 7)

Matters to Ponder

- What do you think is the economic impact on a typical coca farmer in Colombia, Peru, or other Andean nation, as Plan Colombia is carried out? What do you think would be the implications of encouraging alternative economic development in this region (such as encouraging farmers to switch to an alternative crop)?
- How does Plan Colombia help ensure the continuation of a democratic government in that nation?
- What you do think about the possibility of political instability in Colombia spreading beyond its borders, creating potentially dangerous political problems across northern South America and the rest of Latin America?

Further Sources to Seek Out

McKay, Lesley (2001, August/September). The coca wars: Bolivia's women farmers refuse to pay the price for U.S. drug policies. *Ms. Magazine,* pp. 15–18.

Orth, Maureen (2002, March). Afghanistan's deadly habit. *Vanity Fair,* pp. 150–152, 165–172, 177–178. An insightful analysis of the status of opium poppy cultivation in post-Taliban Afghanistan.

Rosenberg, Tina (2001, April 12). The great cocaine quagmire. *Rolling Stone,* pp. 51–54. A detailed critique of U.S. interdiction efforts in Colombia, written by a foreign-affairs editorial writer for the *New York Times.*

Stanton, John J. (2001, May). War on drugs: U.S. has no "exit strategy." *National Defense,* pp. 18–20. An insightful look at drug interdiction policies in foreign countries, written from a military-operations perspective.

U.S. aid to Colombia: Partnership for democracy or a "new Vietnam"? Is the Clinton Administration policy toward Colombia sound? (2001, February). *Congressional Digest.* The entire issue of this respected monthly Washington periodical is devoted to the arguments for and against Plan Colombia and a detailed examination of U.S. interdiction policy for illegal drugs.

Web Sites to Explore

www.dea.gov
The web site for the Drug Enforcement Administration, where statistics and reports on drug interdiction efforts can be found.

www.drcnet.org
The web site for the Drug Reform Coordination Network, with articles and references criticizing drug interdiction programs.

Question: Should We Encourage Needle Exchange Programs for Intravenous Drug Abusers?

Illicit drug use has never been a safe lifestyle, to put it mildly. The reality of street drugs is that the buyer has no way of knowing what he or she has bought until the drug has been used, and then frequently it is too late. Obviously, no federal agency has been charged with assuring safety and effectiveness. Few if any illicit drug sellers make any pretense of being ethical businesspeople, their only objective being to make money and avoid prosecution by the law. On occasion, the drugs they sell are diluted with either inert or highly dangerous ingredients. Adulterated heroin, for example, may contain a large proportion of milk sugar as a harmless filler and a dash of quinine to simulate the bitter taste of real heroin, when the actual amount of heroin being sold is far less than the "standard" street dosage. At the other extreme, the content of heroin may be unexpectedly high and may lead to a lethal overdose, or it may contain animal tranquilizers, arsenic, strychnine, insecticides, or other highly toxic contaminants. Even if drugs are procured from a friend or someone known to the user, these risks remain. Neither seller nor buyer is likely to know the exact ingredients. The dangers of acute toxicity (physical harm manifested immediately or soon after the drug is ingested by the body) are always present.

Some risks are inherent in specific forms of heroin abuse and cannot be reduced by anything less than avoiding heroin itself. In the case of intravenous (IV) heroin abuse, in which heroin is injected into a vein (as opposed to snorted through the nose or smoked), the act of drug taking raises special concerns and consequences, some of which can be lethal. Whether the drug is heroin or some other substance, IV drug administration is dependent upon the use of a syringe and needle to deliver the drug into a vein and therefore directly into the bloodstream. In doing so, the IV drug abuser allows the passage of contaminants and toxins that would normally be excluded from affecting the body.

On the one hand, this method of drug administration produces a highly desirable "rush," since the impact on the brain through this route of drug administration is among the fastest possible (with the possible exception of inhaling a drug). The effects of abused drugs delivered in this way, often called mainlining, are felt in the brain in less than fifteen seconds. In a medical setting, IV injections of medications provide not only rapid effects in cases of emergency but also control over the dosage of the medication and the opportunity to administer multiple drugs at the same time.

On the other hand, specific life-threatening risks are incurred. The principal problem is that the effects of drugs are virtually irreversible. In the event of a mistake or unexpected reaction, there is no turning back unless some other drug (an antidote) is available that can counteract the first one. In addition, repeated injections through a particular vein may cause the vein to collapse or develop a dangerous blood clot. Whether one is considering a drug of abuse or an accepted medication, all intravenous injections, by definition, require a needle to pierce the skin and enter body tissue. As a result, there is an inherent risk of bacterial or viral infection if the needle is not sterile. In a medical setting, precautions are of course taken that needles are sterile and conditions are hygienic. In the case of street drugs, however, none of these circumstances hold. Moreover, the common practice of sharing needles among i.v. drug abusers is a perfect scenario for the spread of infectious hepatitis and, in particular, human immunodeficiency virus (HIV).

The spread of AIDS from HIV contamination after needle sharing has remained a major societal problem since the beginning of the AIDS epidemic in the 1980s. In New York, for example, 60 percent of IV drug users have tested HIV-positive, and the prevalence among similar populations in regions of the world as disparate as Europe and Asia are only slightly less. Approximately, one-third of all new AIDS cases in the United States in 1998 were found to be related directly or indirectly to drug use involving needles. A direct relationship refers to AIDS cases who were self-injecting drugs; an indirect relationship refers to AIDS cases who had either heterosexual or homosexual contact with an injecting drug user.

The question then remains whether needle-sharing behavior can be reduced in some significant way. The principal response has been to establish a procedure for administering individual sterile needles to IV drug abusers, thus preventing the sharing of needles. Such programs are usually referred to as needle exchange programs, since the drug abuser exchanges his or her used needle for a sterile one provided by the program.

Some critics have argued that such programs broadcast the message that it is OK to do drugs in the first place and that it is impossible for a drug abuser to quit drug-taking behavior in general. Others who favor sterile needle exchange programs argue that the most critical consideration is the restriction of the spread of AIDS. They see the programs (illegal in many communities but ongoing despite their illegal status) as a specific tactic in the overall strategy of "harm reduction" in drug-taking behavior, as opposed to "zero tolerance." Three selections in this chapter present these differing points of view. In the first selection, David Vlahov and Benjamin Junge view the establishment of needle exchange programs as a necessary public health effort. The second selection, published by the Center for AIDS Prevention Studies in San Francisco, supports and expands the perspective of the first one. However, the third selection, by Joe Loconte, expresses the view that needle exchange programs do more harm than good and that they present a major obstacle against ending an individual's pattern of drug-taking behavior. The larger issues of the "harm-reduction" approach in U.S. drug control policy will be explored in Chapter 4.

REFERENCE

Levinthal, Charles F. (2002). *Drugs, behavior, and modern society* (3rd ed.). Boston: Allyn and Bacon.

SELECTION 8

The following selection is written by David Vlahov and Benjamin Junge for the governmental publication *Public Health Reports* (June 1998). Vlahov is a Professor of Epidemiology and Medicine at the Johns Hopkins School of Hygiene and Public Health. Junge is Senior Research Coordinator with the Department of Epidemiology at the Johns Hopkins School of Hygiene and Public Health. Both have directed the evaluation of the Baltimore Needle Exchange Program.

■ The Role of Needle Exchange Programs in HIV Prevention

DAVID VLAHOV AND BENJAMIN JUNGE

Injecting drug users (IDUs) are at high risk for infection by human immunodeficiency virus (HIV) and other blood-borne pathogens. In the United States, IDUs account for nearly one-third of the cases of acquired immunodeficiency syndrome (AIDS), either directly or indirectly (heterosexual and perinatal cases of AIDS where the source of infection was an IDU). IDUs also account for a substantial proportion of cases of hepatitis B (HBV) and hepatitis C (HCV) virus infections. The primary mode of transmission for HIV among IDUs is parenteral, through direct needle sharing or multiperson use of syringes. Despite high levels of knowledge about risk, multiperson use of needles and syringes is due primarily to fear of arrest and incarceration for violation of drug paraphernalia laws and ordinances that prohibit manufacture, sale, distribution, or possession of equipment and materials intended to be used with narcotics. It is estimated that in 1997 there were approximately 110 needle exchange programs (NEPs) in North America. In part, because of the ban on the use of Federal funds for the operation of needle exchange, it has been difficult to evaluate the efficacy of these programs. This [selection] presents data from the studies that have evaluated the role of NEPs in HIV prevention.

Evidence for the efficacy of NEPs comes from three sources: (1) studies originally focused on the effectiveness of NEPs in non-HIV blood-borne infections, (2) mathematical modeling of data on needle exchange on HIV seroincidence, and (3) studies that examine the positive and negative impact of NEPs on HIV and AIDS. Case-control studies have provided powerful data on the positive effect of NEPs on reduction of two blood-borne viral infections (HBV and HCV). For example, a case-control study in Tacoma, Washington, showed that a six-fold increase in HBV and a seven-fold increase in HCV infections in IDUs were associated with nonuse of the NEP.

The first federally funded study of needle exchange was an evaluation of the New Haven NEP, which is legally operated by the New Haven Health Department. Rather than relying on self-report of reduced risky injection drug use, this study utilized mathematical and statistical modeling, using data from a syringe tracking and testing system. Incidence

Vlahov, David, and Junge, Benjamin (1998, June). The role of needle exchange programs in HIV prevention. *Public Health Reports.* Washington, DC: U.S. Government Printing Office. References omitted.

of HIV infection among needle exchange participants was estimated to have decreased by 33% as a result of the NEP.

A series of Government-commissioned reports have reviewed the data on positive and negative outcomes of NEPs. The major reports are from the National Commission on AIDS; the U.S. General Accounting Office; the Centers for Disease Control/ University of California; and the National Academy of Sciences. The latter two reports are used in this [selection].

The aggregated results support the positive benefit of NEPs and do not support negative outcomes from NEPs. When legal restrictions on both purchase and possession of syringes are removed, IDUs will change their syringe-sharing behaviors in ways that can reduce HIV transmission. NEPs do not result in increased drug use among participants or the recruitment of first-time drug users. . . .

Injecting drug users (IDUs) are at risk for human immunodeficiency virus (HIV) and other blood-borne infections. The principal mode of transmission is parenteral through multiperson use of needles and syringes. The mechanism of contamination is through a behavior called registering, whereby drug users draw back on the plunger of a syringe after venous insertion to ensure venous placement before injecting drug solutions. Strategies to prevent or reduce parenteral transmission of HIV infection need to focus on reducing, if not eliminating altogether, the multiperson use of syringes that have been contaminated. The principle underlying these strategies has been stated clearly in the recommendations of the 1995 National Academy of Sciences Report on preventing HIV infection as follows: "For injection drugs the once only use of sterile needles and syringes remains the safest, most effective approach for limiting HIV transmission." This principle was echoed in the 1996 American Medical Association's booklet *A Physician's Guide to HIV Prevention* and in 1995 in the booklet of the U.S. Preventive Services Task Force *Guide to Clinical Preventive Services.* More recently, this principle has been codified in a multi-agency *HIV Prevention Bulletin.*

The first line of prevention is to encourage IDUs to stop using drugs altogether. However, for drug users who cannot or will not stop drug use, owing to their addiction, other approaches are needed. Two major approaches have been developed to provide sufficient sterile needles and syringes to drug users to reduce transmission of HIV and other blood-borne infections. The first is needle exchange programs (NEPs), and the second is modification of syringe prescription and paraphernalia possession laws or ordinances. Hereafter, we will refer to the latter as deregulation of prescription and paraphernalia laws.

NEPs

There are now more than 110 NEPs in the United States. By comparison, there are 2000 or more outlets in Australia and hundreds in Great Britain. The exchange programs are varied in terms of organizational characteristics. Some operate out of fixed sites; others are mobile. Some are legally authorized; others are not. Funding, staffing patterns, policies, and hours of operation vary considerably among the different programs.

Despite different organizational characteristics, the basic description and goals of NEPs are the same. They provide sterile needles in exchange for contaminated or used needles to increase access to sterile needles and to remove contaminated syringes from circulation in the community. Equally important, needle exchanges are there to establish contact with otherwise hard-to-reach populations to deliver health services, such as HIV testing and counseling, as well as referrals to treatment for drug abuse.

Over time, numerous questions have arisen about NEPs, such as whether these programs encourage drug use and whether they result in lower HIV incidence. These questions have been summarized and examined in a series of published reviews and Government-sponsored reports. The Government-sponsored reports include those from the National Commission on AIDS in 1991, the U.S. General Accounting Office in 1993, the University of California and Centers for Disease Control (CDC) Report in 1993, and the National Academy of Sciences in 1995.

As to whether NEPs increase drug use among participants, the 1993 California report examined published reports that involved comparison groups (Table 3.1). Because the sampling and data collection methods varied considerably among studies, the summary has been reduced here to show whether needle exchange was associated with a beneficial, neutral, or adverse effect. Of the eight reports that examined the issue of injection frequency, three showed a reduction in injection frequency, four showed a mixed or neutral effect (no change), and one initially recorded an increase in injection frequency.

In terms of attracting youth or new individuals into NEPs in the United States, programs that have no minimum age restriction have reported that recruitment of participants who are younger than 18 years old was consistently less than 1%; this low rate of use was noted in studies that were conducted in San Francisco and New Haven and in our recent studies in Baltimore. However, recent studies also have shown that new injectors who are adolescent or young adults also are at extremely high risk for HIV infection. In response to this problem, Los Angeles has recently developed an NEP specifically directed at new initiates into injection drug use (P. Kerndt, personal communication, February 10, 1996).

Another question is whether the presence of NEPs in a community conveys a message to youth that condones and encourages drug use. This issue is particularly difficult to study. In 1993, the authors of the University of California-CDC report examined longitudinal national drug use indicator data (data from the DAWN Project), which monitors emergency-room mentions of drug-abuse-related admissions. Comparisons of data before and

TABLE 3.1   Summary of Studies of Behavioral Change Within NEPS

Outcome Measures	Beneficial NEP Effect	Mixed or Neutral NEP Effect	Adverse NEP Effect
Drug risk:			
Sharing frequency	10	4	—
Give away syringes	3	1	1
Needle cleaning	3	1	—
Injection frequency	3	4	1
Sex risk:			
Number of partners	2	1	—
Partner choice	1	1	—
Condom use	1	1	1

after the opening of needle exchanges and between cities with and without NEPs showed no significant trends.

The only systematic study to date of trends in drug use within a community, following the opening of a needle exchange comes from Amsterdam. Using data on admissions to treatment for drug abuse, Buning and colleagues noted that the proportion of drug users younger than 22 declined from 14% in 1981 to 5% in 1986; the NEP opened in 1984. The opening of the needle exchange increased neither the proportion of drug users overall nor the proportion of those younger than 22 years. Thus, the currently available data argue against the belief that needle exchange encourages drug use.

Another issue is whether needle exchanges will result in more contaminated syringes found on the street. If a needle exchange is designed as a one-for-one exchange, the answer is no. In Baltimore, a carefully designed systematic street survey showed no increase in discarded needles following the opening of an NEP. An update following two years of surveys has shown a similar trend of no increase.

Findings of behavioral change associated with needle exchange are varied. A number of published studies have compared levels of risky behavior among IDUs participating and those not participating in needle exchange. As the University of California-CDC report noted, methods varied considerably among these published reports, so that the summary here (Table 3.1) sorts the studies into whether and how the needle exchange has shown an effect—risk reduction, no effect, or adverse effect.

In terms of drug risks, Table 3.1 shows that there were 14 studies that looked at the frequency of needle sharing, the most dangerous behavior in terms of drug-related risk of HIV transmission. In those studies, 10 showed a reduction in needle sharing frequency, four had no effect, and none showed any increase in needle sharing.

Similar trends were noted for the practice of giving away syringes: three showed a reduction in this practice, one no effect, and one an increase. Three out of four studies reporting on this needle cleaning showed a positive effect. Finally, in terms of sexual risk behavior, few studies overall have examined the impact of needle exchange on sexual risks. Sexual transmission among IDUs is an important area that merits further investigation.

The next question about NEPs is whether such programs actually reduce the incidence of HIV infection in IDUs. While the idea of using only sterile needles makes the question of efficacy seem obvious, the real question centers on how effective the programs are in practice and how subject such programs are to the ubiquitous "law of unintended consequences."

Studies of the impact of needle exchange on the incidence of HIV infection in the United States are few, primarily because funding for such evaluations is relatively recent and sample size requirements are large. The first study (shown in Table 3.2) was conducted by Hagan and colleagues in Tacoma, Washington. In that city, the prevalence and, therefore, the incidence of HIV were extremely low. A needle exchange was initiated with the goal of maintaining HIV incidence at a low level. Two case-controlled analyses used hepatitis B and hepatitis C virus infection as outcome variables because the epidemiology of these two viruses is similar to HIV, although transmission of hepatitis is more efficient than HIV In these studies, needle exchange participation was associated with more than an 80% reduction in the incidence of hepatitis infection. Over time, HIV prevalence has not risen.

In terms of HIV studies, Kaplan and Heimer at Yale utilized information about HIV test results of washes from syringes returned to the New Haven Needle Exchange Program

TABLE 3.2   Impact of NEPs on Incidence of Blood-Borne Infections in the United States

Author	City	Design	Outcome	Percent Reduction
Hagan et al.	Tacoma	Case-control	HBV	83
			HCV	86
Kaplan et al.	New Haven	Mathematical modeling based on testing of syringes returned to NEP	HIV	33
Des Jarlais et al.	New York	Prospective study of seroconversion; NEP is external cohort and IDUs in neighboring regions	HIV	70

by constructing an elegant statistical model to estimate that needle exchange reduced HIV incidence by 33%. This model has been reviewed by three independent statistical reviewers who have judged the model sound in estimates as reasonable or even conservative.

More recently, Des Jarlais and colleagues from New York City published a prospective study of seroconversion between attendees and nonattendees of needle exchange. In this study, they estimated a 70% reduction in HIV incidence. Several other studies are ongoing in San Francisco, Chicago, and Baltimore, but their findings are too preliminary to present at this time.

In terms of HIV seroconversion studies from needle exchanges with comparison groups from outside the United States, data are available from Amsterdam and Montreal. In Amsterdam, data from a case-control study nested within an ongoing cohort study identified a slightly increased risk of HIV seroconversion with needle exchange use. However, when the analyses were examined by calendar time, the needle exchange was initially protective, but the association reversed over time. The authors attributed their results to the needle exchange losing lower risk users to pharmacy access over time, leaving a core of highest risk users within the exchange.

More recently a study was published using a case-control analysis nested within a cohort study in Montreal. Of 974 HIV seronegative subjects followed an average of 22 months, 89 subjects seroconverted. Consistent use of needle exchange compared with nonuse was associated with an odds ratio for HIV seroconversion of 10.5, which remained elevated even during multivariate adjustment. The authors concluded that NEPs were associated with higher HIV rates and speculated that the exchange may have facilitated formation of new social networks that might have permitted broader HIV transmission. In an accompanying commentary, Lurie criticized the Montreal study saying that the more likely explanation for the findings was that powerful selection forces attracted the most risky IDUs as evidenced by substantial differences in the baseline data for the exchangers vs. nonexchangers: exchangers had higher injection frequencies, were less likely to have a history of drug abuse treatment, were more likely to share needles and use shooting galleries, and had a high HIV prevalence. Lurie attributed the differences to the hours and locations of the exchange (late night in the red-light district) attracting only a select subset of users.

In Vancouver, Strathdee reported on HIV incidence in a cohort of IDUs of whom 92% were enrolled in needle exchange. The incidence of 18.6 (100 person-years) was associated with low education, unstable housing, commercial sex, borrowing needles, injecting with others, and frequent use of needle exchange. The related study by Archibald and colleagues demonstrates a selection of higher risk individuals into needle exchange in Vancouver.

The point to consider is what accounts for the discrepancy between the U.S. and non-U.S. studies. From a methodological perspective, selection factors could be operating. For example, in Vancouver, a study compared characteristics of exchangers with those of nonexchangers, or high frequency vs. low frequency exchangers; this study showed that the high frequency exchangers were more likely to engage in high risk activities. While the Vancouver study showed that self-selection into needle exchange results in leaving a comparison group that is not similar in other respects, the data do suggest that needle exchange has been successful in recruiting high risk users.

At another level, the U.S. studies involve evaluation of a needle exchange in comparison with people who do not have access to an NEP or to sterile needles through other sources. In contrast, the Canadian and Dutch studies have involved comparisons that do have an alternative source for sterile needles, principally through pharmacies; their studies may have selected into the needle exchange the people who cannot get needles from pharmacies. The effectiveness of NEPs depends on understanding who constitutes the comparison group.

More recently, an ecological analysis was published with serial HIV seroprevalence data for 29 cities with NEPs and 52 cities without such programs. The results, although subject to a possible ecological fallacy, indicated a 5.8% decline in HIV prevalence per year in cities with NEPs and a 5.9% increase in cities without exchange.

Deregulating Syringe Prescription and Paraphernalia Laws

In 1992, Connecticut changed the state laws to permit sale and possession of up to 10 syringes at a time. The CDC, in conjunction with the state of Connecticut, conducted initial studies that examined whether IDUs utilized pharmacies and discovered that they did. The CDC and the state of Connecticut then examined how pharmacy utilization affected needle-sharing behaviors in the two samples of IDUs that were interviewed: 52% reported sharing needles before the law changed, and 31% did so after the law changed. While these data are encouraging, data on needle disposal and HIV incidence are not yet available.

Summary

Access to sterile needles and syringes is an important, even vital, component of a comprehensive HIV prevention program for IDUs. The data on needle exchange in the United States are consistent with the conclusion that these programs do not encourage use and that needle exchanges can be effective in reducing HIV incidence. Other data show that NEPs help people stop drug use through referral to drug treatment programs. The studies outside of the United States are important for reminding us that unintended consequences can occur. While changes in needle prescription and possession laws and regulations have shown promise, the identification of organizational components that improve or hinder effectiveness of needle exchange and pharmacy-based access are needed.

SELECTION 9

The following selection is a publication of the Center for AIDS Prevention Studies (CAPS) and the AIDS Research Institute, University of California, San Francisco, Thomas J. Coates, Director. It reinforces the position of the previous selection, encouraging needle exchange programs among IV drug abusers.

■ *Does IV Needle Exchange Work?*

Why Do We Need Needle Exchange?
More than a million people in the U.S. inject drugs frequently, at a cost to society in health care, lost productivity, accidents, and crime of more than $50 billion a year.[1] People who inject drugs imperil their own health. If they contract HIV or hepatitis, their needle-sharing partners, sexual partners and offspring may become infected.

It is estimated that half of all new HIV infections in the U.S. are occurring among injection drug users (IDUs).[2] For women, 61% of all AIDS cases are due to injection drug use or sex with partners who inject drugs. Injection drug use is the source of infection for more than half of all children born with HIV.[3]

Injection drug use is also the most common risk factor in persons with hepatitis C infection. Up to 90% of IDUs are estimated to be infected with hepatitis C, which is easily transmitted and can cause chronic liver disease. Hepatitis B is also transmitted via injection drug use.[4]

Needle exchange programs (NEPs) distribute clean needles and safely dispose of used ones for IDUs, and also generally offer a variety of related services, including referrals to drug treatment and HIV counseling and testing.

Why Do Drug Users Share Needles?
The overwhelming majority of IDUs are aware of the risk of the transmission of HIV and other diseases if they share contaminated equipment. However, there are not enough needles and syringes available and even these are often not affordable to IDUs.

Getting IDUs into treatment and off drugs would eliminate needle-related HIV transmission. Unfortunately, not all drug injectors are ready or able to quit. Even those who are highly motivated may find few services available. Drug treatment centers frequently have long waiting lists and relapses are common.

Most U.S. states have paraphernalia laws that make it a crime to possess or distribute drug paraphernalia "known to be used to introduce illicit drugs into the body."[5] In addition, ten states and the District of Columbia have laws or regulations that require a prescription to buy a needle and syringe. Consequently, IDUs often do not carry syringes for fear of

A publication of the Center for AIDS Prevention Studies (CAPS) and the AIDS Research Institute, University of California, San Francisco, Thomas J. Coates, Director. Reproduction of this text is encouraged; however, copies may not be sold, and the Center for AIDS Prevention Studies at the University of California, San Francisco, should be cited as the source of this information. For additional copies of this and other HIV Prevention Fact Sheets, please call the National Prevention Information Network at 800/458–5231. Comments and questions about this Fact Sheet may be e-mailed to CAPSWeb@psg.ucsf.edu.

police harassment or arrest. Concern with arrest for carrying drug paraphernalia has been associated with sharing syringes and other injection supplies.[6]

In July 1992, the state of Connecticut passed laws permitting the purchase and possession of up to ten syringes without a prescription and making parallel changes in its paraphernalia law. After the new laws went into effect, the sharing of needles among IDUs decreased substantially, and there was a shift from street needle and syringe purchasing to pharmacy purchasing.[7] However, even where over-the-counter sales of syringes are permitted by law, pharmacists are often unwilling to sell to IDUs, emphasizing the need for education and outreach to pharmacists.

What's Being Done?

Around the world and in more than 80 cities in 38 states in the U.S., NEPs have sprung up to address drug-injection risks. There are currently 113 NEPs in the U.S. In Hawaii, the NEP is funded by the state Department of Health. In addition to needle exchange, the program offers a centralized drug treatment referral system and a methadone clinic, as well as a peer-education program to reach IDUs who do not come to the exchange. Rates of HIV among IDUs have dropped from 5% in 1989 to 1.1% in 1994–96. From 1993–96, 74% of NEP clients reported no sharing of needles, and 44% of those who did report sharing reported always cleaning used needles with bleach.[8]

Harm Reduction Central in Hollywood, CA, is a storefront NEP that targets young IDUs aged 24 and under. The program provides needle exchange, arts programming, peer-support groups, HIV testing and case management and is the largest youth NEP in the U.S. Over 70% of clients reported no needle-sharing in the last 30 days, and young people who used the NEP on a regular basis were more likely not to share needles.[9]

Does Needle Exchange Reduce the Spread of HIV? Encourage Drug Use?

It is possible to significantly limit HIV transmission among IDUs. One study looked at five cities with IDU populations where HIV prevalence had remained low. Glasgow, Scotland; Lund, Sweden; New South Wales, Australia; Tacoma, WA; and Toronto, Ontario, all had the following prevention components: beginning prevention activities when levels of HIV infection were still low; providing sterile injection equipment through NEPs; and conducting community outreach to IDUs.[10]

A study of 81 cities around the world compared HIV infection rates among IDUs in cities that had NEPs with cities that did not have NEPs. In the 52 cities without NEPs, HIV infection rates increased by 5.9% per year on average. In the 29 cities with NEPs, HIV infection rates decreased by 5.8% per year. The study concluded that NEPs appear to lead to lower levels of HIV infection among IDUs.[11]

In San Francisco, CA, the effects of an NEP were studied over a five-year period. The NEP did not encourage drug use either by increasing drug use among current IDUs, or by recruiting significant numbers of new or young IDUs. On the contrary, from December 1986 through June 1992, injection frequency among IDUs in the community decreased from 1.9 injections per day to 0.7, and the percentage of new initiates into injection drug use decreased from 3% to 1%.[12]

Hundreds of other studies of NEPs have been conducted, and all have been summarized in a series of eight federally funded reports dating back to 1991. Each of the eight reports has concluded that NEPs can reduce the number of new HIV infections and do not appear to lead to increased drug use among IDUs or in the general community.[13, 14, 15]

These were the two criteria that by law had to be met before the federal ban on NEP service funding could be lifted. This is a degree of unanimity on the interpretation of research findings unusual in science. Five of the studies recommended that the federal ban be lifted and two made no recommendations. In the eighth report the Department of Health and Human Services decided that the two criteria had been met, but failed to lift the ban. The Congress has since changed the law, continuing to ban federal funding for NEPs, regardless of whether the criteria are met.

Is Needle Exchange Cost-Effective?

Yes. The median annual budget for running a program was $169,000 in 1992. Mathematical models based on those data predict that needle exchanges could prevent HIV infections among clients, their sex partners, and offspring at a cost of about $9,400 per infection averted.[16] This is far below the $195,188 lifetime cost of treating an HIV-infected person at present.[17] A national program of NEPs would have saved up to 10,000 lives by 1995.[13]

What Must Be Done?

Efforts to increase the availability of sterile needles must be a part of a broader strategy to prevent HIV among IDUs, including expanded access to drug treatment and drug-use prevention efforts. Although the U.S. federal government has acknowledged that NEPs reduce rates of HIV infection and do not increase drug use rates, it still refuses to provide funding for NEPs.[15] Therefore, advocacy activity at the state and local community level is critical. However, the federal government should play a more active role in advocating for NEPs publicly, even if it doesn't fund them.

States with prescription laws should repeal them; those with paraphernalia laws should revise them insofar as they restrict access to needles and syringes. Local governments, Community Planning Groups and public health officials should work with community groups to develop comprehensive approaches to HIV prevention among IDUs and their sexual partners, including NEPs and programs to increase access to sterile syringes through pharmacies.

Says Who?

1. Rice, D. P., Kelman, S., and Miller, L. S. Estimates of economic costs of alcohol and drug abuse and mental illness, 1985 and 1988. *Public Health Reports.* 1991;106:280–92.

2. Holmberg, S. D. The estimated prevalence and incidence of HIV in 96 large U.S. metropolitan areas. *American Journal of Public Health.* 1996;86:642–654.

3. Centers for Disease Control and Prevention (CDC). *HIV/AIDS Surveillance Report.* 1998;9:12.

4. Alter, M. J., and Moyer, L. A. The importance of preventing hepatitis C virus infection among injection drug users in the United States. *Journal of Acquired Immune Deficiency Syndromes and Human Retrovirology.* 1998; 18(Suppl 1):S6–10.

5. Gostin, L. O., Lazzarini, Z., Jones, T. S., et al. Prevention of HIV/AIDS and other blood-borne diseases among injection drug users: a national survey on the regulation of syringes and needles. *Journal of the American Medical Association.* 1997;277:53–62.

6. Bluthenthal, R. N., Kral, A. H., Erringer, E. A., et al. Drug paraphernalia laws and injection-related infectious disease risk among drug injectors. *Journal of Drug Issues.* (in press).

7. Groseclose, S. L., Weinstein, B., Jones, T. S., et al. Impact of increased legal access to needles and syringes on practices of injecting-drug users and police officers–Connecticut, 1992–1993. *Journal of Acquired Immune Deficiency Syndromes.* 1995;10:82–89.

8. Vogt, R. L., Breda, M. C., Des Jarlais, D. C., et al. Hawaii's statewide syringe exchange program. *American Journal of Public Health.* 1998;88:1403–1404.

9. Kipke, M. D., Edgington, R., Weiker, R. L., et al. HIV prevention for adolescent IDUs at a storefront needle exchange program in Hollywood, CA. Presented at 12th World AIDS Conference, Geneva, Switzerland. 1998. Abstract #23204.

10. Des Jarlais, D. C., Hagan, H., Friedman, S. R., et al. Maintaining low HIV seroprevalence in populations of injecting drug users. *Journal of the American Medical Association.* 1995;274:1226–1231.

11. Hurley, S. F., Jolley, D. J., and Kaldor, J. M. Effectiveness of needle-exchange programmes for prevention of HIV infection. *Lancet.* 1997;349:1797–1800.

12. Watters, J. K., Estilo, M. J., Clark, G. L., et al. Syringe and needle exchange as HIV/AIDS prevention for injection drug users. *Journal of the American Medical Association.* 1994; 271:115–120.

13. Lurie, P., and Drucker, E. An opportunity lost: HIV infections associated with lack of a national needle-exchange programme in the USA. *Lancet.* 1997;349:604–608.

14. Report from the NIH Consensus Development Conference. February 1997.

15. Goldstein, A. Clinton supports needle exchanges but not funding. *Washington Post.* April 21, 1998:A1.

16. Lurie, P., Reingold, A. L., Bowser, B., et al. The health impact of needle exchange programs in the United States and abroad. Prepared for the Centers for Disease Control and Prevention. October 1993.

17. Holtgrave, D. R., and Pinkerton, S. D. Updates of cost of illness and quality of life estimates for use in economic evaluations of HIV prevention programs. *Journal of Acquired Immune Deficiency Syndromes and Human Retrovirology.* 1997;16:54–62.

Prepared by Peter Lurie (Public Citizen's Health Research Group, CAPS) and Pamela DeCarlo (CAPS)

SELECTION 10

The following selection is an essay written by Joe Loconte for the Heritage Foundation journal *Policy Review* (July–August, 1998). Loconte is Deputy Editor of *Policy Review* and author of *Seducing the Samaritan: How Government Contracts Are Reshaping Social Security* (1997).

■ *Killing Them Softly*

JOE LOCONTE

The Clinton administration says giving clean needles to drug users will slow the spread of AIDS and save lives. But former addicts—and the specialists who treat them—say their greatest threats come from the soul-destroying culture of addiction.

In a midrise office building on Manhattan's West 37th Street, about two blocks south of the Port Authority bus terminal, sits the Positive Health Project, one of 11 needle-exchange outlets in New York City. This particular neighborhood, dotted by X-rated video stores, peep

Loconte, Joe (1998, July–August). Killing them softly. *Policy Review.* Washington, DC: Heritage Foundation, pp. 14–22. Reprinted with permission.

shows, and a grimy hot dog stand, could probably tolerate some positive health. But it's not clear that's what the program's patrons are getting.

The clients are intravenous (IV) drug users. They swap their used needles for clean ones and, it is hoped, avoid the AIDS virus, at least until their next visit. There's no charge, no hassles, no meddlesome questions. That's just the way Walter, a veteran heroin user, likes it.

"Just put me on an island and don't mess with me," he says, lighting up a cigarette.

A tall, thinnish man, Walter seems weary for his 40-some years. Like many of the estimated 250,000 IV drug users in this city, he has spent years shooting up and has bounced in and out of detoxification programs. "Don't get the idea in your mind you're going to control it," he says. "I thought I could control it. But dope's a different thing. You just want it." Can he imagine his life without drugs? "I'm past that," he says, his face tightening. "The only good thing I do is getting high."

Heroin First, Then Breathing

Supporters of needle-exchange programs (NEPs), from AIDS activists to Secretary of Health and Human Services Donna Shalala, seem to have reached the same verdict on Walter's life. They take his drug addiction as a given, but want to keep him free of HIV by making sure he isn't borrowing dirty syringes. Says Shalala, "This is another life-saving intervention." That message is gaining currency, thanks to at least 112 programs in 29 states, distributing millions of syringes each year.

Critics say free needles just make it easier for addicts to go about their business: abusing drugs. Ronn Constable, a Brooklynite who used heroin and cocaine for nearly 20 years, says he would have welcomed the needle-exchange program—for saving him money. "An addict doesn't want to spend a dollar on anything else but his drugs," he says.

Do needle exchanges, then, save lives or fuel addiction?

The issue flared up earlier this year when Shalala indicated the Clinton administration would lift the ban on federal funding. Barry McCaffrey, the national drug policy chief, denounced the move, saying it would sanction drug use. Fearing a political debacle, the White House upheld the federal ban but continues to trumpet the effectiveness of NEPs. Meanwhile, Representative Gerald Solomon and Senator Paul Coverdell are pushing legislation in Congress to extend the prohibition indefinitely.

There is more than politics at work here. The debate reveals a deepening philosophical rift between the medical and moral approaches to coping with social ills.

Joined by much of the scientific community, the Clinton administration has tacitly embraced a profoundly misguided notion: that we must not confront drug abusers on moral or religious grounds. Instead, we should use medical interventions to minimize the harm their behavior invites. Directors of needle-exchange outlets pride themselves on running "nonjudgmental" programs. While insisting they do not encourage illegal drug use, suppliers distribute "safe crack kits" explaining the best ways to inject crack cocaine. Willie Easterlins, an outreach worker at a needle-stocked van in Brooklyn, sums up the philosophy this way: "I have to give you a needle. I can't judge," he says. "That's the first thing they teach us."

This approach, however well intentioned, ignores the soul-controlling darkness of addiction and the moral freefall that sustains it. "When addicts talk about enslavement, they're not exaggerating," says Terry Horton, the medical director of Phoenix House, one of the nation's largest residential treatment centers. "It is their first and foremost priority. Heroin first, then breathing, then food."

It is true that needle-sharing among IV drug users is a major source of HIV transmission, and that the incidence of HIV is rising most rapidly among this group—a population of more than a million people. Last year, about 30 percent of all new HIV infections were linked to IV drug use. The Clinton administration is correct to call this a major public health risk.

Nevertheless, NEP advocates seem steeped in denial about the behavioral roots of the crisis, conduct left unchallenged by easy access to clean syringes. Most IV drug users, in fact, die not from HIV-tainted needles but from other health problems, overdoses, or homicide. By evading issues of personal responsibility, the White House and its NEP allies are neglecting the most effective help for drug abusers: enrollment in tough-minded treatment programs enforced by drug courts. Moreover, in the name of "saving lives," they seem prepared to surrender countless addicts to life on the margins—an existence of scheming, scamming, disease, and premature death.

Curious Science

Over the last decade, NEPs have secured funding from local departments of public health to establish outlets in 71 cities. But that may be as far as their political argument will take them: Federal law prohibits federal money from flowing to the programs until it can be proved they prevent AIDS without encouraging drug use.

It's no surprise, then, that advocates are trying to enlist science as an ally. They claim that numerous studies of NEPs prove they are effective. Says Sandra Thurman, the director of the Office of National AIDS Policy, "There is very little doubt that these programs reduce HIV transmission." In arguing for federal funding, a White House panel on AIDS recently cited "clear scientific evidence of the efficacy of such programs."

The studies, though suggestive, prove no such thing. Activists tout the results of a New Haven study, published in the *American Journal of Medicine,* saying the program reduces HIV among participants by a third. Not exactly. Researchers tested needles from anonymous users—not the addicts themselves—to see if they contained HIV. They never measured "seroconversion rates," the portion of participants who became HIV positive during the study. Even Peter Lurie, a University of Michigan researcher and avid NEP advocate, admits that "the validity of testing of syringes is limited." A likely explanation for the decreased presence of HIV in syringes, according to scientists, is sampling error.

Another significant report was published in 1993 by the University of California and funded by the U.S. Centers for Disease Control. A panel reviewed 21 studies on the impact of NEPs on HIV infection rates. But the best the authors could say for the programs was that none showed a higher prevalence of HIV among program clients.

Even those results don't mean much. Panel members rated the scientific quality of the studies on a five-point scale: one meant "not valid," three "acceptable," and five "excellent." Only two of the studies earned ratings of three or higher. Of those, neither showed a reduction in HIV levels. No wonder the authors concluded that the data simply do not, and for methodological reasons probably cannot, provide clear evidence that needle exchanges decrease HIV infection rates.

The Missing Link

The most extensive review of needle-exchange studies was commissioned in 1993 by the U.S. Department of Health and Human Services (HHS), which directed the National Academy of Sciences (NAS) to oversee the project. Their report, "Preventing HIV Transmission: The Role of Sterile Needles and Bleach," was issued in 1995 and set off a political firestorm.

"Well-implemented needle-exchange programs can be effective in preventing the spread of HIV and do not increase the use of illegal drugs," a 15-member panel concluded. It recommended lifting the ban on federal funding for NEPs, along with laws against possession of injection paraphernalia. The NAS report has emerged as the bible for true believers of needle exchange.

It is not likely to stand the test of time. A truly scientific trial testing the ability of NEPs to reduce needle-sharing and HIV transmission would set up two similar, randomly selected populations of drug users. One group would be given access to free needles, the other would not. Researchers would follow them for at least a year, taking periodic blood tests.

None of the studies reviewed by NAS researchers, however, were designed in this way. Their methodological problems are legion: Sample sizes are often too small to be statistically meaningful. Participants are self-selected, so that the more health-conscious could be skewing the results. As many as 60 percent of study participants drop out. And researchers rely on self-reporting, a notoriously untrustworthy tool.

"Nobody has done the basic science yet," says David Murray, the research director of the Statistical Assessment Service, a watchdog group in Washington, DC. "If this were the FDA applying the standard for a new drug, they would [block] it right there."

The NAS panel admitted its conclusions were not based on reviews of well-designed trials. Such studies, the authors agreed, *simply do not exist.* Not to worry, they said: "The limitations of individual studies do not necessarily preclude us from being able to reach scientifically valid conclusions." When all of the studies are considered together, they argued, the results are compelling.

"That's like tossing a bunch of broken Christmas ornaments in a box and claiming you have something nice and new and usable," Murray says. "What you have is a lot of broken ornaments." Two of the three physicians on the NAS panel, Lawrence Brown and Herbert Kleber, agree. They deny their report established anything like a scientific link between lower HIV rates and needle exchanges. "The existing data is flawed," says Kleber, executive vice president for medical research at Columbia University. "NEPs may, in theory, be effective, but the data doesn't prove that they are."

Some needle-exchange advocates acknowledge the dearth of hard science. Don Des Jarlais, a researcher at New York's Beth Israel Medical Center, writes in a 1996 report that "there has been no direct evidence that participation is associated with a lower risk" of HIV infection. Lurie, writing in the *American Journal of Epidermiology,* says that "no one study, on its own, should be used to declare the programs effective." Nevertheless, supporters insist, the "pattern of evidence" is sufficient to march ahead with the programs. . . .

Death-Defying Logic

Critics of needle exchanges are forced to admit there's a certain logic to the concept, at least in theory: Give enough clean needles to an IV drug user and he won't bum contaminated "spikes" when he wants a fix.

But ex-addicts themselves, and the medical specialists who treat them, say it isn't that simple. "People think that everybody in shooting galleries worries about AIDS or syphilis or crack-addicted babies. That's the least of people's worries," says Jean Scott, the director of adult programs at Phoenix House in Manhattan. "While they're using, all they can think about is continuing to use and where they're going to get their next high."

Indeed, the NEP crowd mistakenly assumes that most addicts worry about getting AIDS. Most probably don't: The psychology and physiology of addiction usually do not allow them the luxury. "Once they start pumping their system with drugs, judgment disappears. Memory disappears. Nutrition disappears. The ability to evaluate their life needs disappears," says Eric Voth, the chairman of the International Drug Strategy Institute and one of the nation's leading addiction specialists. "What makes anybody think they'll make clean needles a priority?"

Ronn Constable, now a program director at Teen Challenge International in New York, says his addiction consumed him 24 hours a day, seven days a week. Addicts call it "chasing the bag": shooting up, feeling the high, and planning the next hit before withdrawal. "For severe addicts, that's all they do," Constable says. "Their whole life is just scheming to get their next dollar to get their next bundle of dope."

Ernesto Margaro fed his heroin habit for seven years, at times going through 40 bags—or $400—a day. He recalls walking up to a notorious drug den in the Bedford-Stuyvestant section of Brooklyn with a few of his friends. A man stumbled out onto the sidewalk and collapsed. They figured he was dying.

Margaro opened a fire hydrant on him. "When he finally came to, the first thing we asked him was where he got that dope from," he says. "We needed to know, because if it made him feel like that, we were going to take just a little bit less than he did."

This is typical of the hardcore user: The newest, most potent batch of heroin on the streets, the one causing the most deaths, is in greatest demand. "They run around trying to find out who the dead person copped from," says Scott, a drug treatment specialist with 30 years' experience. "The more deaths you have, the more popular the heroin is. That's the mentality of the addict."

Needle Entrepreneurs

Some younger addicts may at first be fearful of the AIDS virus, though that concern probably melts away as they continue to shoot up. But the hardcore abusers live in a state of deep denial. "I had them dying next to me," Constable says. "One of my closest buddies withered away. I never thought about it."

Needle-exchange programs are doing brisk business all over the country: San Diego, Seattle, Denver, Baltimore, Boston, and beyond. San Francisco alone hands out 2.2 million needles a year. If most addicts really aren't worried about HIV, then why do they come?

In most states, it is difficult to buy drug paraphernalia without a prescription. That makes it hard, some claim, to find syringes. But drug users can get them easily enough on the streets. The main reason they go to NEPs, it seems, is that the outlets are a free source of needles, cookers, cotton, and bleach. They're also convenient. They are run from storefronts or out of vans, and they operate several days a week at regular hours.

And they are hassle-free. Users are issued ID cards that entitle them to carry drug paraphernalia wherever they go. Police are asked to keep their distance lest they scare off clients.

Most programs require that users swap their old needles for new equipment, but people aren't denied if they "forget" to bring in the goods. And most are not rigid one-for-one exchanges. Jose Castellar works an NEP van at the corner of South Fifth Street and Marcy Avenue in Brooklyn. On a recent Thursday afternoon, a man walked up and mechanically dropped off 18 syringes in a lunch sack. Castellar recognized him as a regular, and gave him back 28—standard procedure. "It's sort of like an incentive," he explains.

It's the "incentive" part of the program that many critics find so objectionable. An apparently common strategy of NEP clients is to keep a handful of needles for themselves and sell the rest. Says Margaro, "They give you five needles. That's $2 a needle, that's $10. That's your next fix. That's all you're worried about."

It may also explain why many addicts who know they are HIV positive—older users such as Walter—still visit NEPs. Nobody knows how many there are, because no exchanges require blood tests. In New York, health officials say that perhaps half of the older IV addicts on the streets are infected.

Defenders admit the system is probably being abused "An addict is an addict. He's going to do what he needs to maintain his habit," says Easterlins, who works a van for ADAPT, one of New York City's largest needle-exchange programs. Naomi Fatt, ADAPT's executive director, is a little more coy. "We don't knowingly participate" in the black market for drug paraphernalia, she says. And if NEP clients are simply selling their syringes to other drug users? "We don't personally care how they get their sterile needles. If that's the only way they can save their lives is to get these needles on the streets, is that really so awful?" . . .

Good and Ready?

Keeping drug users free of AIDS is a noble—but narrow—goal. Surely the best hope of keeping them alive is to get them off drugs and into treatment. Research from the National Institute for Drug Abuse (NIDA) shows that untreated opiate addicts die at a rate seven to eight times higher than similar patients in methadone-based treatment programs.

Needle suppliers claim they introduce addicts to rehab services, and Shalala wants local officials to include treatment referral in any new needle-exchange programs. But program staffers are not instructed to confront addicts about their drug habit. The assumption: Unless drug abusers are ready to quit on their own, it won't work.

This explains why NEP advocates smoothly assert they support drug treatment, yet gladly supply users with all the drug-injection equipment they need. "The idea that they will choose on their own when they're ready is nonsense," says Voth, who says he's treated perhaps 5,000 abusers of cocaine, heroin, and crack. "Judgment is one of the things that disappears with addiction. The worst addicts are the ones least likely to stumble into sobriety and treatment."

According to health officials, most addicts do not seek treatment voluntarily, but enter through the criminal-justice system. Even those who volunteer do so because of intense pressure from spouses or employers or raw physical pain from deteriorating health. In other words, they begin to confront some of the unpleasant consequences of their drug habit.

"The only way a drug addict is going to consider stopping is by experiencing pain," says Robert Dupont, a clinical professor of psychiatry at Georgetown University Medical

School. "Pain is what helps to break their delusion," says David Batty, the director of Teen Challenge in Brooklyn. "The faster they realize they're on a dead-end street, the faster they see the need to change." . . .

Reducing Harm

Needle-exchange advocates chafe at the thought of coercing drug users into treatment. This signals perhaps their most grievous omission: They refuse to challenge the self-absorption that nourishes drug addiction.

In medical terms, it's called "harm reduction"—accept the irresponsible behavior and try to minimize its effects with health services and education. Some needle exchanges, for example, distribute guides to safer drug use. A pamphlet from an NEP in Bridgeport, Connecticut, explains how to prepare crack cocaine for injection. It then urges users to "take care of your veins. Rotate injection sites. . . ."

"Harm reduction is the policy manifestation of the addict's personal wish," says Satel, "which is to use drugs without consequences." The concept is backed by numerous medical and scientific groups, including the American Medical Association, the American Public Health Association, and the National Academy of Sciences.

In legal terms, harm reduction means the decriminalization of drug use. Legalization advocates, from financier George Soros to the Drug Policy Foundation, are staunch needle-exchange supporters. San Francisco mayor Willie Brown, who presides over perhaps the nation's busiest needle programs, is a leading voice in the harm-reduction chorus. "It is time," he has written, "to stop allowing moral or religious tradition to define our approach to a medical emergency."

It is time, rather, to stop medicalizing what is fundamentally a moral problem. Treatment communities that stress abstinence, responsibility, and moral renewal, backed up by tough law enforcement, are the best hope for addicts to escape drugs and adopt safer, healthier lifestyles.

Despite different approaches, therapeutic communities share at least one goal: drug-free living. Though they commonly regard addiction as a disease, they all insist that addicts take full responsibility for their cure. Program directors aren't afraid of confrontation, they push personal responsibility, and they tackle the underlying causes of drug abuse.

The Clinton administration already knows these approaches are working. NIDA recently completed a study of 10,010 drug abusers who entered nearly 100 different treatment programs in 11 cities. Researchers looked at daily drug use a year before and a year after treatment. Longterm residential settings—those with stringent anti-drug policies—did best. Heroin use dropped by 71 percent, cocaine use by 68 percent, and illegal activity in general by 62 percent.

NEP supporters are right to point out that these approaches are often expensive and cannot reach most of the nation's estimated 1.2 million IV drug users. Syringe exchanges, they say, are a cost-effective alternative.

NEPs may be cheaper to run, but they are no alternative; they offer no remedy for the ravages of drug addiction. The expense of long-term residential care surely cannot be greater than the social and economic costs of failing to liberate large populations from drug abuse. . . .

Brave New World?

Whether secular or religious, therapeutic communities all emphasize the "community" part of their strategy. One reason is that addicts must make a clean break not only from their drug use, but from the circle of friends who help them sustain it. That means a 24-hour-a-day regimen of counseling, education, and employment, usually for 12 to 24 months, safely removed from the culture of addiction.

This is the antithesis of needle-exchange outlets, which easily become magnets for drug users and dealers. Nancy Sosman, a community activist in Manhattan, calls the Lower East Side Harm Reduction Center and Needle Exchange Program "a social club for junkies." Even supporters such as Bruneau warn that NEPs could instigate "new socialization" and "new sharing networks" among otherwise isolated drug users. Some, under the banner of AIDS education, hail this function of the programs. Allan Clear, the executive director of New York's Harm Reduction Coalition, told one magazine, "There needs to be a self-awareness of what an NEP supplies: a meeting place where networks can form."

Meanwhile, activists decry a lack of drug paraphernalia for eager clients. They call the decision to withhold federal funding "immoral." They want NEPs massively expanded, some demanding no limits on distribution. Says one spokesman, "The one-to-one rule in needle exchange isn't at all connected to reality." New York's ADAPT program gives out at least 350,000 needles a year. "But to meet the demand," says Fatt, "we'd need to give out a million a day."

A million a day? Now that would be a Brave New World: Intravenous drug users with lots of drugs, all the needles they want, and police-free zones in which to network. Are we really to believe this strategy will contain the AIDS virus?

This is not compassion, it is ill-conceived public policy. This is not "saving lives," but abandoning them—consigning countless thousands to drug-induced death on the installment plan. For when a culture winks at drug use, it gets a population of Walters: "Don't get the idea in your mind you're going to control it."

Looking at Both Sides—The Debate Continues

The core arguments with regard to the promotion of needle exchange programs are aptly represented in the following two excerpts from selections in this chapter:

> Efforts to increase the availability of sterile needles must be a part of a broader strategy to prevent HIV among IDUs [intravenous drug users], including expanded access to drug treatment and drug-use prevention efforts. Although the U.S. federal government has acknowledged that NEPs [needle-exchange programs] reduce HIV infection and do not increase drug use rates, it still refuses to provide funding for NEPs. Therefore, advocacy activity at a state and local community level is critical. (from the Center for AIDS Prevention Studies, San Francisco, selection 9)

> Critics [of NEPs] say free needles just make it easier for addicts to go about their business: abusing drugs. . . . Joined by much of the scientific community, the Clinton administration has tacitly embraced a profoundly misguided notion: that we must not confront drug abusers

on moral or religious grounds. Instead, we should use medical interventions to minimize the harm their behavior invites. . . . This approach, however well intentioned, ignores the soul-controlling darkness of addiction and the moral freefall that sustains it. . . . NEP advocates seem steeped in denial about the behavioral roots of the crisis, conduct left unchallenged by easy access to clean syringes. (from Loconte's article, selection 10)

Matters to Ponder

- How would you feel if a friend of yours became an IV heroin abuser and continued his or her drug-taking behavior through a needle-exchange program in your community?
- How do you feel about Loconte's assertion that needle-exchange programs do not address the root cause of drug addiction? If this is true, what other factors, do you think, are involved?

Further Sources to Seek Out

Infectious diseases and drug abuse. (1999, August). *NIDA Notes* (a publication of the National Institute on Drug Abuse, National Institutes of Health, U.S. Department of Health and Human Services), p. 15. An excellent summary of aspects of needle-exchange programs from a public-health perspective.

Lurie, P., and Druiker, E. (1997). An opportunity lost: HIV infections associated with lack of a national needle-exchange programme in the USA. *Lancet, 349,* pp. 604–608. An analysis of HIV-infection prevention, as viewed from a medical perspective.

National Institute on Drug Abuse. (1995). *Cooperative agreement for AIDS community-based outreach/intervention research program, 1990–present.* Rockville, MD: National Institute on Drug Abuse. A summary of the role of needle-exchange programs in the context of AIDS intervention, as of the mid-1990s.

Web Sites to Explore

www.caps.ucsf.edu
The web site for the Center for AIDS Prevention Studies and the AIDS Research Institute, University of California, San Francisco, where needle exchange program information can be found.

www.drcnet.org
The web site for the Drug Reform Coordination Network, for a variety of publications related to harm-reduction approaches in drug abuse, including needle exchange programs.

Question: Should Harm Reduction Be Our Overall Goal in Fighting Drug Abuse?

To say that we are waging a "war on drugs" is, in effect, communicating how serious we are in dealing with the problems of drug abuse in the United States. Using the metaphor of warfare, we recognize that there is an acknowledged enemy (drug abuse), there are victims or casualties (us), resources at our disposal to fight the necessary battles (federal and state governments, communities, parents, etc.) and there is a high price to pay (in excess of $18 billion of federal funds each year). The operating plan of battle is established by the set of federal penalties currently in place for drug trafficking, according to each of the five schedules of controlled substances (Table 4.1) and marijuana (Table 4.2).

The implications of this real-life struggle, such as our overall strategy and ultimate goals, are also drawn in metaphorical terms. Do we want total victory and complete annihilation of the enemy? Or do we want some kind of negotiated settlement, some type of compromise, that gives us some semblance of peace and tranquility? If it is the former, then we require a total elimination, often expressed as "zero tolerance" of abusive drug-taking behavior in America. If it is the latter, then we require a good deal less. We desire, in that case, only a reduction of the harmful consequences of abusive drug-taking behavior, knowing fully well that a total elimination is unrealistic. This is essentially our dilemma, and the core issue for this chapter. What does the American public really want? Which way should we direct our drug policies?

The harm-reduction approach in drug policy has its historical roots in the libertarian philosophy of the nineteenth-century philosopher John Stuart Mill who argued that the state did not have the duty to protect individual citizens from harming themselves. As Mill expressed it,

> The only purpose for which power can be rightfully exercised over any member of a civilised community, against his will, is to prevent harm to others. His own good, either physical or moral, is not a sufficient warrant. . . .Over himself, over his own body and mind, the individual is sovereign.

On the other hand, it is readily evident that drug-taking behavior does indeed harm other people. We can look to the violence of illicit drug trafficking and the disruption in the lives of drug abusers' family and friends. The question, according to those advocating a harm-

TABLE 4.1 Current Federal Penalties for Drug Trafficking, According to Each of Five Controlled Substance Schedules (CSS)

CSS	2nd Offense Penalty	1st Offense Penalty	Quantity	Drug	Quantity	1st Offense Penalty	2nd Offense Penalty
I and II	Not less than 10 years. Not more than life. If death or serious injury, not less than life. Fine or not more than $4 million individual, $10 million other than individual.	Not less than 5 years. Not more than 40 years. If death or serious injury, not less than 20 years. Not more than life. Fine of not more than $2 million individual, $5 million other than individual.	10–99 or 100–999 gm mixture	Methamphetamine	100 gm or more or 1 kg[a] or more mixture	Not less than 10 years. Not more than life. If death or serious injury, not less than 20 years. Not more than life. Fine of not more than $4 million individual, $10 million other than individual.	Not less than 20 years. Not more than life. If death or serious injury, not less than life. Fine of not more than $8 million individual, $20 million other than individual.
			100–999 gm mixture	Heroin	1 kg or more mixture		
			500–4,999 gm mixture	Cocaine	5 kg or more mixture		
			5–49 gm mixture	Cocaine base	50 gm or more mixture		
			10–99 gm or 100—999 gm mixture	PCP	100 gm or more or 1 kg or more mixture		
			1–10 gm mixture	LSD	10 gm or more mixture		
			40–399 gm mixture	Fentanyl	400 gm or more mixture		
			10–99 gm mixture	Fentanyl analogue	100 gm or more mixture		

	Drug	Quantity	1st Offense Penalty	2nd Offense Penalty
	Others[b]	Any	Not more than 20 years. If death or serious injury, not less than 20 years, not more than life. Fine $1 million on individual, $5 million not individual.	Not more than 30 years. If death or serious injury, life. Fine $2 million individual, $10 million not individual.
III	All	Any	Not more than 5 years. Fine not more than $250,000 individual, $1 million not individual.	Not more than 10 years. Fine not more than $500,000 individual, $2 million not individual.
IV	All	Any	Not more than 3 years. Fine not more than $250,000 individual, $1 million not individual.	Not more than 6 years. Fine not more than $500,000 individual, $2 million not individual.
V	All	Any	Not more than 1 year. Fine not more than $100,000 individual, $250,000 not individual.	Not more than 2 years. Fine not more than $200,000 individual, $500,000 not individual.

[a]Law as originally enacted stated 100 gm. Congress requested technical correction to 1 kg.

[b]Does not include marijuana, hashish, or hash oil.

Note: Trafficking penalties distinguish between Schedule 1 drugs excluding marijuana (above) and marijuana itself (Table 4.2, page 72).

Source: Drug Enforcement Administration, U.S. Department of Justice. Reprinted from Levinthal, Charles F. (2002). *Drugs, behavior, and modern society* (3rd edition). Boston: Allyn and Bacon, Table 17.1. Reprinted with permission.

TABLE 4.2   Current Federal Penalties for Drug Trafficking for Marijuana and Other Cannabis Products

Quantity	Description	1st Offense	2nd Offense
1,000 kg or more; or 1,000 or more plants	Marijuana Mixture containing detectable quantity[a]	Not less than 10 years, not more than life. If death or serious injury, not less than 20 years, not more than life. Fine not more than $4 million individual, $10 million other than individual.	Not less than 20 years, not more than life. If death or serious injury, not less than life. Fine not more than $8 million individual, $20 million other than individual.
100 kg to 1,000 kg; or 100–999 plants	Marijuana Mixture containing detectable quantity	Not less than 5 years, not more than 40 years. If death or serious injury, not less than 20 years, not more than life. Fine not more than $2 million individual, $5 million other than individual.	Not less than 10 years, not more than life. If death or serious injury, not less than life. Fine not more than $4 million individual, $10 million other than individual.
50 to 100 kg 10 to 100 kg 1 to 100 kg 50–99 plants Less than 50 kg Less than 10 kg Less than 1 kg	Marijuana Hashish Hashish Oil Marijuana Marijuana Hashish Hashish Oil	Not less than 20 years. If death or serious injury, not less than 20 years, not more than life. Fine $1 million individual, $5 million other than individual. Not more than 5 years. Fine not more than $250,000, $1 million other than individual.	Not more than 30 years. If death or serious injury, life. Fine $2 million individual, $10 million other than individual. Not more than 10 years. Fine not more than $500,000 individual, $2 million other than individual.

[a]Includes hashish and hashish oil.

Source: Drug Enforcement Administration, U.S. Department of Justice. Reprinted from Levinthal, Charles F. (2002). *Drugs, behavior, and modern society* (3rd edition). Boston: Allyn and Bacon, Table 17.1. Reprinted with permission.

reduction strategy, is to look for policies that reduce the harm that drugs do, both directly to the drug user and indirectly to others.

On the opposite end of the debate are advocates for a drug policy that is based upon the goal of absolute deterrence, brought about by law enforcement. Sociologist Erich Goode has put it this way:

> . . . .they do not believe simply that law enforcement is more likely to "contain" or keep a given activity at a lower level than no enforcement at all. Even further, they believe (or, at

least, in their speeches, they state) that law enforcement, if not restrained by loopholes, technicalities, and restrictions, will actually reduce that activity, ideally, nearly to zero. In short, we *can* win the war on drugs, the cultural conservative asserts, if we have sufficient will, determination, and unity.

Those who argue that a reduction of the harmful consequences of abusive drug-taking behavior is the optimal strategy can be seen as following a middle path between, on one hand, those who advocate stronger law enforcement and interdiction efforts to eliminate all drugs and, on the other hand, those who advocate an approach in which presently illegal drugs are legalized and thus made available to the American public. Drug problems, as the harm-reductionists argue, are more a result of the harsh and absolutist system of prohibitions now in place than the drugs themselves. As expressed in the introduction to this book, there is no doubt that the misery endured by drug-dependent individuals, their families and associates, and society in general is immense. The debate is in the strategy that is best suited to contend with the horrific conditions in which we now live.

Robert J. MacCoun, in an influential essay written in 1998, "Toward a psychology of harm reduction," has examined two major criticisms leveled at harm-reduction advocates:

- Does harm reduction literally send the wrong message? As he has expressed it, " . . . if we provide heroin users with clean needles, they might infer that we don't expect them to quit using heroin—if we did, why give them needles? Arguably, this perception could undermine their motivation to quit."
- Does harm reduction make drugs more attractive? MacCoun writes, " . . . if the perceived risks were motivating (drug abusers) to behave somewhat self-protectively, a reduction in risk should lead them to take fewer precautions than before, raising the probability of their unsafe conduct to a higher level."

We will return to the MacCoun essay at the end of this chapter.

Obviously, strong emotional factors are at play here, as we will see in the three selections in this chapter. In the first selection, Bruce D. Glasscock expresses the perspective of a law enforcement officer. In the second selection, Robert J. MacCoun and Peter Reuter address the success or failure of policies by other nations with respect to drug-taking behavior. The harm-reduction position is argued by the noted pharmacologist Avram Goldstein, from the second edition (2001) of his influential 1994 book *Addiction: From Biology to Drug Policy.*

REFERENCES

Goode, Erich (1997). *Between politics and reason: The drug legalization debate.* New York: St. Martin's Press. Quotation on page 58.

How did we get here? History has a habit of repeating itself (2001, July 28–August3). *The Economist,* pp. 4–5. Quotation of John Stuart Mill on page 5.

MacCoun, Robert J. (1998). Toward a psychology of harm reduction. *American Psychologist, 53,* 1199–1208. Quotations on pages 1202 and 1203.

SELECTION 11

The following selection is congressional testimony of Bruce D. Glasscock, Chief of the Plano, Texas, Police Department and 2nd Vice President of the International Association of Chiefs of Police, before the House Committee on Government Reform, Subcommittee on Criminal Justice, Drug Policy, and Human Resources, Washington, DC, on July 13, 1999.

■ *Congressional Testimony in Opposition to Drug Legalization*

BRUCE D. GLASSCOCK

Good Morning, Mr. Chairman and Members of the Subcommittee.

My name is Bruce Glasscock; I am the Chief of the Plano, Texas, Police Department and also serve as 2nd Vice President of the International Association of Chiefs of Police. I am pleased to be here this morning to share my experience in combating drug abuse and my views on the question of drug legalization. The issue of drug legalization is of great concern to those of us in the law enforcement community. It is my belief the nature of our profession provides law enforcement officials with a unique insight into the ravages caused by the abuse of narcotics and other dangerous drugs. These experiences have clearly demonstrated to me that this Nation should not be considering legalizing drugs, but rather we should increase our efforts to combat drug traffickers and assisting those individuals who have become addicted on drugs to break the cycle of addiction.

Over the last few years, my position as Chief of the Plano Police Department has provided me with a firsthand look at the problems and dangers that accompany drug abuse. The recent heroin overdose death of former Dallas Cowboy Mark Tuinci received extensive national media coverage; unfortunately, it was not the first such occurrence in Plano. Our community was faced with a series of events involving heroin overdoses that resulted in our taking an aggressive plan of action in dealing with drug abuse. In June 1995 the City of Plano experienced its first heroin-related death. Additionally, between 1995 and 1996, our detectives noted an increase in burglaries being committed by heroin addicts to support their addictions. During this same time period local hospitals reported they were seeing about 6 overdoses a week, some of which resulted in death. Between 1995 and YTD 1999, there were 18 heroin overdose deaths related to Plano in some fashion—1 in 1995; 3 in 1996; 9 in 1997; 3 in 1998; and 2 deaths so far in 1999. The victims of these deaths were not your stereotypical drug addicts. The average age was 20 years old (range 14–36); most were young adolescent white males; most considered your average "All American Kid." Because of the rise in incidences of heroin overdoses, in early 1997 the Plano Police Department adopted a multifaceted strategy to attack the heroin crisis.

Testimony by Bruce D. Glasscock, Chief of the Plano, Texas, Police Department and 2nd Vice President of the International Association of Chiefs of Police, before the House Committee on Government Reform, Subcommittee on Criminal Justice, Drug Policy, and Human Resources, Washington, DC, July 13, 1999.

First, we undertook aggressive enforcement action to identify and prosecute those responsible for supplying the heroin. The police department joined with the DEA, FBI, Texas Department of Public Safety, and other local law enforcement agencies in a coordinated effort.

Because of this effort, 29 individuals were indicted on federal charges of conspiring to distribute heroin and cocaine, as well as charges of contributing to heroin overdose deaths. Another of our enforcement actions involved an undercover operation in our senior high schools, which resulted in the arrest of 37 individuals on 84 cases of narcotics violations. We believe our enforcement actions have greatly reduced the amount of heroin being sold in the Plano community and the number of heroin overdoses.

The second part of this strategy involved using education as a means to reduce the demand for heroin. The DEA's Demand Reduction Specialist, who provided us with guidance in demand reduction, spoke at community meetings, helped utilize the media effectively, and assisted us in this effort. During this time our department hosted several community meetings, the largest occurring in November of 1997. This meeting was attended by more than 1,800 citizens and was televised and covered by the national and local media as well as the city cable television network. Our education efforts would not have been successful if it were not for the cooperation of the Plano Community Task Force, Plano's Promise, and many other community organizations not affiliated with the police department. These community organizations provided education programs with high school groups, PTA's, neighborhood associations, church and parent groups. In addition to the above-mentioned strategies, our department is involved with several organizations that are working to continue the fight against drug abuse. These organizations strive to prevent drug usage through education, as well as intervention. The department is currently involved with the Kick Drugs Out of America Program, which is a school-based program designed to teach children the skills needed to resist drug and gang-related pressure. This program is in addition to the police department-run D.A.R.E. program, which also teaches elementary school children the risks of drugs and how to resist peer pressure.

We are currently working with a nonprofit organization in Florida that offers home drug-testing kits to families. This organization, Drug Free America, offers a free and anonymous way for parents to find out if their children are using drugs. If the child tests positive for drugs, Drug Free America provides the family with support organizations in or near the community to help with intervention efforts.

Our statistics show a clear reduction in the number of heroin overdose deaths, as well as hospitals reporting a reduction in overdose cases, which leads to the conclusion our strategy is working. Our continuing investigations also show a reduced availability of heroin on the streets in our community. Unfortunately, the battle is not over. Our drug risk assessment continues to show the North Texas area is a major hub for shipment and distribution of a variety of illegal drugs by Mexican drug traffickers. These drugs include methamphetamine, heroin, cocaine, and marijuana.

The porous Texas/Mexico border has 1,241 miles of frontier that challenges all our local, state, and federal resources. Since the enactment of the North American Free Trade Agreement (NAFTA) the major ports of entry have experienced approximately a

30 percent increase in legitimate commercial and passenger traffic. The number of vehicles inspected has increased, but the overall inspection rate has decreased, affording new opportunities for smuggling. Our statistics show, since passage of NAFTA in 1992, Texas had the highest volume of drug trafficking in the nation. All of this directly impacts local communities located along the NAFTA transportation corridors and will continue to do so.

This massive effort represents what just one city faces and has gone through to combat the flow of drugs into its community in order to protect its citizens. Plano is not unique; similar scenarios are being repeated in communities throughout the nation. Combined strategies like the ones I have just described to you are expensive, complex to manage, and sometimes controversial. However, they are working. Unfortunately, if those who favor legalization have their way, our efforts to reduce crime and protect our children from the horrors of drug abuse will be wasted. It is a simple fact: increased drug abuse and increased crime go hand in hand. It makes no difference whether users can purchase their drugs legally or not, they must still find a way to pay for them. And the way most drug addicts finance their habits is through crime. Eventually they will do one of two things—"they will either steal or deal." This is not just speculation on my part; in 1996 a study conducted by the National Institute of Justice clearly demonstrated drug users are more likely to be involved in criminal activities.

The findings in this study indicated that a median 68 percent of arrestees test positive for at least one drug at arrest, and the same study conducted in 1995 revealed that 31 percent of both male and female arrestees reported that they were under the influence of drugs or alcohol at the time they committed crimes. That year's report also indicated that 28 percent of inmates arrested for homicides were under the influence of drugs when they committed that crime.

In 1986, during the midst of the crack epidemic, violent crime reached a level of 617 violent crimes per 100,000 citizens. As we experienced a continuing escalation of drug-related violence, this figure rose in 1993 to 746 violent crimes for every 100,000 citizens. In response, an outraged public joined together with government leaders to challenge the escalating violent crime. As a result of these efforts vigorous new enforcement programs were implemented in the 1990s that have begun to reverse this trend. In recent years, we have seen a decrease in the violent crime rate in many communities—such as New York City, Boston, and Houston—attributable to aggressive law enforcement efforts and the incarceration of criminals. We know vigorous law enforcement actions aimed at criminal activity, including illegal drug use, can have a material effect on reducing violent crime in our communities. After making progress against violent crime during the past several years, we should not erode these gains by instituting policies such as the legalization of drugs, which we know will increase drug use and drug-related crime.

In addition, aside from the fact that legalization will lead to an increase in the level of crime and violence in our communities, increased drug use has terrible consequences for our citizens in other ways. Drug-related illness, death, and crime are estimated to cost Americans almost $67 billion a year. That translates into every American having to pay $1,000 per year to carry the costs of health care, extra law enforcement, car crashes, crime, and lost productivity due to drug use.

Drug use also impacts on the productivity of America's workers. Seventy-one percent of all illicit drug users are 18 or older and employed. In a study conducted by the U.S. Postal Service, the data collected shows that among drug users, absenteeism is 66 percent higher and health benefits utilization is 84 percent greater in dollar terms when compared against other workers. Disciplinary actions are 90 percent higher for employees who are drug users, as compared to non-drug users.

Public safety is another critical area that is impacted by drug abuse. A 1993 National Highway Traffic Safety Administration study reported that 18 percent of 2,000 fatally injured drivers from seven states had drugs other than alcohol in their systems when they died.

I trust it is clear by now why other law enforcement officials and I believe the legalization of drugs is the wrong course for our Nation to take. Drug legalization will lead to increased crime; a decline in economic productivity; significantly increase the burden on an already strained health care system; endanger those traveling on our roadways; and, perhaps most tragically, sends a message to our children that drug use is acceptable.

The Partnership for a Drug Free America reported the results of a recent survey showing that as young Americans perceive that drugs are dangerous, drug use drops proportionately. Conversely, as young Americans get the message that social disapproval drops, as they hear the legalization debate, drug use increases. Drug use in America was reduced significantly between the year 1985 through 1992. Since 1992, and until recently, the amount of antidrug messages has decreased. As recently retired DEA Administrator Tom Constantine once said, ". . .as a nation we took our eye off the ball and began to get complacent about drugs—drug use among young people began to rise again in 1992." The legalization movement and the growing destigmatization of drugs, along with the confusing message we are giving our young people, will result in further decreases in the perceptions of risk, and I believe a concurrent increase in drug use among our youth.

Within this atmosphere it is very difficult—if not impossible—to reach children and convince them that doing drugs is bad. We must not make it easier or more acceptable for today's young people to start down the slippery slope from drug experimentation to drug addiction. We, as a nation, must continue to clearly, and unequivocally, state that drug use is dangerous, drug use is unhealthy, and drug use is illegal.

This concludes my statement. I thank you for the opportunity to appear here today and I will be happy to answer any questions you may have.

SELECTION 12

The following selection is the Congressional testimony of Robert J. MacCoun and Peter Reuter, before the House Committee on Government Reform, Subcommittee on Criminal Justice, Drug Policy, and Human Resources, Washington, DC, on July 13, 1999. MacCoun is Professor of Public Policy and Law at the University of California at Berkeley and Reuter is Professor of Public Affairs and Criminology at the University of Maryland. Both are consultants to RAND's Drug Policy Research Center.

▪ *Congressional Testimony in Favor of a Harm-Reduction Policy*

ROBERT J. MACCOUN AND PETER REUTER

Thank you for the opportunity to testify. I ask that my written statement be entered into the record. Professor Reuter and I have spent almost a decade analyzing the likely consequences of alternative legal regimes for the currently illicit drugs. We have examined (a) data on policies and outcomes in Western Europe and Australia; (b) historical American experiences with legal cocaine and heroin, and with the prohibition of alcohol; and (c) experiences controlling other vices, including gambling, prostitution, tobacco, and alcohol. Our research will be published in a book next year by Cambridge University Press. Decriminalization, legalization, and harm reduction are three distinct concepts. Unfortunately, these terms are often used interchangeably in the policy debate. From a policy standpoint it is unhelpful to blur these distinctions because these three strategies differ in their likely benefits and their likely risks. The empirical base for projecting consequences of a change in law is strongest for marijuana decriminalization, weaker for marijuana legalization, and quite weak for the decriminalization or legalization of cocaine or heroin. There is a fairly sizeable body of evidence regarding needle exchange, a form of harm reduction, but we will not discuss that topic due to time limitations.

Marijuana Decriminalization in the United States and Australia

In brief, decriminalization refers to the elimination or substantial reduction of penalties for possession of modest quantities of the drug in question. Depending on the jurisdiction, possession may or may not be punished by a civil fine; multiple offenses or serious offenses may trigger criminal prosecution. But it is important to emphasize that in a decriminalization regime, the sale and manufacture of the drug remains illegal and is criminally prosecuted. Marijuana has been decriminalized in 11 U.S. states, in some regions of Australia, and in the Netherlands, Italy, and Spain. Italy and Spain have also decriminalized possession of heroin and cocaine; the Netherlands and Australia have not.

   Several lines of evidence—on the deterrent effects of marijuana laws and on decriminalization experiences in the United States, the Netherlands, and Australia—suggest that eliminating (or significantly reducing) criminal penalties for first-time possession of small quantities of marijuana has either no effect or a very small effect on the prevalence of marijuana use. There are several statistical analyses of survey data on marijuana use in decriminalization and nondecriminalization states. Survey analyses in decriminalizing states have found either no change in marijuana use, or an increase that was slight and temporary. Decriminalization was not associated with any detectable changes in adolescent attitudes toward marijuana. Most cross-state comparisons have found no difference in adolescent marijuana use in decriminalization vs. nondecriminalization states.

Testimony by Robert J. MacCoun and Peter Reuter, before the House Committee on Government Reform, Subcommittee on Criminal Justice, Drug Policy, and Human Resources, Washington, DC, July 13, 1999. Footnotes omitted.

These actual changes in marijuana laws and their enforcement were fairly subtle; arrest rates for marijuana possession are the same in those U.S. states that decriminalized and those that did not, though in the decriminalization states the penalties are presumably less severe. When MacCoun asks his undergraduate students at Berkeley whether they are in favor of California removing penalties for the possession of small amounts of marijuana about two-thirds say yes and the rest are opposed. Almost none know that it already occurred 25 years ago.

But the conclusion that cannabis decriminalization in the U.S. had little or no effect is bolstered by evidence from a similar policy change in two regions of Australia. Studies of decriminalization in South Australia and in the Australian Capital Territory report no changes in marijuana use associated with this legal change, and no differences in marijuana use between these regions and nondecriminalization regions of Australia.

Dutch Cannabis Policy

Our statements about marijuana decriminalization should not be generalized to marijuana legalization. Legalization goes well beyond the decriminalization of user possession to allow some form of legally regulated sales or distribution. We know of only one contemporary example that comes close to marijuana legalization, and that's the Dutch model of de facto legalization.

Dutch cannabis policy and its effects are routinely mischaracterized by both sides in the U.S. drug debate. Much of the confusion hinges on a failure to distinguish between two very different aspects of Dutch policy—decriminalization of personal possession vs. the nonprosecution of commercial sales and promotion.

In compliance with international treaty obligations, Dutch law states unequivocally that cannabis is illegal. Yet in 1976 the Dutch adopted a formal written policy of nonenforcement for violations involving possession or sale of up to 30 grams (5 grams since 1995) of cannabis—a sizable quantity, since one gram is probably sufficient for three joints. Not only are prosecutors forbidden to act against users but a formal written policy regulates the technically illicit sale of those small amounts in licensed coffee shops and nightclubs. The Dutch implemented this system of quasi-legal commercial availability to avoid excessive punishment of casual users and to weaken the link between soft and hard drug markets; the coffee shops allow marijuana users to avoid street dealers, who may also traffic in other drugs.

In a 1997 article in *Science* magazine, we argued that Dutch policy evolved from a decriminalization regime (mid-1970s to mid-1980s) to a commercialization regime (mid-1980s to 1995), and that these two phases appear to have had quite different consequences. The initial decriminalization phase had no detectable impact on levels of cannabis use, consistent with evidence from the U.S. and Australia. Survey data showed literally no increase in youth or adult use from 1976 to about 1984, and Dutch rates were well below those in the U.S. Marijuana was not very accessible, being sold or traded in just a few obscurely placed outlets.

But between 1980 and 1988, the number of coffee shops selling cannabis in Amsterdam increased tenfold; the shops spread to more prominent and accessible locations in the central city and began to promote the drug more openly. Coffee shops now account for perhaps a third of all cannabis purchases among minors, and supply most of the adult market.

As commercial access and promotion increased, the Netherlands saw rapid growth in the number of cannabis users, an increase not mirrored in other nations. Whereas 15 percent of 18–20 year olds reported having used marijuana in 1984, the figure had more than doubled to 33 percent in 1992. That increase might have been coincidental—the data permit only weak inferences—but it is consistent with other evidence (from alcohol, tobacco, and legal gambling markets) that the commercial promotion of vice increases consumption. Since 1992 the Dutch figure has continued to rise but that growth is paralleled in the United States and most other rich Western nations despite very different drug policies—apparently another of those inexplicable shifts in global youth culture. The rise in marijuana use has not led to a worsening of the Dutch heroin problem.

Though the Netherlands had an epidemic of heroin use in the early 1970s, there has been almost no recruitment since 1976. Heroin and cocaine use are not particularly high by European standards and a smaller fraction of marijuana users go on to use cocaine or heroin in Holland than in the U.S. There is no evidence that the Dutch cannabis policy has resulted in any increase in property crime or violence, and claims that it has are simply not plausible.

The Dutch have made a policy choice; less black market activity at the retail level and less police intrusiveness in ordinary life in exchange for higher levels of marijuana use. Whether that is the right choice depends on one's views about the dangers of marijuana use. At any rate, it seems likely that the Dutch might have achieved their goals with a less extreme policy; e.g., South Australia allows home cultivation of small quantities of marijuana, but not commercial sales or promotion.

Alternative Policies for Heroin and Cocaine

Much less is known about the consequences of alternative drug laws for heroin or cocaine. There is no instance of legal commercial access to cocaine or heroin in a modern industrialized nation. Spain and Italy have decriminalized these drugs but do not produce suitable statistics for analysis. Few British doctors exercise their privilege of prescribing heroin for addict maintenance; contrary to widespread claims, this program was already greatly curtailed before the heroin epidemic of the 1970s. Switzerland reports significantly improved health and reduced criminality among participants of their heroin prescription program, though more rigorous testing is still needed. Thus we can offer only a theoretical analysis that highlights the tradeoffs involved in legalizing heroin or cocaine.

Critics of current U.S. policies argue that many if not most of the harms associated with drugs are actually caused by our drug prohibition, or by the way it is enforced. Defenders of prohibition counter that legalization would significantly increase drug use and drug addiction in American society. Both arguments are at least partially correct.

First, it is almost certainly true that many of the harms currently associated with heroin and cocaine are due to the fact that those drugs are illegal. Prohibition deserves much of the blame for the crime and violence around illicit drug markets, for a large fraction of all drug overdoses and drug-related illnesses, and for corruption and violations of civil liberties.

Second, other harms are clearly due to the drugs themselves and the influence they have on the user's health and behavior. Legalization would eliminate the harms caused by prohibition, but it would not eliminate the harms caused by drug use.

And third, as we argued with respect to Dutch coffee shops, we believe that legalization would significantly increase the number of drug users and the quantity of drugs consumed. We limit this conclusion to legalization in the form of commercial availability; the available evidence does not suggest that medical prescription, decriminalization, or harm reduction programs increase drug use to any appreciable degree.

So on the one hand, legalization would probably reduce the adverse consequences (to the user and to others) associated on average with each drug-taking episode. And on the other hand, legalization would increase the number of incidents of drug use, by increasing the number of users and possibly by increasing the amounts they would use.

Thus, the choice between drug control models involves a central tradeoff. If average harm went down under legalization without an increase in use, we'd clearly be better off than we are today. But if legalization produced a significantly large increase in total use, total drug harm would go up, even if each incident of use became somewhat safer. Because Total Drug Harm = Average Harm Per Use × Total Use, total harm can rise even if average harm goes down.

At present there is no firm basis for predicting the relative magnitude of these effects. Thus, legalization is a very risky strategy for reducing drug-related harm.

But it is unhelpful to dichotomize the debate into two polar extremes: Our current heavily punitive approach vs. an alcohol-type free adult market in drugs. In fact, there are a whole range of policy alternatives in between those extremes. For example, harm reduction interventions like needle exchange aim to reduce the harmful consequences of drug use. Contrary to recent claims, harm reduction does not imply legalization, and in fact many harm reduction advocates explicitly reject legalization. What is often overlooked is that in Europe, harm reduction is being implemented entirely within prohibition regimes. The drawbacks of legalization do not imply that our current version of prohibition is the optimal drug strategy; it may well be possible to implement prohibition in less harmful ways.

SELECTION 13

The following selection is a portion of Chapter 20 from Avram Goldstein's book *Addiction: From Biology to Drug Policy* (2nd ed.; pp. 307–316), published by Oxford University Press, New York, in 2001. Goldstein is Professor Emeritus of Pharmacology at Stanford University. His many honors for contributions to drug research and treatment include membership in the National Academy of Sciences and its Institute of Medicine and the Pacesetter Award for Research from the National Institute on Drug Abuse.

■ *New Strategies for Rational Drug Policy*

AVRAM GOLDSTEIN

What should be the purpose of government policy on addictive drugs? What should we be trying to accomplish, and why? It is certainly in the interest of society as a whole to reduce the amount of damage done by drug addiction. This means preventing youngsters from being drawn into using addictive drugs in the first place. It means cutting down the amount of drug use by people already addicted, improving their physical and mental health, and trying to free them of their addiction. It also means reducing the harm caused to others as a result of drug use by addicts. At the same time we have to take care that implementing drug policy does not cause more harm to individuals and society than do the drugs themselves. To strike the right balance requires careful, thoughtful analysis, with a recognition that changes come slowly, that there are no quick fixes.

In [the discussion that follows], I propose general policies that apply to the drug addiction problem as a whole. . . . Many of the proposals offered herein were developed in a lengthy scholarly article coauthored with my Canadian colleague Dr. Harold Kalant and published in the 28 September 1990 issue of the journal *Science* (vol. 249, pp. 1513–1521).

1. Consider drug addiction to be primarily a public health problem. Drug policies have too often been driven by public panic and media hysteria, to which politicians respond by whatever actions they think will be reassuring in the immediate crisis. This pattern does not address the real need. It is time to return the drug problem to the domain of medicine and public health, where it belongs. For many reasons, it is logical to approach drug addiction as if it were an infectious disease. Such concepts as incidence, prevalence, relative immunity, and genetic and environmental influences on susceptibility can be applied to both. Attempts at prevention, eradication, education, treatment, relapse prevention, and containment are comparable. And important for preventing the spread of drug addiction is the fact that—as with infectious diseases— it is primarily the newly infected who transmit the condition to their peers. Quarantine, which has sometimes been used in severe and life threatening epidemics, can be an effective tool (especially for diseases that are transmitted readily by casual contact); but it always raises ethical and legal issues concerning the degree to which it is permissible to restrict the personal liberties of those who are infected in order to protect those who are not.

The argument that the analogy of addiction to infectious disease is false because people are passive victims of infectious disease but actively seek out addictive drugs was discussed at length [previously]. There it was pointed out that in both cases human behavior is responsible, at least in part. The person who gets AIDS or hepatitis through promiscuous unprotected sex and the person who gets lung cancer through addictive smoking are both responsible for the public health burden they place on society.

The public health approach rests on the philosophy of harm reduction. This is an attitude, a way of approaching difficult and sometimes intractable problems, which is commonplace in public health and medical practice. It is the very opposite of rigid, judgmental attitudes based on concepts of morality. The reorientation of thinking that is proposed here would counter the kind of simplistic "drug war" mentality that has been so unproductive in the past. The slogan "war on drugs," however, has much to recommend it. It is appropriate in the same way that we might speak of a war on AIDS, a war on cancer, or a war on poverty. The metaphor implies that there is a serious threat to our society, that national resources need to be mobilized, that a united nation can best accomplish what is called for, that large investments of money and energy will be required, that the effort commands a high priority, that the best minds need to be tapped for solutions, that "business as usual" will not do.

Bearing in mind the warning . . . about misuse of the term, true "harm reduction" should be the central strategy in the war on drugs. Physicians recognize that some diseases can neither be eradicated nor cured. They simply do the best they can to minimize the harm, acknowledging that not every problem has a totally satisfactory solution. Illustrative is the physician's approach to a chronic disabling disease like rheumatoid arthritis. No cure is yet known, but the pain and disability can be managed moderately well with appropriate medications. The condition is subject to relapses, even after long periods of remission—a noteworthy similarity to the drug addictions.

The key to treating such conditions is to avoid unrealistic expectations and to accept small victories gratefully. It is important not to regard relapse as failure, but rather as a challenge to reinstitute and improve the treatment. Although it would be lovely if by some magical means we could wipe out all drug addictions, that is just not going to happen. Once we recognize and accept that reality, we can go forward to craft realistic policies for reducing the harm done by each addictive drug to the addicts and to society.

In recognition of the importance of the drug addiction problem to the nation's health, a special agency was established in the executive branch of government—the Office of National Drug Control Policy (ONDCP). An important role of this office is to coordinate the activities of the many federal agencies with responsibilities related to drug abuse and addiction. The annual National Drug Control Strategy document and other ONDCP publications are invaluable sources of data on all aspects of our drug problem and the activities being pursued to bring it under control. ONDCP also provides an important pulpit for educating the public; and positions expounded by ONDCP have often coincided with those advocated in this book. Especially significant have been repeated pronouncements by General Barry McCaffrey, director of ONDCP, to the effect that national drug policy must be driven by science, not by ideology. But a weakness imposed by Congress is distinctly unscientific and needs to be remedied; conspicuously absent from the authorized mission of ONDCP are nicotine and alcohol (except as concerns children, for whom these drugs are illegal). Finally, ONDCP is playing a leadership role in drawing up specific recommendations for rational and consistent harm-reduction policies through legislative, executive, and judicial actions at federal, state, and local levels of government.

The principal improvement needed, overall, is a shift in emphasis from supply reduction to demand reduction activities. With more than $18 billion federal dollars now (in the 2000 budget) expended annually on the drug problem, a way needs to be found more quickly to reverse the overall imbalance of expenditures, which continues to be nearly 70 to 30 in favor of supply reduction over demand reduction.

2. Make demand reduction the primary strategy. Throughout history, societies have attempted to eliminate one addictive drug or another (whichever was most abhorrent to the dominant culture) by harsh punitive measures—even capital punishment for the users. Sometimes such measures have been effective, but whether truly draconian policies might work is really an academic question for Americans. American society is built on respect for human rights, as enshrined in the U.S. Constitution's Bill of Rights. To sacrifice those principles for the sake of reducing or even eliminating (if it were possible) drug addiction would not—I hope and trust—be acceptable to the majority of citizens. Without infringing on constitutional liberties, the best hope of making a significant impact on the drug problem is to reduce demand, and to do so patiently and systematically, through two approaches.

First, expand prevention education, continuing and accelerating the current trend toward honest, health-based, elementary and secondary education about all addictive drugs. Get rid of the misleading terms "alcohol and drugs" and "nicotine and drugs," which imply that alcohol and nicotine are not drugs, whereas they are actually the ones that cause the greatest harm to public health. Moreover, they are the gateway drugs, the ones that children and adolescents use first, after which some progress to marijuana, then to cocaine and heroin. Educate in an evenhanded manner about the effects of all the addictive drugs. "Just say no!" is useful and necessary, but by no means sufficient. Teach why saying no is a wise policy. Teach that children should not use any addictive drugs because—whatever their legal status—they are harmful to health and can lead to uncontrolled use and all the consequences of the addicted state. Concerning those drugs that are illicit, every child, at the appropriate grade level, should be taught respect for the law in a context of learning the history and basis of the drug laws and the political processes for debating and changing the laws in a democratic society.

Second, make treatment readily and universally available. This is one of the most reliable and cost-effective ways of reducing demand for drugs. The number of funded treatment "slots" presently falls far short of meeting the demand. Every day an addict spends in treatment is a day of reduced drug use and of reduced crime (to the extent that criminal activity was motivated by the need to support the addiction). As discussed in preceding chapters, research has confirmed this socially beneficial effect of treatment on drug-related crime. In addition, since the addict's motivation to enter treatment is often weak, finding a treatment facility and being admitted rapidly to treatment must be made easy. The Dutch have set a good example of how to do this.

3. Address the spread of AIDS and other infectious diseases by intravenous drug users. We need to continue dealing with the role of intravenous drug use (primarily of cocaine, amphetamines, and heroin) in the spread of AIDS and hepatitis. The AIDS virus (HIV) accidentally found a foothold nearly 20 years ago in the community of gay men in the United States; but it soon spread, through heterosexual contacts, to an increasing number of women. The spread of HIV among intravenous drug users affects all of society, for the virus will not confine itself to the addict group any more than it has to the gay community. Prostitutes, especially, play a role in the spread of HIV and other sexually transmitted diseases, and prostitution is a common means of financial support for addicts. Providing sterile needles and condoms to all addicts is a policy already instituted in many communities, and it ought to be implemented everywhere. The data show convincingly that providing sterile needles and syringes does not recruit new users.

It is true that there is still no strong scientific proof that needle exchanges and condom distribution will stop the spread of HIV among intravenous drug users. However, the public health approach to a death-dealing virus must be based on whatever partial evidence is available, on common sense, and on the need to teach the facts about intravenous drug use, AIDS, and hepatitis. Unfortunately, powerful forces are opposed to this simple public health measure because of worry about "sending the wrong kind of message." It seems to me that the wrong kind of message would be, "We don't care whether these diseases continue to spread or not." With respect to needle exchanges, as for some other aspects of drug policy, we have much to learn from countries like the United Kingdom and the Netherlands.

Even more important than needle exchanges in stemming the spread of AIDS and hepatitis is expansion of methadone maintenance programs to accommodate all heroin addicts who are willing to enroll. It is a well-established fact that when addicts are stabilized on an adequate dosage of methadone in a well-run program with ancillary services, they drastically reduce or discontinue their intravenous drug use and thus their sharing of needles.

4. Address the problem of fetal damage caused by addictive drugs. The special problem of addictive drug use by pregnant women will need urgent and very careful consideration. This issue is of major concern to society for both humanitarian and economic reasons. Drugs used by a pregnant woman affect in several ways how her fetus will develop and thus how much of a burden that child may ultimately be on society. First, there are the obvious congenital malformations, such as are seen in fetal alcohol syndrome. Second, evidence (though still inconclusive) from both animal and human studies suggests the possibility of permanent damage to the developing brain, resulting in mental retardation and behavioral abnormalities that may only be evident years later. Third, both because of drug effects and because the addicted woman is unlikely to maintain her own health during pregnancy, the infant is likely to be born prematurely and of low birth weight, causing an array of adverse health consequences. Fourth, the newborn baby is likely to be dependent on the addictive drug and require special detoxification treatment.

What to do about this problem is a thorny question. Pregnant addicts ought to be afforded free treatment for their drug addiction, coupled with free prenatal care; those are good cost-effective investments for society. But should we do more? Can a case be made for compulsion—for allowing the interests of society to override the civil liberties of the pregnant woman? Long-acting injectable contraceptives could be made available; some argue that court-ordered compulsory contraception may be appropriate in some cases. Mandatory diagnostic procedures could provide findings that might justify abortion of a severely damaged fetus. Public debate is needed about how to develop disincentives to pregnancy in untreated addicts, and about the degree to which the interest of society in healthy babies justifies government intervention. The birth of a drug-damaged child is not only a tragedy; it can also be considered a crime against humanity—provided, of course, that effective alternatives to drug use are made universally available to female addicts of childbearing age.

5. Enact and implement laws that support social norms. Advocates of drug legalization often argue as though legal restrictions and drug education were mutually exclusive. They point to the salutary progress in the United States in reducing the prevalence of nicotine addiction. "See," they say, "the harmful use of an addictive drug is best reduced through education, through health consciousness, in short, through voluntary actions rather than through governmental intrusions." But "rather than" implies a false dichotomy, which distorts what actually happened with tobacco smoking.

The historic decline in smoking over the last 25 years illustrates how laws and education complement each other. Biomedical science led the way in providing irrefutable evidence of the damage to health—evidence summarized in the 1964 Surgeon General's Report. Then, as education made people more aware of the health hazards, and made non-smokers more aware of their rights, people gradually became more accepting of increased regulation. As an example, the ban on smoking in commercial air travel was first instituted on flights of two hours or less, then later extended to all domestic flights. Regulation of smoking in restaurants began with establishment of smoking and nonsmoking sections, but now, in many places, has given way to a total prohibition. As awareness grew, and with more nonsmokers and former smokers in the population, tougher regulations became acceptable, such as prohibition of smoking in all public facilities and in the workplace. Increased taxation as a means of reducing consumption has also gained acceptability. Much more needs to be done, but we see here a working model of how regulations can promote attitudinal change, and how attitudinal change, in turn, can make ever tougher regulations more acceptable. These examples also illustrate how regulations short of complete prohibition can be effective without significantly criminalizing an addictive behavior. At the same time, educational efforts emphasizing harm reduction should be directed at hard-core addicts who continue to resist total abstinence.

6. Consider actual crime—whether or not drug-related—to be primarily a law enforcement problem. For the purpose of this discussion I exclude the "crime" of drug possession for personal use. By actual crime I mean burglary, robbery, theft, shoplifting, and embezzlement, as well as large-scale drug trafficking, gun battles over turf, and all manner of other violent offenses. These should be dealt with on their own terms and not be allowed to detract from the public health approach to the majority of addicts. Violent crime and property crime, whatever their causes, must be dealt with so that innocent citizens can enjoy the right to live in a safe neighborhood, to go about their peaceful pursuits without fear. In short, we should deal with drug-related crime as we deal with any criminal activity. Being addicted does not exculpate actual crime.

A constructive policy will distinguish between the victims and the predators, between the addicts on the one hand and the traffickers who are the real criminals on the other. And the law can distinguish easily between the health problems of addicts and the serious criminal actions associated with addictive drugs. There is a precedent in the way we handle a legally available drug, alcohol. Numerous control measures are directed principally at the traffickers—the manufacturers, advertisers, and distributors. For example, those who manufacture alcohol illicitly, who distribute it without paying the taxes, or who sell it to minors, are subject to criminal sanctions. But users are affected by the law only to the extent that their drug use results in rowdy behavior, drunk driving, assault, or other violations of the rights of others—behaviors that are in themselves criminal.

The objection is often raised that on the street it is impossible to make a clear distinction between users and traffickers because so many users of illicit drugs are also sellers. I find this a specious argument. The major traffickers deal in such large quantities that their status is unambiguous. The fact is, however, that major traffickers are difficult to apprehend; it is much easier to expend police efforts on street addicts, who typically divide and sell some of their own heroin, cocaine, or marijuana. Admittedly, going after the "big fish" is easier said than done, and to do it effectively will require tackling the pervasive problem of corruption at all levels of the law enforcement system.

The laws on possession of illicit drugs ought to be modified so that we stop filling the jails and prisons with hapless users, as in our present revolving-door system. This applies especially to youngsters, experimenting for the first time, who only need a firm slap on the wrist, not criminal sanctions or treatment. In this regard, one of the unfortunate consequences of the panic-driven policies of recent years has been the establishment of mandatory minimum sentences for drug offenders. This misguided approach has deprived judges of the discretionary power to distinguish, in the case of illicit drugs, between major and minor crimes, between significant and trivial offenses. A great many judges have urged restoring judicial discretion in sentencing. In short, the common sense principle of letting the punishment fit the crime needs to be reestablished in the field of drug offenses. The system of drug courts should be expanded quickly, so that first offenders can be offered the option of closely monitored treatment instead of jail.

7. Increase funding for basic and applied research. This recommendation may be discounted as self-serving, coming as it does from a researcher. History teaches us, however, that investment in biomedical research pays off handsomely. The more we know, the better we can apply our knowledge to solve problems. Basic research yields the understanding that permits us to fashion novel practical solutions, without which there would be only guesswork and superstition. Applied research teaches us how best to develop and implement novel practical solutions.

Consider the development of methadone maintenance. Many years of basic research on the biological actions of opiates were needed before—in Germany before World War II—methadone could be synthesized as a morphine substitute for pain relief. As the chemical structure of methadone is not even close to that of morphine, it never would have been developed were it not for the deep understanding, generated over many years of basic research, of those special properties of the morphine molecule that are responsible for its biological effects. The idea of using methadone for maintenance treatment because of its long duration of action depended on much prior research concerning how drugs are metabolized and eliminated from the body. Finally, rigorous applied research was needed to demonstrate that methadone really works in heroin addicts, that it is both safe and efficacious.

Both basic and applied research deserve support as part of any coordinated attack on drug addiction. The mechanisms of research funding should be reviewed, to see if there is need for greater leadership at the federal level to ensure that the most important problems in addiction are attacked as promptly as new knowledge and new technology permit. Numerous unsolved problems call for solution. For example, we are desperately in need of treatment for cocaine addiction. Why is no satisfactory pharmacotherapy yet available? Because it is only recently that basic neurobiology research is showing us where and how cocaine acts in the brain. We might soon be able to learn how to prevent the paranoid psychosis that results from heavy binge use of cocaine or amphetamines. If we understood more about the neurochemistry of craving, we might be able to develop anticraving medications, and thus address the all-important relapse problem. If we knew more about the brain damage caused by chronic use of addictive drugs, we might learn how to prevent or repair that damage. We might even learn how to prevent or reverse the destructive effects of alcohol or cocaine on brain development in the unborn child.

Finally, the Human Genome Project opens the way to learning why some people are so much more vulnerable than others to addiction. That knowledge may prove useful in targeting prevention measures toward children who are at high risk. Even more important, whenever we discover a previously unknown gene that influences vulnerability to addiction, we will find out that gene's normal function in the brain. That means discovering receptors, neurotransmitters, regulatory proteins, and brain pathways that play a role in drug addiction, that can become novel targets for pharmacotherapy.

Looking at Both Sides—The Debate Continues

The following excerpt is taken from an influential essay, "The psychology of harm reduction" by psychologist Robert J. MacCoun, which appeared in the *American Psychologist* in 1998. His conclusions have been widely cited by professionals on both sides of this issue and are presented here.

> . . . I have tried to take a frank look at the arguments against harm reduction, and I have suggested that, like most policy interventions, the approach has potential pitfalls. Not every harm-reduction intervention will be successful, and some might even increase aggregate harm. . . . I conclude by offering five hypotheses about how harm reduction might be more successful—successful both in reducing aggregate harm and in attracting and retaining a viable level of political support.
>
> 1. Harm-reduction interventions should have the greatest political viability when they can demonstrate a reduction in average harm—especially harms that affect nonusers—without increasing drug use levels. Interventions that lead to increases in drug use are likely to encounter stiff opposition, even if they yield demonstrable net reductions in aggregate harm. . . .
> 2. Because the compensatory behavioral mechanism is triggered by perceived changes in risk [meaning that people will be least inclined to engage in a behavior if they perceive that behavior to be risky], harm-reduction efforts seem least likely to increase drug use when those harms being reduced were already significantly underestimated, discounted, or ignored by users and potential users. . . .
> 3. Similarly, interventions involving safe-use information or risk-reducing paraphernalia should be less likely to increase total use, and hence be more politically viable, when they are highly salient for heavy users but largely invisible to potential initiates to drug use [meaning that needle-exchange programs should be well-known to chronic IV drug users but get little or no publicity outside that restricted community]. . . .
> 4. Reducing users' consumption levels should generally provide harm reduction, an important strategy for achieving use reduction when heavy users refuse to become abstinent.
> 5. Whenever feasible, harm-reduction interventions should be coupled with credible primary and secondary prevention efforts, as well as low-threshold access to treatment.
>
> This last point is a truism among many harm-reduction providers. Still, a few in the harm-reduction movement are uncomfortable with the notion that harm-reduction programs should urge users to stop their drug use. . . . Americans who oppose harm reduction are unlikely to change their views until they feel their fears have been taken seriously.

Matters to Ponder

- What do you think about the idea (promoted by opponents to a harm-reduction approach) that harm reduction is only a "Trojan horse" leading insidiously to a more radical option of drug legalization?
- What do you think about the position that harm reduction should be better applied to potentially harmful drugs that are already legal (specifically, tobacco products and alcohol) rather than focus on harm reduction for drugs that are presently illegal?
- Would you feel differently about a harm-reduction approach to heroin and cocaine abuse than a harm-reduction approach to marijuana? If so, why?

Further Sources to Seek Out

Goldstein, Avram. (2001). *Addiction: From biology to drug policy* (2nd ed.). New York: Oxford University Press. Chapter 20 (New strategies for rational drug policy) provides an insightful analysis of harm reduction with respect to a wide range of drugs, legal and illegal.

MacCoun, Robert J. (1998, November). Toward a psychology of harm reduction. *American Psychologist,* pp. 1199–1208. The entire article is worth reading, as one of the definitive analyses of harm-reduction policy and its potential consequences on society.

Web Sites to Explore

www.dea.gov
The web site for the Drug Enforcement Administration, opposing harm-reduction programs in favor of a zero-tolerance approach.

www.drugpolicy.org
The web site for the Drug Policy Alliance (formerly the Lindesmith Center–Drug Policy Foundation), a leader in the advocacy for a harm-reduction approach to drug abuse.

5 Question: Should Drug and Alcohol Dependence Be Considered a Brain Disease?

In the minds of many people, the abuse of alcohol and other drugs is viewed as a kind of moral defect. Alan Leshner, former Director of the National Institute on Drug Abuse (NIDA), has referred to this unfortunate attitude in the following way:

> The most beneficent public view of drug addicts is as victims of their societal situation. However, the more common view is that drug addicts are weak or bad people, unwilling to lead moral lives and control their behavior and gratifications. . . . (M)any people believe that addicted individuals do not even deserve treatment. This stigma, and the underlining moralistic tone, is a significant overlay on all decisions related to drug use and drug users.

For individuals holding this view, the opposing position that drug dependence (the more widely accepted term for drug addiction) is actually a chronic and relapsing brain disease, characterized by compulsive drug seeking and use, represents a jarring and uncomfortable concept. "Not only does acute drug use modify brain functioning in critical ways," says Leshner, "but prolonged drug use causes pervasive changes in brain function that persist long after the individual stops taking the drug." Television commentator Bill Moyers has likened this process in a series of documentaries on drug dependence to a "hijacking of the brain."

During the nineteenth century in the United States, people in the temperance movement set out to achieve their goal of eliminating alcohol use not by addressing the plight of the drinker but rather by turning their rage and scorn on the drug itself. Their position was that alcohol was the work of the devil. When we hear of the phrase "demon rum," we have to recognize that many Americans during this period took the phrase quite literally. Liquor was demonized as a direct source of evil in the world.

The social institution that represented this evil was the local saloon. These establishments were vilified, particularly by women, as the source of all the trouble alcohol could bring, a significant threat to the stability of their community. One historian has put it this way:

> Bars appeared to invite family catastrophe. They introduced children to drunkenness and vice and drove husbands to alcoholism, they also caused squandering of wages, wife beat-

ing, and child abuse; and, with the patron's inhibitions lowered through drink, the saloon led many men into the arms of prostitution (and not incidentally, contributed to the alarming spread of syphilis).

In the modern era, we continue to focus our wrath on the drugs themselves rather than drug-taking behavior. We may find it comfortable to talk about "bad drugs" (as opposed to "good drugs" like the medications we take for disease), but the distinction often breaks down. Do we mean that a "bad drug" is necessarily illegal? If so, then where do we put alcohol and tobacco products, both legal commodities in the United States with clearly undesirable consequences in their use? How do we deal with the possibility of certain medications being diverted from their intended medical use and misused by individuals who do not have the medical symptoms for which these drugs were developed to treat?

If a drug, for example, were totally without any redeeming value (let us say it was extremely poisonous like some particularly toxic mushroom), most people would simply avoid it; adults would caution their children of the consequences and instruct them to avoid any contact. It would have no street value (other than perhaps to a terrorist or psychopath), and no one would seriously object to measures that restricted access to it. It would be a totally "bad" drug, but few people would care about it at all.

When we characterize heroin and cocaine as "bad drugs," we have to be careful about what we are saying. Essentially, our society has balanced the perceived risks inherent in the *recreational use* of heroin or cocaine against any potential benefits. In other words, we are focusing on the consequences of drug-taking behavior rather than the characteristics of the drug itself. Heroin as well as other opiates such as opium and morphine are excellent painkillers; cocaine is an excellent local anesthetic. Society has decided, however, that these positive applications in medicine are outweighed by the negative consequences for the public, on both a personal and social level, thus requiring significant restrictions and controls.

Focusing our attention on drug-taking behavior rather than drugs themselves has been argued as a more productive way of addressing the problems of drug abuse in America. A bizarre but true story from the mid-1970s illustrates the need to make this distinction. At that time, a number of male patients were being treated for alcoholism in a Veteran's Administration hospital in California. In one ward, a patient was observed moving his bed into the men's room. Shortly afterward, several of his fellow patients, one by one, did the same.

What was behind this curious behavior? Evidently, these men, deprived of alcohol after years of alcohol abuse, had discovered that drinking enormous amounts of water, more than seven gallons per day, produced a "high" by altering the acid-to-base balance of their blood. They had found a medically dangerous way (they could have died in the process) but nonetheless psychologically effective way of getting drunk. The fact that they were also urinating approximately the same amount of water each day accounted for their decision to move closer to the toilets. The point of the story is that, in this case, water had become a psychoactive substance with a druglike effect without technically being a drug at all.

Even when we focus on drug-taking behavior, however, we are still confronted with difficult questions to answer. Do we attribute the drug-taking behavior to something beyond individual free will (analogous to people contracting a respiratory illness by no fault of their own) or do we attribute it to a conscious decision made by the individual. This is the issue addressed in this chapter. We begin with an interview with Alan Leshner on the arguments for a "brain disease" concept of alcohol and drug dependence. Opposing this viewpoint is the position of Sally L. Satel, who argues that a disease-centered concept of dependence removes the abuser from all sense of personal responsibility and represents a significant obstacle in solving drug-related problems in our society. The last selection, by Craig Lambert, examines the assumptions behind drug-taking behavior, in light of recent brain research.

REFERENCES

Lender, Mark E., and Martin, James R. (1982). *Drinking in America: A history.* New York: Free Press. Quotation on page 107.

Leshner, Alan I. (1998, October). Addiction is a brain disease—and it matters. *National Institute of Justice Journal,* pp. 2–6. Quotations on pages 3 and 4.

Levinthal, Charles F. (2002). *Drugs, behavior, and modern society* (3rd ed.). Boston: Allyn and Bacon.

Moyers, Bill. (1998). The hijacked brain. Part 2 of the five-part PBS series, "Close to home: Moyers on addiction." New York: WNET-TV.

Toby, Jackson. (1998, Winter). Medicalizing temptation. *The Public Interest,* pp. 64–78.

SELECTION 14

The following selection is an interview with Alan Leshner, former Director of the National Institute on Drug Abuse, conducted by Jerry Stilkind, Contributing Editor to the *USIA Electronic Journal.* In the interview, Leshner discusses current perspectives on drug use, addiction, and treatment. His position is that dependence-producing drugs change the brain in fundamental ways, leading to compulsive, uncontrollable drug-seeking and drug-taking behavior. In 2001, Leshner was appointed Chief Executive Officer of the American Association for the Advancement of Science.

■ *Addiction Is a Brain Disease*

AN INTERVIEW WITH DR. ALAN LESHNER,
DIRECTOR OF THE NATIONAL INSTITUTE ON DRUG ABUSE

QUESTION: Are there particular personality types or socioeconomic conditions that predominate among those who try a drug in the first place?

LESHNER: There are different ways to approach this question. One is to recognize that there are 72 risk factors for drug abuse and addiction that have been identified.

Interview with Alan Leshner, Director of the National Institute on Drug Abuse. *USIA Electronic Journal, 2* (3), June, 1997.

They're not equally important. They operate either at the level of the individual, the level of the family or the level of the community. These are, by the way, the same risk factors for everything else bad that can happen—poverty, racism, weak parenting, peer-group pressure, and getting involved with the wrong bunch of kids, for example. What these risk factors do is increase the probability that people with certain characteristics will, in fact, take drugs.

But you cannot generalize because the majority of people who have a lot of risk factors never do use drugs. In spite of the importance of these risk factors, they are not determinants.

So, what determines whether, say, Harry will use drugs, and whether Harry will become addicted to drugs? They're not the same question. Whether or not Harry will use drugs has to do with his personal situation—is he under stress, are his peers using drugs, are drugs readily available, what kind of pressure is there to use drugs, and does Harry have a life situation that, in effect, he wants to medicate? That is, does Harry feel that if he changed his mood he would feel better, he would have a happier life? People, at first, take drugs to modify their mood, their perception, or their emotional state. They don't use drugs to counteract racism or poverty. They use drugs to make them feel good. And we, by the way, know a tremendous amount about how drugs make you feel good, why they make you feel good, the brain mechanisms that are involved.

Now, there are individual differences, not only in whether or not someone will take drugs, but in how they will respond to drugs once they take them. A Harvard University study published a few weeks ago demonstrated that there is a genetic component to how much you like marijuana. That's very interesting because the prediction, of course, is that the more you like it the more you would be prone to take it again, and the greater the probability you would become addicted. And so there's a genetic component to your initial response to it—whether you like it or not—and also to your vulnerability to becoming addicted once you have begun taking it. We know far more about this for alcohol than we do about other drugs.

Q: Do you mean that the genetic make-up of one person may be such that he gets more of a kick from taking cocaine than another individual? Is that what you mean by vulnerability?

LESHNER: There's no question that there are individual differences in the experience of drug-taking—not everybody becomes addicted equally easily. There's a myth that I was taught when I was a kid, and that was if you take heroin once, you're instantly addicted for the rest of your life. It's not true. Some people get addicted very quickly, and other people become addicted much less quickly. Why is that? Well, it's probably determined by your genes, and by other unknown factors like your environment, social context, and who you are.

Q: Is this true for people around the world—in the United States, Western Europe, India, Colombia?

LESHNER: The fundamental phenomenon of getting addicted is a biological event and, therefore, it's the same everywhere, and the underlying principles that describe the vulnerability, or the propensity to become addicted, are universal.

Q: What is addiction? How is it created in the body?

LESHNER: There has long been a discussion about the difference between physical addiction, or physical dependence, and psychological dependence, behavioral forms of addiction. That is a useless and unimportant distinction. First of all, not all drugs that are highly addicting lead to dramatic physical withdrawal symptoms when you stop taking them. Those that do—alcohol and heroin, for example—produce a physical dependence, which means that when you stop taking them you have withdrawal symptoms—gastrointestinal problems, shaking, cramps, difficulty breathing in some people and difficulty with temperature control.

Drugs that don't have those withdrawal symptoms include some of the most addicting substances ever known—crack cocaine and methamphetamine are the two most dramatic examples. These are phenomenally addicting substances, and when you stop taking them you get depressed, you get sad, you crave the drug, but you don't have dramatic—what we call "florid"—withdrawal symptoms.

Second, when you do have those dramatic withdrawal symptoms with alcohol and heroin, we have medicines that pretty well control those symptoms. So, the important issue is not of detoxifying people. What is important is what we call clinical addiction, or the clinical manifestation of addiction, and that is compulsive, uncontrollable drug seeking and use. That's what matters. People have trouble understanding that uncontrollable, compulsive drug seeking—and the words "compulsive" and "uncontrollable" are very important—is the result of drugs changing your brain in fundamental ways.

Q: How do drugs change the brain? What is it that makes you feel good and wants you to have more?

LESHNER: Let's, again, separate initial drug use from addiction. Although addiction is the result of voluntary drug use, addiction is no longer voluntary behavior, it's uncontrollable behavior. So, drug use and addiction are not a part of a single continuum. One comes from the other, but you really move into a qualitatively different state. Now, we know more about drugs and the brain than we know about anything else and the brain. We have identified the receptors in the brain for every major drug of abuse. We know the natural compounds that normally bind to those receptors in the brain. We know the mechanisms, by and large, by which every major drug of abuse produces its euphoric effects.

Q: Including tobacco, alcohol, marijuana?

LESHNER: Tobacco, alcohol, marijuana, cocaine, heroin, barbiturates, inhalants—every abusable substance. We know a phenomenal amount. What we also know is that each of these drugs has its own receptor system—its own mechanism of action. But in addition to having idiosyncratic mechanisms of action, each also has common mechanisms of action. That common mechanism of action is to cause the release of dopamine, a substance in the base of the brain, in what is actually a circuit called the mesolimbic reward pathway. That circuit has a neurochemical neurotransmitter, which is dopamine.

We believe that the positive experience of drugs comes through the mesolimbic-dopamine pathway. We know that because if you block activation of that dopamine pathway, animals who had been giving themselves drugs no longer give themselves drugs. In addition to that, about a week ago, *Nature* magazine (a British science and medicine journal) published a study showing that the greater the activation of the dopamine system following the administration of cocaine the greater the experience of the high. So we know that this is a critical element, and we know that every addicting substance modifies dopamine levels in that part of the brain. That is to say, alcohol, nicotine, amphetamines, heroin, cocaine, marijuana—all produce dopamine changes in the nucleus accumbens, in the mesolimbic pathway in the base of the brain.

We also know that in the connection between the ventral tegmentum and the nucleus accumbens—in the mesolimbic circuit—that at least cocaine, heroin, and alcohol produce quite similar changes at the biochemical level. That is, not only in terms of how much dopamine is produced but also in the similar effects these substances have long after you stop using the drug. So the point here is that we are close to understanding the common essence of addiction in the brain and we care about this because it tells us how to develop medications for drug addiction. That is the goal—how to treat drug addiction.

Q: But over time, doesn't the brain of an addict release less and less dopamine? So how does he continue to feel good? How does he get his high if dopamine levels are reduced, rather than increased?

LESHNER: Here is another indication of the difference between drug use and addiction. Initially, taking drugs increases dopamine levels, but over time, it actually has the reverse effect. That is, dopamine levels go down. And one of the reasons that we believe that most addicts have trouble experiencing pleasure is that dopamine is important to the experience of pleasure, and when the levels are low you don't feel so good. But once addicted, an individual actually does not take the drug to produce the high.

It is the case in heroin addiction that, initially, they take the drug for the high, but ultimately they take the drug to avoid being sick. The same is true, to some degree, in crack cocaine addiction. That is, we find that people coming off crack cocaine get depressed very badly, and so they are, in effect, medicating themselves, giving themselves crack cocaine to avoid the low. What they're trying to do is pump their dopamine levels up, which doesn't happen, but they keep trying to do it.

Q: Perhaps we should assure people that a certain level of dopamine is normally produced in the brain by pleasurable foods, or activities, and is necessary for human life. Is that correct?

LESHNER: Dopamine is a very important substance in many different ways. It is, for example, involved in motor function. In order to maintain motor function, you must have a minimal amount of dopamine. Parkinson's disease is a deficit in dopamine levels, which results in motor problems. Both schizophrenia and depression have dopamine components to them, mostly schizophrenia. In fact, antipsychotic drugs work on dopamine levels. And so, what you need to be doing is balancing your dopamine, not raising it or lowering it. You're trying to maintain dopamine at a normal level. And again, we think that people who are addicted have trouble experiencing pleasure because their dopamine systems are altered.

Q: If the working of the brain changes during addiction, is this alteration permanent, or can other drugs administered by physicians, or behavioral changes in various programs, bring the brain back to an unaddicted, unaffected state?

LESHNER: Drugs of abuse have at least two categories of effects. One is what I will call "brain damage." That is, they literally destroy cells or functions in the brain. For example, if you use inhalants, you literally destroy brain tissue. If you use large doses of methamphetamine, we believe you literally destroy both dopamine and serotonin neurons. In most cases, however, we believe changes in the brain associated with addiction are reversible in one way or another, or they can be compensated for. We know that the brain of an addicted individual is substantially different from the brain of a nonaddicted individual, and we have many markers of those differences—changes in dopamine levels, changes in various structures and in various functions at the biochemical level. We know some of those changes, like the ability to produce dopamine, recover over time. What we don't know is if they recover to fully normal.

Secondly, we know that some medications can compensate, or can reverse some effects. If the change is reversible, your goal is to reverse. If it's not reversible, but you still need to get that person back to normal functioning, you need a mechanism to compensate for the change.

Q: That moves us into the question of prevention and treatment programs. First, what kinds of prevention programs are known to work?

LESHNER: One problem in the prevention of drug abuse is that people think in terms of programs, rather than in terms of principles. But the truth is, like anything else that you study scientifically, stock programs that you apply anywhere around the world in exactly the same way do not work. Rather what you want are guiding principles. And we have now supported over 10 years of research into prevention, and have actually been able to derive a series of principles of what works in prevention, and have just issued the first ever science-based guide to drug-abuse prevention. And some of those principles are fairly obvious once you state them, but if you don't say them you don't do them. For example, prevention programs need to be culturally appropriate. Well, people say that all the time, and then they look at a prevention program and they say, "Oh good, I'm going to just take that one and put it in my country." Then they're shocked when it doesn't work. Well, you need to have the cultural context to whatever you do.

Another obvious principle is that programs need to be age appropriate. Everyone knows that youngsters early in adolescence are a different species from those late in adolescence. So, you need to deal with them differently. The messages have to be different. The advertisement industry has done a very good job with that.

In addition, people frequently like "one-shot" prevention programs. Go in, do something, and then the problem's solved. Well, they never work. You need to have sustained efforts with what we call "boosters." You make your first intervention, then you go back and give another intervention, and then another, and finally you successfully inoculate the individual. There are a whole series of principles outlined in a pamphlet we recently published—"Preventing Drug Use Among Children and Adolescents: A Research Based Guide"—and a checklist against which you could rate programs.

Q: Is this booklet on your web site?

LESHNER: Yes. You can find this prevention booklet by going to *www.nida.nih.gov* and looking under publications. You can download the whole thing.

Q: Which have been found more effective in treating addicts—behavioral or medical programs? Or do they need to complement each other?

LESHNER: I believe that addiction is a brain disease, but a special kind of brain disease—a brain disease that has behavioral and social aspects. Therefore, the best treatments are going to deal with the biological, the behavioral, and the social-context aspects. Now that's difficult for people to understand, I think, but it's a very important principle. We have studies that show that although behavioral treatment can be very effective, and biological treatment can be very effective, combining the two makes them more effective. In addition to that, remember that people who are addicted typically have been addicted for many, many years, and, therefore, they have to almost relearn how to live in society. And that's a part of treatment.

Q: Such a comprehensive approach sounds pretty expensive. Is it more expensive than a prevention program?

LESHNER: The question boils down to whether you're going to try to compare treating an individual once addicted, which involves doing a cost-benefit analysis of what that individual's habit is costing society, versus a massive prevention program that might cost only three cents per person but which only affects the one or two people who would have used the drug in the first place. So, it's not a comparison that you can actually make. However, I can tell you that even the most expensive treatments—inpatient, therapeutic communities that cost, depending on the particular kind of program, between $13,000 and $20,000 a year per person—are a lot less than imprisoning people. Incarceration costs $40,000 a year per person. So the cost-benefit ratio always is in favor of the treatment approach.

Q: How many drug addicts are there in the United States and around the world?

LESHNER: We believe that there are about 3.6 million individuals in the United States who are addicted to heroin, crack cocaine, amphetamine, marijuana—the illegal drugs. So, at least that many are in need of treatment. Then heavy users add to that number. It's impossible to know exactly the total number who are in need of treatment, but it's probably between four and six million people. I don't know what the comparable figures are internationally.

SELECTION 15

The following selection is an essay written by Sally L. Satel for the journal *The Public Interest* (Fall, 1999), expressing opposition to the concept of drug dependence as a chronic and relapsing disease related to processes of the brain. An earlier version of this article appeared in a pamphlet titled "Is addiction a brain disease?" coauthored with Frederick Goodwin and published by the Ethics and Public Policy Center in its *Medical Science and Society* series.

■ *The Fallacies of No-Fault Addiction*

SALLY L. SATEL

On November 20, 1995, more than 100 substance-abuse experts gathered in Chantilly, Virginia, for a meeting organized by the government's top research agency on drug abuse. One topic for discussion was whether the agency, the National Institute on Drug Abuse (NIDA), which is part of the National Institutes of Health, should declare drug addiction a disease of the brain. Overwhelmingly, the assembled academics, public-health workers, and state officials declared that it should.

At the time, the answer was a controversial one, but, in the three years since, the notion of addiction as a brain disease has become widely accepted, thanks to a full-blown public education campaign by NIDA. Waged in editorial board rooms, town-hall gatherings, Capitol Hill briefings and hearings, the campaign reached its climax last spring when media personality Bill Moyers catapulted the brain-disease concept into millions of living rooms with a five-part PBS special called "Moyers on Addiction: Close to Home." Using imaging technology, Moyers showed viewers eye-catching pictures of addicts' brains. The cocaine-damaged parts of the brain were "lit up"—an "image of desire" was how one of the researchers on Moyers' special described it.

These dramatic visuals lend scientific credibility to NIDA's position. But politicians—and, in particular, President Clinton's drug czar, General Barry McCaffrey, who has begun reciting the brain-disease rhetoric—should resist this medicalized portrait. First, it reduces a complex human activity to a slice of damaged brain tissue. Second, and more importantly, it vastly underplays the paradoxically voluntary nature of addictive behavior. As a colleague said: "We could examine brains all day and by whatever sophisticated means we want, but we would never label someone a drug addict unless he acted like one."

No-Fault Addiction

The idea of a "no-fault" disease did not originate at NIDA. For the last decade or so it was vigorously promoted by mental-health advocates working to transform the public's understanding of severe mental illness. Diseases like schizophrenia and manic depressive illness, they properly said, were products of a defective brain, not bad parenting. Until the early

Satel, Sally L. (1999, Fall). The fallacies of no-fault addiction. Shortened version reprinted with permission of the author from *The Public Interest*, No. 134 (Fall, 1999), © 1999 by National Affairs, Inc.

1980s, when accumulated neuroscientific discoveries showed, irrefutably, that schizophrenia was marked by measurable abnormalities of brain structure and function, remnants of the psychiatric profession and much of the public were still inclined to blame parents for their children's mental illness.

NIDA borrowed the brain-disease notion from the modern mental-health movement, understandably hoping to reap similar benefits—greater acceptance of its efforts and of its own constituent sufferers, that is, addicts. By focusing exclusively on the brain, NIDA ironically diminishes the importance of its own research portfolio, which devotes an ample section to behavioral interventions. It may well be that researchers will someday be able to map the changes in brain physiology that accompany behavioral changes during recovery. Nevertheless, it is crucial to recognize that the human substrate upon which behavioral treatments work, first and foremost, is the will.

Some of those experts that met in Chantilly would say that emphasizing the role of will, or choice, is just an excuse to criminalize addiction. Clinical experience in treating addicts, however, suggests that such an orientation provides therapeutic grounds for optimism. It means that the addict is capable of self-control—a much more encouraging conclusion than one could ever draw from a brain-bound, involuntary model of addiction.

What Does Brain Disease Mean?

A recent article in the journal *Science,* "Addiction Is a Brain Disease, and It Matters," authored by NIDA director Alan I. Leshner, summarizes the evidence that long-term exposure to drugs produces addiction: Taking drugs elicits changes in neurons in the central nervous system that compel the individual to take drugs. Because these changes are presumed to be irreversible, the addict is perpetually at risk for relapse.

> Virtually all drugs of abuse have common effects, either directly or indirectly, on a single pathway deep within the brain. . . . Activation of this pathway appears to be a common element in what keeps drug users taking drugs. . . . The addicted brain is distinctly different from the non-addicted brain, as manifested by changes in metabolic activity, receptor availability, gene expression and responsiveness to environmental cues. . . . That addiction is tied to changes in brain structure and function is what makes it, fundamentally, a brain disease.

Others are less dogmatic. Harvard biochemist Bertha Madras acknowledges a virtual library of documented, replicable brain changes with drug exposure, but she also points out that there have been no scientific studies correlating them with behavior. This missing connection, upon which the addiction-as-a-brain-disease argument clearly depends, has prompted some very unsympathetic reactions. John P. Seibyl, a psychiatrist and nuclear radiologist at Yale University School of Medicine, has called the notion of predicting behavior from brain pathology "modern phrenology."

Not even Alcoholics Anonymous, the institution most responsible for popularizing the disease concept of addiction, supports the idea that drug-induced brain changes determine an addict's behavior. AA employs disease as a metaphor for loss of control. And even though AA assumes that inability to stop drinking, once started, is biologically driven, it does not allow this to overshadow AA's central belief that addiction is a symptom of a spiritual defect, and can thus be overcome through the practice of honesty, humility, and acceptance.

The brain-disease advocates, of course, operate by an entirely different frame of reference. To them, "addiction" means taking drugs compulsively because the brain, having already been changed by drugs, orders the user to do so. As Moyers put it on "Meet the Press," drugs "hijack the brain . . . relapse is normal." The brain-disease advocates assume a correlation between drug-taking behavior and brain-scan appearance, though one has yet to be clearly demonstrated, and speculate, based on preliminary evidence, that pathological changes persist for years. A physiological diagnosis, to stretch the meaning of that word, should of course yield a medicinal prescription. So, brain-disease advocates seem confident, despite evidence to the contrary, that a neuroscience of addiction will give rise to pharmaceutical remedies. Meanwhile, the search for a cocaine medication, having begun with such high hopes, has come up empty. And there is good reason to wonder if this enterprise will ever bear fruit. Even the widely used medication for heroin addiction—methadone—is only partly helpful in curtailing drug use. It fails to remedy the underlying anguish for which drugs like heroin and cocaine are the desperate remedy.

Addicted to Politics

The dispute over whether addiction is a brain disease isn't merely a dispute among doctors. It is, for many reasons, political. The efforts of NIDA do not simply aim to medicalize addiction, presumably a medical concern, but to destigmatize the addict, clearly a sociopolitical concern. This is also the agenda of the newly formed group Physician Leadership on National Drug Policy. "Concerted efforts to eliminate stigma" should result in substance abuse being "accorded parity with other chronic, relapsing conditions insofar as access to care, treatment benefits and clinical outcomes are concerned," a statement from the Leadership group says. These sentiments have been echoed by the Institute of Medicine, a quasi-governmental body that is part of the National Academy of Sciences. "Addiction . . . is not well understood by the public and policymakers. Overcoming problems of stigma and misunderstanding will require educating the public, health educators, policymakers and clinicians, highlighting progress made, and recruiting talented researchers into the field."

Indeed, the politics of drug addiction have begun to strain the logic of drug-addiction experts. In their *Lancet* article, "Myths About the Treatment of Addiction," researchers Charles O'Brien and Thomas McLellan state that relapse to drugs is an inherent aspect of addiction and should not be viewed as a treatment failure. They sensibly point out that in long-term conditions—for example, asthma, diabetes, and hypertension—relapse is often the result of the patient's poor compliance with proper diet, exercise, and medication. But then they jump to the conclusion that since the relapse of some addicts follows from poor compliance too, addiction is like any other disease. This is incorrect. Asthmatics and diabetics who resist doctor's orders share certain characteristics with addicts. But asthmatics and diabetics can also deteriorate spontaneously on the basis of unprovoked, unavoidable primary, physical reasons alone; relapse to addiction, by contrast, invariably represents a voluntary act in conscious defiance of "doctor's orders." The bottom line is that conditions like asthma and diabetes are not developed through voluntary behavior. An asthmatic does not choose to be short of breath. Addicts, however, choose to use drugs.

Analogies aside, calling addiction a chronic and relapsing disease is simply wrong. Treatment-outcome studies do support the claim, but data from the large Epidemiologic Catchment Area (ECA) study, funded by the National Institute of Mental Health, show that in the general population remission from drug dependence (addiction) and drug abuse is the norm. Contra publicist Bill Moyers and researchers O'Brien and McLellan, relapse is not. According to ECA criteria for remission—defined as no symptoms for the year just prior to the interview—59 percent of roughly 1,300 respondents who met lifetime criteria were free of drug problems. The average duration of remission was 2.7 years, and the mean duration of illness was 6.1 years with most cases lasting no more than 8 years.

Yet, if NIDA and other public-health groups can change how the public views addiction, tangible political gains will follow. Such groups aim at securing more treatment and services for addicts, expanded insurance coverage, and increased funding for addiction research. These are not unreasonable aims insofar as substandard quality of care, limited access to care, and understudied research questions remain serious problems. But the knee-jerk reflex to decry stigma has been naively borrowed from the mental-health community. Stigma deters unwanted behaviors, and it enforces societal norms. Destigmatizing addicts (recasting them as chronic illness sufferers) threatens one of the most promising venues for anti-addiction efforts: the criminal justice system. The courts and probation services can impose sanctions that greatly enhance retention and prevent relapse. . . .

A Medical Cure for Addiction?

One of NIDA's major goals has been the development of a cocaine medication by the turn of the century. Now with two years to go, no magic bullet is in sight. To date, over 40 pharmaceuticals have been studied in randomized controlled trials in humans for cocaine abuse or dependence. Some of these were intended to block craving, others to substitute for cocaine itself, but none have yet been found even minimally effective. The NIDA director has downgraded predictions about the curative power of medication, promoting it as potentially "complementary" to behavioral therapy.

The basic problem with putative anticraving medications is their lack of specificity. Instead of deploying a surgical strike on the neuronal site of cocaine yearning, these medications end up blunting motivation in general and may also depress mood. Likewise, experiments with cocaine-like substances have proven frustrating. Instead of suppressing the urge to use the drug, they tend to work like an appetizer, producing physical sensations and emotional memories reminiscent of cocaine itself, triggering a hunger for it.

If a selective medication could be developed, it might be especially helpful to cocaine addicts who have abstained for a time but who experience sudden spontaneous bursts of craving for cocaine, a feeling that is often reported as alien, coming "out of nowhere," and uncoupled from a true desire to use cocaine. Such craving may be triggered by environmental cues (e.g., passing through the neighborhood where the addict used to get high). Generally, the addict learns his idiosyncratic cues, avoids them, and arms himself with exercises and strategies (e.g., immediately calling a 12-step sponsor) that help him fight the urge. It is always conceivable that a medication could help in terms of suppressing the jolt of desire and, ultimately, uncoupling the cue from the conditioned response.

Another pharmacological approach to cocaine addiction has been immunization against the drug's effect. In late 1995, scientists reported the promising effects of a cocaine vaccine in rats. The animals were inoculated with an artificial cocaine-like substance that triggered the production of antibodies to cocaine. When actual cocaine was administered, the antibodies attached to the molecules of cocaine, reducing the amount of free drug available in the bloodstream to enter the brain.

The vaccine is still being developed for use in humans, but the principle behind its presumed effect is already being exploited by an available anti-heroin medication called naltrexone. Naltrexone blocks opiate molecules at the site of attachment to receptors on the neuron. This way, an addict who administers heroin feels no effect. Uncoupling the desired response (getting high) from the action intended to produce it (shooting up) is called "extinction," and, according to behaviorist theory, the subject will eventually stop administering a drug if he no longer achieves an effect. Though naltrexone is effective, most heroin addicts reject it in favor of methadone's calming effect.

Optimism surrounding the pharmaceutical approach to drug dependence stems, in fact, from the qualified success of methadone, an opioid painkiller developed by German chemists during World War II. It was first tested in 1964 as a substitute for heroin in the United States, and now about 19 percent of the nation's estimated 600,000 heroin addicts are enrolled in methadone-maintenance clinics. Numerous studies have documented the socioeconomic benefits of methadone: significant reductions in crime, overdoses, unemployment, and, in some regions, HIV.

Unlike heroin, which needs to be administered every four to eight hours to prevent withdrawal symptoms, methadone requires only daily dosing. "Successful methadone users are invisible," the director of the Beth Israel Medical Center in New York City told the *New York Times*. Between 5 percent and 20 percent remain on the medication for over 10 years, and many are indeed invisible. An example mentioned in the *Times* article is Jimmie Maxwell, an 80-year-old jazz trumpet player who has stayed clean for the past 32 years by taking methadone every day. Unfortunately, people like Maxwell, who lead an optimal life and are otherwise drug-free, represent perhaps 5 percent to 7 percent of methadone patients. Moreover, patients in methadone maintenance are frequently not drug-free; as many as 35 percent to 60 percent also use cocaine or other illicit drugs or black-market sedatives. During a six-year follow-up, D. Dwayne Simpson of the Institute of Behavioral Research at Texas Christian University found over half of all patients were readmitted to their agency at some point.

This should come as little surprise. Methadone will only prevent withdrawal symptoms and the related physiological hunger for heroin, but it alone can't medicate the psychic deficits that led to addiction, such as deep-seated inabilities to tolerate boredom, depression, stress, anger, loneliness. The addict who initiated heavy drug use in his teens hasn't even completed the maturational tasks of adolescence, let alone prepared himself psychologically to solve the secondary layer of troubles that accumulated over years of drug use: family problems, educational deficiencies, disease, personal and economic losses. Only a fraction of heroin addicts become fully productive on methadone alone.

The biological view of addiction conceals an established fact of enormous and pressing clinical relevance: The course of addictive behavior can be influenced by the very consequences of the drug taking itself. Indeed, when the addict reacts to aversive sequelae of drug use—economic, health, legal, and personal—by eventually quitting drugs, reducing use, changing his pattern of use or getting help, he does so voluntarily. Rather than being the inevitable, involuntary product of a diseased brain, the course addiction follows may represent the essence of a free will. Consequences can inspire a change in voluntary behavior, irrespective of its predictability or biological underpinnings. Involuntary behavior cannot be changed by its consequences. A review of the clinical features of addiction will help illustrate the mix of voluntary and involuntary behaviors associated with addiction, belying the claim that addiction is a brain disease.

Harnessing the Will to Stay Clean

It is especially common for heroin-dependent individuals to become immune to the euphoric effect of the drug yet still seek the drug to keep from going into withdrawal. Upon cessation of heroin, a predictable pattern of gross physiological symptoms appears. The same is true of cessation of other opioid drugs including Demerol, morphine, Percocet, codeine, as well as alcohol. To picture this one only need recall actor Jack Lemmon in the movie, "Days of Wine and Roses," his body wracked with tremors, sweating, anxious, desperate for a drink after running out of whisky. Or Frank Sinatra in "Man with the Golden Arm," the heroin addict suffering painful muscle cramps and powerful cravings for heroin after his last fix wore off.

Unlike heroin and alcohol, cocaine does not produce such serious physical withdrawal symptoms. The heavy cocaine addict typically uses the drug in a driven, repetitive manner for 24 to 72 hours straight. Cocaine wears off very quickly and, as it fades, the yearning for more is overpowering. Each fresh hit quells the intense craving. The process winds down only when the addict becomes exhausted, runs out of money, or becomes paranoid, a potential effect of cocaine and other stimulants, such as methamphetamine. He then "crashes" into a phase of agitated depression and hunger followed by sleep for 12 to 36 hours. Within hours to days after awakening, he experiences powerful urges to use the drug again, and the cycle resumes.

A regular user in the midst of a cocaine binge or experiencing heroin withdrawal cannot readily stop using if drugs are available. He is presumably in the "brain-disease" state, when use is most compulsive, neuronal disruption most intense. True, even purposeful behavior can occur in this state—for example, the attempt, sometimes violent, to get money or drugs is highly goal-directed. But, at the same time, addicts in such an urgent state will ignore their screaming babies, frantically gouge themselves with dirty needles, and ruin families, careers, and reputations.

Nonetheless, most addicts have broken the cycle many times. Either they decide to go "cold turkey" or end up doing so, unintentionally, by running out of drugs or money or landing in jail. Some heroin addicts admit themselves to the hospital to detoxify because they want to quit, others to reduce the cost of their habit, knowing they'll be more sensitive to the effects of heroin afterward. This latter trip to the hospital, while motivated by an effort to pursue drug use more efficiently, is nonetheless a purposeful move that, under other circumstances, might be taken by the addict to re-exert control.

In the days between binges, cocaine addicts make many deliberate choices including (potentially) the choice to stop using. Heroin-dependent individuals, by comparison, use the drug several times a day but can be quite functional in all respects as long as they have stable access to some form of opiate drug in order to prevent withdrawal symptoms. Certainly, some addicts may "nod off" in abandoned buildings, true to stereotype, if they consume more opiate than the amount to which their body has developed tolerance, but others can be "actively engaged in activities and relationships," according to ethnographers Edward Preble and John J. Casey, Jr. "The brief moments of euphoria after each administration constitute a small fraction of their daily lives. The rest of the time they are aggressively pursuing a career . . . hustling."

According to the Office of National Drug Control Policy, as many as 46 percent of drug users not in treatment reported exclusively legal sources of income, and 42 percent reported both legal and illegal. The National Institute of Justice found that between 33 percent and 67 percent of arrested drug users indicate "full and part time work" as their main source of income. It is reasonable to assume that individuals who are most heavily involved in drug use participate least in the legitimate economy. Nonetheless, the fact that many committed drug users do have jobs shows that addiction does not necessarily preclude purposeful activity.

The temporal architecture of an addict's routine reveals periods in which the individual is capable of reflection and deliberate behavior. During the course of a heroin addict's day, for example, he may feel rather calm, and his thoughts might be quite lucid, if he is confident of access to drugs and if he is using it in doses adequate to prevent withdrawal symptoms, but not large enough to sedate. Likewise, there are periods within a cocaine addict's week when he is neither engaged in a binge nor wracked with intense craving for the drug. During such moments, does anyone believe the addict is the victim of a brain disease?

Society's Expectations

Thus, when properly "fixed," the heroin addict might rationally decide to enter a detoxification program or enter a methadone-maintenance program. And between binges the cocaine addict could decide to enter a treatment program or move across town away from the visual cues and the personal associations that provoke craving. Yes, the addict can do such things. But if asked to do so at any given moment, will he?

Probably not. Even those who wish most passionately for a better life may fear coping without drugs. It gets worse: The addict may believe a better life is just not possible. Yet, chances are that some would say "yes" to the possibility of overcoming their addiction. And this can be encouraged behaviorally through rewards and punishments. For example, society could decide to make some necessities—welfare payments, employment, public housing, or child custody—contingent on abstinence. A systematic plan that closes absolutely all avenues of support to those who can't or won't stop using drugs—allowing them only elective treatment or, once arrested for nonviolent drug-related crime, court-ordered treatment— would be too radical, unfair even.

For one thing, the treatment system—especially residential treatment for both voluntary and criminally coerced addicts—would need to be greatly expanded to accommodate those who did not curtail use under pressure alone. Moral objections to refusing addicts access to many public goods and services—or, better, administering small punishments or rewards contingent on performance—would need to be overcome. According to a behavioral model of addiction, it is not unethical. Society can and should legitimately place expectations and demands on addicts because their "brain disease" is not a persistent state. Furthermore, experimental evidence shows that addicts can control drug taking.

In his book, *Heavy Drinking: The Myth of Alcoholism as a Disease,* philosopher Herbert Fingarette cites numerous independent investigations conducted under controlled conditions showing the degree to which alcoholics are capable of regulating themselves. Researchers found, for example, that the amount of alcohol consumed was related to its cost and the effort required to obtain it. Once offered small payments, subjects were able to refuse freely available alcohol. And, after drinking an initial "priming" dose, the amount of alcohol subsequently consumed was inversely proportionate to size of the payment. Other experiments showed that the drinkers' beliefs and attitudes about alcohol influenced how much they consumed. This is potentially very significant to drug addiction; for example, the demand for heroin and cocaine is elastic, responding to price.

The story of the returning Vietnam servicemen is a revealing natural experiment that "changed our views of heroin" according to epidemiologist Lee Robins and colleagues who wrote the now classic paper on the subject, "Vietnam Veterans Three Years After Vietnam." They found that only 14 percent of men who were dependent on heroin in Vietnam—and who failed a publicized urine test at departure because they did not stop using—resumed regular heroin use back home. The rest had access to heroin, and had even used some occasionally, but what made them decide to stop for good, Robins found, was the "sordid" culture surrounding heroin use, the drug's price, and fear of arrest. . . .

Taking Control

Labeling addiction a chronic and relapsing brain disease is mere propaganda. By downplaying the volitional dimension of addiction, the brain-disease model detracts from the great promise of strategies and therapies that rely on sanctions and rewards to shape self-control. And by reinforcing a dichotomy between punitive and clinical approaches to addiction, the brain-disease model devalues the enormous contribution of criminal justice to combating addiction. The fact that many, perhaps most, addicts are in control of their actions and appetites for circumscribed periods of time shows that they are not perpetually helpless victims of chronic disease. They are the instigators of their own addiction, just as they can be the agents of their own recovery.

SELECTION 16

The following selection, written by Craig Lambert for *Harvard Magazine* (March/April 2000), captures the current understanding of the relationship between drug dependence and the brain. Lambert is Deputy Editor of *Harvard Magazine.*

■ *Deep Cravings*

New Research on the Brain and Behavior Clarifies the Mysteries of Addiction

CRAIG LAMBERT

The bombshell dropped in 1976, when "The Natural History of Chipping" appeared in the *American Journal of Psychiatry.* In their article, Norman Zinberg, then clinical professor of

Lambert, Craig (2000, March–April). Deep cravings: New research on the brain and behavior clarifies the mystery of addiction. *Harvard Magazine,* pp. 60–68. Shortened version, reprinted with permission.

psychiatry at Harvard, and his research assistant R. C. Jacobson described five case studies, representative of 54 identified long-term heroin users who had regularly injected the drug for from two to 23 years, yet had never become addicts. These "chippers," whose existence Zinberg had noted as early as 1964, actively developed social rituals and usage strategies that permitted stable, controlled use of heroin.

That article demolished the received wisdom of decades. Ever since 1898, when Bayer & Co. of Germany, makers of another painkiller, Bayer aspirin, introduced heroin to the pharmaceutical market, popular and scientific mythology had enshrined it as the most addictive of drugs. (The word *heroin,* allegedly referring to heroic feelings stimulated by the drug, was originally a Bayer trademark.) The finding that people could take heroin without forming habits challenged the whole idea that drugs themselves were addictive.

Since then, the ethos has shifted markedly. "The idea of addictive drugs makes no sense," says Howard Shaffer. "It's magical thinking to imagine that drugs have this power." Shaffer, associate professor of psychology in the department of psychiatry and director of the Division on Addictions at Harvard Medical School, has studied both drug addicts and compulsive gamblers and notes, "We don't talk about addictive dice."

The old-fashioned concept of "addictive personality" has also collapsed. Today, the word *addiction* does not appear in standard psychiatric nomenclature. Rather, addiction seems to characterize neither a substance nor a personality type, but a *form of relationship.* Clinicians now speak of addiction to gambling, sex, aerobic exercise, work, day-trading, eating carrots, shopping, even excessive drinking of water. The term is vastly popular: people laughingly refer to themselves as "TV addicts" or "chocoholics." But Bertha Madras, professor of psychobiology in the department of psychiatry, objects: "The word is grossly overused. Addiction is a neurobiological disorder. Clinically, it's a very clear syndrome. If you look at all drug addictions from tobacco to heroin, there's only one clear statement that applies to all of them: uncontrolled use despite negative consequences."

Classically, drug addiction means tolerance (the need for increasing doses to obtain the same effect) and withdrawal (psychic and/or bodily ailments, sometimes lethal, that accompany sudden cessation of use). Both signs indicate *neuroadaptation:* repeated intake of a drug alters the brain in profound ways that both stimulate more drug use and render choice more difficult. Yet "pathological gamblers show physiological signs of tolerance and withdrawal, just like narcotic addicts," says Shaffer. "And hospital patients medicated for pain can develop tolerance and withdrawal, but don't show signs of addiction, such as drug-seeking behavior. We can't be sure if it's the drugs or the behaviors that are changing the brain chemistry." The emerging consensus, he says, is that both factors are at work.

Such riddles suggest why addiction research spans many disciplines, from neurobiology to social policy. The Division on Addictions, founded in 1993, is one of nine such divisions focusing on areas that do not fit well into the Medical School's regular academic departments. Addiction is as old as human history, and remains one of the costliest and most intractable of all social problems. It confounds rationality: millions of addicts persist in their blatantly self-destructive behavior despite the loss of family, friends, jobs, money, and health. (Some studies have shown the death rate for untreated heroin addicts to be as high as 7 percent annually.) To use the analogy of professor of psychiatry George Vaillant '55, M.D. '59, the addict can resemble a cigar smoker in an elevator, oblivious to something that is obvious to everyone else. Research is now beginning to show what makes addicted brains, bodies, minds, and spirits so different.

The Addicted Brain

Most animals will gladly take any drug that humans use, excepting marijuana and certain psychedelics like LSD. "The addictive potential of drugs appears to be reflected in many mammalian species," says Madras, who studies the effects of cocaine on macaque monkey brains at the Harvard-affiliated New England Regional Primate Research Center. Pigeons, rats, and monkeys will all press levers to access cocaine or opiates, suggesting that addiction taps into widely shared neural pathways. This makes sense because psychoactive drugs generally exert their most important effects on older brain structures, those areas sometimes called the "reptile brain." In fact, some current research suggests that these pathways may have evolved even before reptiles appeared.

Biologist Tristan Darland, a postdoctoral fellow in the laboratory of Cabot professor of the natural sciences John Dowling, is currently running experiments on zebra fish—common residents of home aquariums whose brains have enough cortex to let them learn some behaviors, though far less effectively than mammals. Darland begins by having the fish swim for 30 minutes in a tank that has a wick saturated with cocaine at one end. The next day, he returns the zebra fish to the same tank for two minutes, but with no cocaine on the wick. Nonetheless, the fish usually prefer the end of the tank where they encountered the cocaine—and spend 70 to 80 percent of their time there. Even during their initial "conditioning" swim, the fish gravitate toward the cocaine end, but "prior exposure to cocaine evokes a stronger response. Evidently, they see it as pleasurable," Darland explains. Results from more than 100 fish show that at least 85 percent prefer the side they associate with cocaine.

The zebra fish may be undergoing some systematic changes in brain chemistry. Psychoactive drugs alter patterns of communication within the brain, via neurotransmitters (molecules that convey messages in the nervous system). "The chemical structure of drugs happens to resemble the chemical structure of the brain's own neurotransmitters," Madras explains. "I call them 'the great brain impostors.' They target the same communication systems as the brain's natural messages. But the complex communication and control systems in the brain are geared for the natural message, not the impostor. As a result, the brain adapts to, and compensates for, the abnormal signals generated by the drug. Here is where the addictive process begins. Brain adaptation is central to addiction. In the case of drugs that produce physical or psychological withdrawal, there is a compulsion to restore the brain to the status it had when it was awash with drugs."

A central enzymatic pathway in the midbrains of vertebrates produces an important neurotransmitter called dopamine, which occurs at high concentrations in a part of the brain called the nucleus accumbens. "All addictive drugs seem to increase dopamine release in the nucleus accumbens," says Darland. "It's been hypothesized that the dopamine system in potential addicts is somehow different. Addictive drugs cause a big increase in dopamine release, with different mechanisms involved, depending on the drug. Cocaine seems to block dopamine uptake, keeping it in circulation. Morphine apparently shuts off inhibitory neurons in the ventral tegmental area of the brain, where the dopamine pathway begins.

"Dopamine release is associated with eating, with sex—with many pleasurable states. It's a 'feel-good' molecule," Darland continues. "These pathways didn't evolve for the sake of doing drugs. They are there to keep humans procreating and eating."

Draper professor of psychiatry Joseph Coyle says, "It looks like there are some final common pathways through which addictive drugs work, in the nucleus accumbens and the amygdala, and which involve the neurotransmitters dopamine and enkephalin. This leads to some interesting things. It's rare to see an individual who uses only cocaine or heroin; these brain systems are involved in other addictive behaviors. Howard Shaffer, for example, has studied gamblers and finds that you rarely see a person who is *just* a pathological gambler— usually it's a gambler who also smokes and drinks too much, or may have a drug habit. Regarding treatment, it also might explain why Naltrexone, an opiate receptor antagonist, has been shown to be effective in reducing relapse among alcoholics."

To better define the sites in the brain where these molecular firestorms occur, instructor in psychiatry Hans Breiter is using magnetic resonance imaging (MRI) to view patterns of neuronal activity in the brains of cocaine addicts. He has begun to identify the brain centers that become active during *euphoria* (when addicts are high on the drug) and to distinguish them from those that fire when the user experiences *craving* (strong desire for cocaine). Some preliminary data suggest that the same brain centers may show parallel activity in compulsive gamblers, possibly indicating—as Shaffer has suggested—that addictive pathways in the brain can exist independent of drug input.

But the neuroscience of addiction is far from settled. Madras, for example, dissents from the current model that sees drug effects converging on the dopamine system. She cites the different effects of drugs, their different targets in the brain, the inability of one drug to substitute for another (cocaine will not relieve morphine withdrawal, nor is methadone an effective treatment for cocaine addiction), and the fact that adverse circumstances such as fear or electric shock also prompt the release of dopamine. "Dopamine may not be the brain's euphoriant," she says, "but the brain's adrenaline."

"In a sense, these drugs are stressors," explains Gene Heyman, Ph.D. '77, lecturer on psychology in the department of psychiatry. "Besides their hedonic properties, they shock the system when taken in these amounts. Rats on opiates, stimulants, or alcohol reliably show increases in corticosterone, a stress-related hormone. Clinical evidence shows parallel findings with heroin addicts. This suggests that opiates and perhaps other addictive drugs have a short-term effect of easing stress, but a long-term effect of increasing susceptibility to stress." Jack Mendelson, professor of psychiatry, draws a parallel between the hormonal responses caused by cocaine and those associated with thrilling or frightening pursuits like hang-gliding and bungee-cord jumping: "Cocaine triggers major stress hormones like epinephrine [adrenaline], norepinephrine, adrenocorticotropic hormone [ACTH], and serotonin. These are the same ones that surge up during bungee jumping."

Even if these chemical responses are common to all drugs of abuse, they are not uniform in degree among all individuals. Darland and Dowling are now attempting to breed zebra fish with increased cocaine sensitivity, which may help identify genetic predispositions to drug addiction. In humans, several lines of research suggest such genetic sensitivities. In the 1960s and 1970s, Scandinavian researchers followed up families of alcoholics to find that the prevalence of alcoholism was four times greater in individuals from alcoholic backgrounds. The researchers clearly demonstrated that genetic variables, rather than family behavior, were at work. More recent research has indicated that hospital patients of Asian background need relatively higher doses of opiates to relieve pain, suggesting that they may metabolize opioids more rapidly, and hence are perhaps at greater risk for opiate addiction. Differences in gene pools may influence cultural practices. "In France and Italy, children drink wine with meals at early ages, whereas in Ireland they are discouraged from drinking before age 21," says Barry Kosofsky, associate professor of neurology. "Some cultures may fear alcohol more, perhaps due to genetic predispositions for alcoholism."

Not only genes but prenatal environments may incline an organism toward drug sensitivity. Neurotransmitters "sculpt" the brain by controlling its early development. Kosofsky investigates the effect of drugs on the developing brain by studying children born to women addicted to crack cocaine. "The intrauterine environment is critical in terms of brain development," he says. "Alcohol, nicotine, or cocaine in a pregnant woman can all have great impact on the fetal brain." Kosofsky hopes to learn whether exposure to cocaine in the womb will increase the likelihood of someone becoming addicted to cocaine as an adult. "This," he says, "would raise the possibility that infants exposed to drugs before birth are more likely to beget others who are also exposed to drugs in the womb"—creating a kind of nongenetic "inheritance" of drug abuse.

Early experiences with drugs, whether in the womb or as an adult, have ineradicable effects. Drug users often describe a wish to recapture the bliss of their first high. But this goal proves elusive because once the brain has neuroadapted to drugs, it is physiologically and structurally changed. The director of the National Institute on Drug Abuse and many others argue that *voluntary* drug consumption alters the brain in ways that lead to *involuntary* drug consumption. The question of whether drug habits are voluntary or not leads us to ask how people get over their addictions, and raises some of the moral issues surrounding compulsive behavior.

The Ambivalent Addict

Even if we all have the neural wiring to become addicts, only a few of us actually do so. Bertha Madras estimates that 5 to 10 percent of those who experiment with a drug become compulsive users or abusers. (Cigarettes are the exception: data show habituation rates ranging from 10 to 70 percent.) What distinguishes that 5 or 10 percent who get hooked? Some studies indicate that children who have "personality disorders," earn poor grades, or have been sexually abused are at higher risk for drug abuse. Yet Howard Shaffer says, "I don't think there is an addictive personality, nor does the scientific literature support the concept." George Vaillant states flatly, "The 'addictive personality' probably doesn't exist," noting that "addictions tend to distort personality. You can't predict this—alcoholics look like everyone else until they become alcoholics, much as cigarette smokers do." Some theorists postulate that "novelty-seeking" or "sensation-seeking" personalities are prone to drug abuse, but Vaillant observes, "They are seeking the high, not addiction." Similarly, he adds, "People with miserable childhoods may look like addictive personalities, but they are seeking pain relief, not addiction."

Clinical professor of psychiatry Edward Khantzian has written extensively about addiction as a form of self-medication. "The nature of suffering is at times overwhelmingly intense—or elusive, vague, and beyond people's control," he says. "The drug user suddenly feels some control over what had felt uncontrollable. I do think there's a specificity involved. People with a lot of rage and irritability find the opiates very soothing. Stimulants may appeal to those individuals who are dysphoric, deenergized, or depressed. Some say that drugs hijack the reward centers of the brain, but I believe that what is hijacked is the *emotional* brain."

According to clinical instructor in psychiatry Stephen Bergman '66, M.D. '73, "All addictions feed the ego, the self. The ego is insatiable. If you are into your ego, you can never get enough—not enough drugs, sex, money, alcohol, relationships, not enough anything. Enough, that is, to feel 'not bad.' Many of these people don't like it if they have to be in a room by themselves for a while. In 12-step programs, those who recover do it by asking for *help*. The connection has to change, from the self to a *we*. The only thing that helps is getting beyond yourself."

Shaffer's studies of compulsive gamblers may support Bergman's notion. "Gambling at slot machines seems to have more addictive potential than table games like cards, dice, or roulette," he says. "There's a lot of social ritual at the gaming tables, but fewer social controls available at the slot machines. Similarly with compulsive shopping: if you don't shop with other people, there are fewer social controls. The excessive shopper shops alone." Other isolated addicts come readily to mind—the solitary drinker, the solo food binges of the bulimic, the workaholic executive alone in the penthouse office at midnight. Connections with other people interrupt the addictive cycle; they redirect attention away from the self-reinforcing feedback of the addictive activity that can quickly escalate to excessive levels.

Addiction is not all pharmacology, neurotransmitters, and intrapsychic states; the social settings of drug consumption have powerful effects. They can influence basic brain chemistry—which is one reason Gene Heyman rejects the notion that "addictive behavior is insensitive to persuasion, that there's an irresistible urge to take the drug." Heyman agrees that drugs alter the brain, but disputes the idea that they change the brain in ways that make choice impossible—he does not believe, in other words, that neuroadaptation makes drug use involuntary. Exhibit A, he says, is 50 million ex-smokers who have voluntarily ended their intake of nicotine.

Many external factors can influence the choice to use drugs. Culture matters: drug intake is far less prevalent in places where religion plays a major role—Israel, Islamic nations, Mormon communities. Laws, too, have an effect: during Prohibition, the incidence of cirrhosis of the liver, probably the best epidemiological index of alcoholism, plummeted. Social class predicts some use patterns: differential quitting rates for tobacco use have strengthened the correlation between smoking and lower levels of education. Then there are social norms: the precipitous drop in the social desirability of smoking has supported quitters. And money talks: in experimental situations, social psychologists have offered addicts cash rewards—say, $50—for not smoking, drinking, or doing cocaine. "There are powerful positive results—addiction will stop in the short run," Heyman says. "If drug use really is involuntary, it doesn't matter whether it's short- or long-term. You can't pay someone not to have dandruff, not to be depressed, not to hallucinate."

One reason people believe drug use is involuntary is that recovery rates for addicts treated at clinics are quite bad. Within one year of treatment, relapse rates of 67 to 90 percent are common for alcohol, opiate, cocaine, and tobacco users. "But most of the people who become addicted to drugs don't go to clinics," says Heyman. "Actually, only 30 to 40 percent go to clinics. Yet this clinic population has greatly influenced our vision and concept of addiction."

It turns out that addicts who *don't* go to clinics have much *higher* recovery rates. Heyman cites two large community surveys, one from 1980 to 1984 and another from 1990 to 1992, that interviewed a cross-section of the general population and reliably identified individuals who met recognized criteria for drug dependence. "Most of those who had been addicts were no longer addicted," says Heyman. "Fifty-nine to 76 percent had been in remission for the previous year or longer. Smaller scale ethnographic studies of general populations also report high remission rates for addicts, and these results strongly suggest that for most, remission is permanent."

Another fascinating finding is the well-known 1975 study, conducted by Lee Robins of Washington University Medical School in St. Louis, of U.S. servicemen who became heroin addicts in Vietnam. Thousands of men got hooked, and 80 percent of those who initially took heroin more than three times became regular users, taking the drug at least once per week. Those who stayed in Vietnam longer often moved on from sniffing to injection. Yet three years after these veterans returned to the States, more than 90 percent had quit. (This contrasts sharply with relapse rates that often exceed 90 percent for heroin addicts in treatment.) The veterans' success in kicking their habits wasn't simply due to decreased drug availability: half of the Vietnam addicts used heroin at least once after they returned home. But "what's really interesting is what happened to the 6 percent of the Vietnam addicts who went into treatment," Heyman says. "For this group, the relapse rate was about 70 percent! In other words, Vietnam vets who go into treatment look pretty much like other Americans who go into treatment."

The question of how addicts who present themselves for treatment differ from other addicts is not well studied, Heyman says. "What has emerged is that treatment seekers are much more likely to have other psychiatric disorders—depression, schizophrenia, affective disorders, or conduct disorders like sociopathy. These psychiatric syndromes may undermine the mechanisms and processes that assist in recovery." Consider that 30 years ago, there was no apparent correlation between smoking and depression. Today, there is one, Heyman explains—"linked to a selective quit rate as a function of psychiatric disorders."

He suggests we "think of addiction not as compulsion, but ambivalence. Alcoholics often recognize that the alcohol is doing them in, yet they keep right on drinking. These data lead people to conclude that the drinking is involuntary, out of control, since continuing to drink doesn't make sense. Another view is that people are inconsistent and contradictory, and predictably so—it's a slightly starker view of human nature. When talking to his therapist, the guy says he wants to stop. But that's looking at his life as a whole—after all, it's hard to be a heavy drinker, or a heroin or cocaine user, without having tons of problems. Yet at a given instant, when the alcoholic is looking at a glass of wine, the frame of reference is, 'What do I want to do right now?' The situations in which they say they want to stop are different from those in which the drug or substance is presented.

"Humans are inconsistent. Their preferences change with the setting," Heyman continues. "To end an addiction, people need an alternative to drug use, something better to do. The clinic population, people with other psychiatric disorders, have a much harder time changing their situations to ones where drug use is less preferred. If you see it as preference rather than compulsion, you can account for all the data."

Lethal Liquids, and Some Ways Out

One of the foremost scholars doing longitudinal research (studies that follow up subjects over many years) in psychiatry is George Vaillant, who directs the Study of Adult Development, based at Harvard Medical School. Vaillant's 1983 book *The Natural History of Alcoholism,* a milestone in the field, analyzes drinking patterns in two populations of World War II era men: a group from Harvard and another group from working-class, inner-city Boston. Generations of researchers have followed these men as they have aged. "Alcohol is more often the horse and less often the cart than any other social ill I can think of," Vaillant says. "I find it terribly interesting that people are much more concerned with every other form of addiction than they are with alcoholism, which—as a problem to humanity—is as big as all other addictions combined. It costs as much as all infectious and pulmonary disease. And it has more impact on others. Drug addicts harm themselves, but that's small beer compared with 25,000 alcohol-related traffic fatalities per year."

Even though cigarette smoking is the direct cause of 400,000 American deaths annually, while alcohol directly causes only 100,000 deaths, "alcoholism is a major reason that people don't stop smoking," says Vaillant. "Those who keep on smoking after age 50 tend to be alcoholics." In hospitals, alcoholics cost six times as much as other patients. Half of all people who show up in emergency rooms with severe multiple fractures are alcoholics. "But the emergency rooms treating multiple fractures ignore blood alcohol levels," Vaillant says. "The causal link isn't made."

"No other drug of addiction impairs one's aversion to punishment the way alcohol does," he continues. "Yes, compulsive gambling impairs your aversion to being poor, and heroin use impairs your aversion to being arrested. But alcoholism goes across the board. When drinking, people are much more likely to engage in all kinds of dangerous, life-threatening behavior—wife beating, child abuse, unprotected sex with strangers, smoking, drunk driving. You can be five foot two and willing to take on anyone in the bar."

Such imperviousness to punishment also tends to forestall recovery. In any case, "the best intentions in the world don't help you with addiction," says Vaillant. "Will power is not a prognostic factor in recovery. Addiction resides in what is often referred to as our reptilian brain, and—well, alligators don't come when they're called. What *does* matter, over the short term, is hitting bottom and having something to lose—the employed, married, upper-middle-class drinker does better at the Betty Ford Center than the homeless alcoholic. But over the long term, inner-city men recovered twice as often from alcoholism as the Harvard men did. The difference has nothing to do with treatment, intelligence, self-care, or having something to lose. It *does* have to do with hitting bottom. Someone sleeping under the elevated train tracks can at some point recognize that he's an alcoholic, but the guy getting stewed every night at a private club may not."

How, then, to change addictive behavior? We may start with the new understanding of the problem—that the roots of addiction lie in both brain chemistry *and* behavior. "It's a wrong-headed bias to think that these are *either* psychological or biological problems," says Gene Heyman. Both voluntary and involuntary behaviors have biological bases. Successful treatments for addiction need to address both realms at once—say, combining a drug like

Naltrexone, which influences neurotransmitters, with a healthier alternative to the drinking, drugging, or gambling life.

Vaillant's studies have convinced him that there are four factors, common to all addictions, that predict success in breaking a habit.

Find a competing behavior that is less disruptive. "Say a drinker goes to Alcoholics Anonymous, sobers up, and starts drinking a lot of coffee and smoking cigarettes," he says. "Then he quits smoking, by chewing the erasers off pencils and overeating, so he gains weight. Now his problem is obesity, so he winds up hanging around Overeaters Anonymous and drinking a gallon of water a day. It's what teachers call 'redirecting.' You may not be able to stop two four-year-olds from fighting, but you can say, 'Let's go get ice cream cones.' "

An external superego. "If I tell you you'll get liver disease if you keep on drinking, you could care less," Vaillant says. "But if I say that as an M. D. I'm going to do random checks on your urine, you may pay attention. Or if, when you drink Jack Daniels, it bums your stomach. Methadone is an external superego, since it blocks the effect of heroin. Someone who engaged in compulsive sex might not care if it hurt their spouse's feelings, but if there were an electric bracelet that could transmit a shock at crucial moments, that might make a difference."

"I get no kick from cocaine." "It's fascinating that heroin addicts get better when they fall in love with someone new," Vaillant says. "Our brains are wired for falling in love, because that's good for nature—but you can short-circuit that pathway with morphine, nicotine, caffeine. Love gets the whole brain involved. Romantic attachment not only competes with the addiction, but takes place in a nonaddictive way."

Spiritus contra spiritum. "Charismatic religions offer a conversion experience, as described by William James and C. G. Jung. Suddenly you find your higher power, and booze is no longer important," Vaillant explains. "There is also the protective wall of a human community—something that AA, for example, provides. It's important to find a new social group, since you owe money to all your old ones. Religion offers an oceanic high— the sense that a higher power loves you. To the addict, heroin, cocaine, and booze are like mother's milk. Religion is, too."

Looking at Both Sides—The Debate Continues

The core arguments with regard to the conceptualization of drug and alcohol dependence as a brain disease are aptly represented in the following two excerpts.

> Although each drug that has been studied has some idiosyncratic mechanisms of action, virtually all drugs of abuse have common effects, either directly or indirectly, on a single pathway deep within the brain, the mesolimbic reward system. Activation of this system appears to be a common element in what keeps drug users taking drugs. This is not unique to any one drug; all addictive substances affect this circuit.
>
> Not only does acute drug use modify brain function in critical ways, but prolonged drug use causes pervasive changes in brain function that persist long after the individual stops taking the drug. (from the Leshner interview, selection 14)

The dispute over whether addiction is a brain disease isn't merely a dispute among doctors. It is, for many reasons, political. The efforts of NIDA [The National Institute on Drug Abuse] do not simply aim to medicalize addiction, presumably a medical concern, but to destigmatize the addict, clearly a sociopolitical concern. . . . Labeling addiction a chronic and relapsing brain disease is mere propaganda. By downplaying the volitional dimension of addiction, the brain-disease model detracts from the great promise of strategies and therapies that rely on sanctions and rewards to shape self-control. . . . [Addicts] are the instigators of their own addiction, just as they can be the agents of their own recovery. (from Satel's article, selection 15)

Matters to Ponder

- If an addict were to believe in the brain-disease model, do you think he or she would be less inclined to seek out behavioral forms of treatment? Why do you think so?
- Do you think destigmatizing drug abusers has had a beneficial or detrimental effect on the prospects for recovery? Explain your answer in the context of an alcoholic.

Further Sources to Seek Out

Leshner, Alan I. (1997, October 3). Addiction is a brain disease, and it matters. *Science,* pp. 45–47. A summary of the brain-disease perspective.

———. (2001, May). When the question is drug abuse and addiction, the answer is "all of the above." *NIDA Notes, 16* (2), pp. 3–4. An explanation of how successful drug treatment strategies need to take biological, psychological, and sociological perspectives into consideration.

Toby, Jackson. (1998, Winter). Medicalizing temptation. *The Public Interest,* pp. 64–78. A well-written essay expressing opposition to the concept of drug dependence as a brain disease.

Web Sites to Explore

www.nida.nih.gov
The web site for the National Institute on Drug Abuse, with publications expressing the position that a brain-disease concept applies to drug dependence.

www.peele.net
The web site for the writings of Stanton Peele, an influential critic of the brain-disease concept of drug dependence.

Question: Is Alcoholics Anonymous the Best Strategy for the Treatment of Alcoholism?

Alcoholics Anonymous is undoubtedly the best-known treatment program for alcoholics in the world. Founded in 1935, this organization (most often simply referred to as A.A.) has been conceived as a fellowship of alcoholics who wish to rid themselves of their problem drinking by helping one another maintain absolute sobriety. As described in the official A.A. web site, "we attempt—most of us successfully—to create a satisfying way of life without alcohol. For this we find we need the help and support of other alcoholics in A.A."

Complete anonymity to the public is maintained as a condition for participation in any A.A. program, hence its name. Its philosophy is expressed in the famous Twelve Steps, in which members are encouraged to have acknowledged that they have been "powerless over alcohol" and their lives have become unmanageable. Participants pledge to have taken the step to turn their will and their lives over "to the care of God *as we understood Him*" (italics theirs).

Functioning as clients in a type of group therapy, A.A. members are oriented toward a common goal: the maintenance of abstinence from alcohol despite a powerful and continuing craving for it. Meetings are typically dominated by the recounting of members' personal struggles with alcohol, their efforts to stop drinking, and their support for fellow alcoholics in their own struggles. New members are encouraged to pair up with a sponsor, usually a more experienced A.A. member who has successfully completed the Twelve Steps and can serve as a personal source of support on a day-to-day basis. According to Alcoholics Anonymous, no alcoholic is ever cured, only recovered, and the process of recovery continues throughout that person's life. Alcoholism is considered a disease (see Chapter 5 in this book), and relapses from sobriety can occur at any moment.

A.A. has grown to more than 95,000 chapters around the world and an estimated two million members, though a verification of these estimates is difficult since the organization is deliberately structured very loosely. Its sheer size has resulted in a powerful impact not only on the way we deal with alcoholism itself but also on the way we consider treatment for any compulsive behavior. Over the years, twelve-step programs have entered the public lexicon, as a generic concept for treating drug-taking behavior. We now have Al-Anon for the spouses and family of alcoholics going through the program and Alateen as a specialized A.A. program for teenage alcoholics, as well as Gamblers Anonymous, Nicotine

Anonymous, Narcotics Anonymous, and Cocaine Anonymous, as well as Overeaters Anonymous.

A.A. has also spawned alternative treatment programs for alcoholism that deviate from basic A.A. principles. The self-help program Rational Recovery (RR) assumes that people do not need to believe they are "powerless over alcohol" or that they need to submit themselves to a "Power greater than ourselves" (excerpts taken from the Twelve Steps) in order to recover from alcoholism. Instead, the dominant RR philosophy is that individuals have the power themselves to overcome anything, including drinking. The strategy is based upon the principles of Rational Emotive Therapy (RET), developed by the psychologist Albert Ellis, which emphasizes the rooting out of irrational thoughts, emotions, and beliefs that prevent the achievement of personal goals.

Another major difference from A.A. is that RR insists on professional involvement in its programs, with a professional advisor (often a clinical psychologist specializing in addictive behaviors) assisting members in learning the fundamentals of RET. No reference is made to God or a Higher Power; in fact, RR members point out that the objective is "NHP (no higher power) sobriety." The goal in RR is that within a year and a half members will be able to maintain sobriety without going to RR meetings. In contrast, A.A. members are encouraged to continue going to meetings for the rest of their lives, and are in fact judged as a success by the number of A.A. meetings attended.

A more radical approach in self-help treatment of alcoholism is the position taken by Moderation Management (MM). Advocates of MM argue that a disease model does not apply in the case of alcoholism (or drug abuse in general). As sociologist Erich Goode has expressed it, those believing in a nondisease model of alcoholism view alcoholics as " . . . not sick, but . . . rational problem-solving human beings attempting to carve out a meaningful existence in a harsh and seemingly unyielding environment." In the case of MM, the goal is not abstinence from alcohol but rather the moderation of alcohol ingestion. Guidelines for women are no more than nine drinks a week, no more than three a day; for men, the limit is fourteen drinks a week and no more than four on any given day. All MM members are prohibited from drinking and driving.

Two of the three selections in this chapter exemplify the major disagreement with respect to alcoholism treatment. Should alcoholics totally abstain from alcohol (the position of A.A.) or should alcoholics learn to deal with alcohol consumption in a moderate and responsible way so as to avoid the negative consequences of problem drinking (the position of MM)? The first selection spotlights the principles of A.A., its Twelve Steps and Traditions. The second selection, written by Ronald E. Hopson and Bethany Beaird-Spiller, concerns an analysis of how Alcoholics Anonymous, as an organization, functions in the larger context of psychotherapy. The third selection, written by Stanton Peele, argues strenuously against the basic precepts of A.A.

REFERENCES

A.A. World Services. (1998). A newcomer asks. *http://www.alcoholics-anonymous.org.*
Goode, Erich (1999). *Drugs in American society* (5th ed.). New York: McGraw-Hill, p. 350.
Levinthal, Charles F. (2002). *Drugs, behavior, and modern society* (3rd ed.). Boston: Allyn and Bacon.
Shute, Nancy. (1997, September 8). Drinking dilemma. *U.S. News and World Report*, pp. 54–65.

SELECTION 17

The hallmark of Alcoholics Anonymous is the set of principles upon which it operates as an alcoholism treatment. These principles are expressed in the following selection, known as the Twelve Steps and the Twelve Traditions. Each individual in Alcoholics Anonymous is expected to subscribe to these basic beliefs as a condition for his or her recovery. The organization was founded in 1935 by William Griffith Wilson ("Bill W.") and Robert Smith ("Dr. Bob"), who together formulated the Twelve Steps. The Twelve Traditions were adopted by the International Convention of A. A., at Cleveland, Ohio, in 1950.

■ *The Twelve Steps of Alcoholics Anonymous*

In simplest form, the A.A. program operates when a recovered alcoholic passes along the story of his or her own problem drinking, describes the sobriety he or she has found in A.A., and invites the newcomer to join the informal Fellowship.

The heart of the suggested program of personal recovery is contained in Twelve Steps describing the experience of the earliest members of the Society:

1. We admitted we were powerless over alcohol—that our lives had become unmanageable.
2. Came to believe that a Power greater than ourselves could restore us to sanity.
3. Made a decision to turn our will and our lives over to the care of God as we understood Him.
4. Made a searching and fearless moral inventory of ourselves.
5. Admitted to God, to ourselves and to another human being the exact nature of our wrongs.
6. Were entirely ready to have God remove all these defects of character.
7. Humbly asked Him to remove our shortcomings.
8. Made a list of all persons we had harmed, and became willing to make amends to them all.
9. Made direct amends to such people wherever possible, except when to do so would injure them or others.
10. Continued to take personal inventory and when we were wrong promptly admitted it.
11. Sought through prayer and meditation to improve our conscious contact with God *as we understood Him,* praying only for knowledge of His will for us and the power to carry that out.
12. Having had a spiritual awakening as the result of these steps, we tried to carry this message to alcoholics and to practice these principles in all our affairs.

Newcomers are not asked to accept or follow these Twelve Steps in their entirety if they feel unwilling or unable to do so.

They will usually be asked to keep an open mind, to attend meetings at which recovered alcoholics describe their personal experiences in achieving sobriety, and to read A.A. literature describing and interpreting the A.A. program.

A.A. members will usually emphasize to newcomers that only problem drinkers themselves, individually, can determine whether or not they are in fact alcoholics.

At the same time, it will be pointed out that all available medical testimony indicates that alcoholism is a progressive illness, that it cannot be cured in the ordinary sense of the term, but that it can be arrested through total abstinence from alcohol in any form.

■ *A.A. Traditions*

During its first decade, A.A. as a fellowship accumulated substantial experience which indicated that certain group attitudes and principles were particularly valuable in assuring survival of the informal structure of the Fellowship. In 1946, in the Fellowship's international journal, the *A.A. Grapevine,* these principles were reduced to writing by the founders and early members as the Twelve Traditions of Alcoholics Anonymous. They were accepted and endorsed by the membership as a whole at the International Convention of A.A., at Cleveland, Ohio, in 1950.

1. Our common welfare should come first; personal recovery depends upon A.A. unity.
2. For our group purpose there is but one ultimate authority—a loving God as He may express Himself in our group conscience. Our leaders are but trusted servants; they do not govern.
3. The only requirement for A.A. membership is a desire to stop drinking.
4. Each group should be autonomous except in matters affecting other groups or A.A. as a whole.
5. Each group has but one primary purpose—to carry its message to the alcoholic who still suffers.
6. An A.A. group ought never endorse, finance or lend the A.A. name to any related facility or outside enterprise, lest problems of money, property and prestige divert us from our primary purpose.
7. An A.A. group ought to be fully self-supporting, declining outside contributions.
8. Alcoholics Anonymous should remain forever nonprofessional, but our service centers may employ special workers.
9. A.A., as such, ought never be organized; but we may create service boards or committees directly responsible to those they serve.
10. Alcoholics Anonymous has no opinion on outside issues: hence the A.A. name ought never be drawn into public controversy.
11. Our public relations policy is based on attraction rather than promotion; we need always maintain personal anonymity at the level of press, radio, and films.
12. Anonymity is the spiritual foundation of all our traditions, ever reminding us to place principles before personalities.

While the Twelve Traditions are not specifically binding on any group or groups, an overwhelming majority of members have adopted them as the basis for A.A.'s expanding "internal" and public relationships.

SELECTION 18

The following selection is an article written by Ronald E. Hopson and Bethany Beaird-Spiller, published in *Alcoholism Treatment Quarterly* in 1995, examining the functioning of A.A. from the viewpoint of a psychotherapist. At the time of the writing, Ronald E. Hopson was Assistant Professor in the Department of Psychology, University of Tennessee, Knoxville. Bethany Beaird-Spiller was a graduate student at that university.

Why AA Works: A Psychological Analysis of the Addictive Experience and the Efficacy of Alcoholics Anonymous

RONALD E. HOPSON AND BETHANY BEAIRD-SPILLER

ABSTRACT. The therapeutic efficacy of AA, though acknowledged, is little understood. An analysis of the addictive experience is conducted to provide explanatory hypotheses for the success of AA. The addictive experience is characterized by intensity of feelings which cannot be rendered symbolically via language. Out of this mode of experiencing emerges three phenomena: (1) an alteration in the sense of the movement of time; (2) a sense of alienation and lack of connection to others; (3) a lack of sense of agency and the inability for self/affect regulation. These results are brought into dialogue with the AA recovery program and AA is found to specifically address the problematic modes of experiencing characteristic of the addicted person.

The longest standing treatment program for the problem of alcoholism is Alcoholics Anonymous (AA). Despite the varying approaches to the problem of alcoholism, virtually all of the approaches which have been advanced to understand alcoholism include AA as an essential element in the recovery process. What may account for the ubiquitous presence of AA among treatment approaches? What are the essential characteristics of AA which make it arguably the most successful approach for treating alcoholism?

The purpose of the present study is to provide explanatory hypotheses for the success of the AA program, and to contribute to the development of a paradigm for the understanding of alcoholism. Lorenz (1950) has argued that basic to scientific inquiry is the "unprejudiced observation of all there is to be observed" about a phenomenon. This suggests the

Hopson, Ronald E., and Beaird-Spiller, Bethany. (1995). Why AA works: A psychological analysis of the addictive experience and the efficacy of Alcoholics Anonymous. *Alcoholism Treatment Quarterly, 12,* 1–17. © 1995, Haworth Press, Binghamton, NY. Reprinted with permission.

importance and validity of a first-person perspective on the problem of alcoholism. The relative efficacy of AA as a treatment approach developed by persons experienced in the phenomenon of addiction, as well as the current state of understanding of the problem warrant a return to the 'things themselves' (Husserl, 1970).

Present Study

The present study is the second to explore the nature of alcoholism/addiction from the perspective of the alcoholic/addict, and aims to provide empirically based explanatory hypotheses for the success of AA. Previously, Hopson (1993) has discussed the findings reported herein in relation to psychotherapy. The present study focuses upon the relationship between the findings and the structure, function and efficacy of AA.

Procedure

Twenty-one volunteers were recruited at random from a mid-size urban community. Participants were drawn from outpatient alcohol and drug treatment programs. The participants were interviewed about their non-intoxicated experiences during the active phase of their addiction. The participants, ten male, eleven female, ranged in age from 25 years to 61 years with twenty of the participants between the ages of 25 years and 45 years. Seventeen participants were single (five of which had never been married), sixteen were employed, and their educational level ranged from high school graduate to professional/technical training (e.g., nursing). The sample size is characteristic of phenomenologically based research studies which aim not for statistical generalization, but rather to discover and accurately describe the essential attributes of a phenomenon (Polkinghorn, 1989). All participants considered themselves addicted to alcohol and some reported abuse of or addiction to other chemicals (e.g., nicotine, stimulants, narcotics). Donovan and Marlatt (1988) and Kosten and Rounsaville (1986) maintain that there are common elements among addictions which justify grouping several types of compulsive behavior under the term addiction. No differences were noted in the essential description of the addictive experience according to drug of choice. All participants had been through a treatment program though all were not involved in an ongoing self-help group such as AA. Length of abstinence for participants ranged from less than one year (though at least one month) for two persons, while all others had been abstinent between one and ten years including two participants who had been abstinent between eleven and twenty years. All participants considered themselves addicted to alcohol for at least one year and two participants reported being addicted for more than thirty years. Eight participants were involved in their first attempt at sobriety since beginning their alcohol use.

All subjects participated in an approximately hour-long audio-taped, unstructured interview about their non-intoxicated experiences during the active phase of their alcoholism. The interview question was: "Tell me about some times in your life during the time you were drinking. Please be as thorough as possible and describe everything you can about the experience."

A clinical interview technique was used to obtain a description of the addictive experience. In this method, the interviewer asked the participant to describe the experience under consideration in as much detail as possible. Ambiguous descriptions were queried by the interviewer until the interviewer and subject were satisfied that the description was as clear as possible. The interviews were then transcribed. Analysis of the transcripts was done by a team of phenomenological researchers, to obtain a thorough description of the essential characteristics of the addictive experience (Husser, 1970; Merleau-Ponty, 1962; Valle & Halling, 1989). The team of researchers, consisting of graduate students and faculty, read each transcript to determine the thematic structure of the reported experiences. Diversity of perspectives are an important element of this approach. Themes are arrived at through synthesis of the multiple perspectives represented by the team thereby enhancing the reliability of the themes. Though alternative themes may be suggested from the text, it is maintained that the themes reported herein are an accurate, psychologically meaningful representation of the addictive experience. (See Messer, Sass and Woolfolk [1988] for a thorough discussion of hermeneutic interpretation of human experience). The following procedure outlined by Polkinghorn (1989), Giorgi (1975), and Thompson, Locander and Pollio (1989) was employed in the analysis:

1. The interview was read aloud in segments or units. A unit is delimited by a change of subject or an elaboration following an inquiry (Dapkus, 1985; Labov & Fanchel, 1977). In the present study, a unit was designated by a question from the interviewer.
2. The units resulting from this procedure were then examined to determine, *in the subject's own words,* the meaning that dominates that unit. The subject's own words or phrases were used to represent the meaning of that unit.
3. Meaning units are then established for the entire transcript. This procedure is followed for each transcript. (Tables detailing the steps of this procedure are available from the first author upon request.)
4. After meaning units are established for all transcripts, these units are progressively collapsed into a smaller number of units (subthemes) still using the subject's own words.
5. The subthemes are synthesized across transcripts into a general description of the addictive experience (themes). "Synthesis involves tying together and integrating the meaning units into a consistent and systematic general description of the psychological structure of the experience under investigation" (Polkinghorn, 1989, p. 56). In order for a theme to be established, it must be represented in every transcript.

The requirement that each theme be found in every subject's transcript insures a high degree of specificity to the addictive phenomena and simultaneously a high degree of generalizability across addicted persons. Generalizability from this perspective requires that other specific experiences reported by addicted persons, though not represented among these transcripts, may be illuminated by themes uncovered in this study. The issue of generalizability is also addressed through comparison of these findings with descriptions of the phenomena in the clinical literature.

Results
The addictive experience may be characterized by problematic modes of experiencing in four areas: (1) Intense feelings for which language is inadequate; (2) A disruption in the experience of time; (3) Alienation from oneself and others; and (4) Lack of sense of agency, self-efficacy and the capacity for self-regulation.

The experience of the alcoholic is characterized by intense feelings. These feelings form the context within which the alcoholic lives. The world is ordered by feelings and the actions of the alcoholic person are organized around an attempt to manage feelings. The feelings are often, though not always, negative and are experienced as potentially overwhelming and always intense.

> Example: During this time in my life there was a lot of pressure on me. On my job. A lot of people were demanding things. . . . I would have all of this anger about them inside of me. It felt like as soon as I stopped drinking there was a lot of pressure on me. All of the reality was there. . . . Everything seemed larger or out of perspective, the feelings and the tasks, all of that I was feeling real good. I thought this is good. I don't know if I actually thought I could handle it then, consciously. But I remember thinking that since I felt so good then, that I would feel even that much better with a drink. . . . Anger was there all of my waking time . . . I could still if I don't keep things in perspective, still real easily get myself tied up into some real intense feelings.

This suggests the alcoholic has difficulty labelling and symbolizing feelings using language (hyposymbolization), as Wurmser (1978) has argued. Sullivan (1953) has observed that the capacity to use language is essential in the development of adequate self-regulatory mechanisms. The magnitude of the feeling state of the addicted person cannot be captured in words, thereby self-regulation may be problematic.

> Example: All of my life I held my feelings inside. I was unable to identify my feelings and whenever I'd come in from work, I might not realize what I was feeling . . . I learned that if I started first of all identifying my feelings and then talking about it . . . I had always gone on the assumption that actions speak louder than words . . . I wasn't able, first of all to figure out what I was feeling and second of all to communicate it.

Within the context of these wordless, intense affective experiences, the sense of temporal flow is disrupted. The experience of intense affect together with a disruption in the sense of movement of time suggests a relationship between time and affective experience as has been proposed by Wallace and Rabin (1960), and Kastenbaum (1965). The usual sense of temporality and flux is interrupted. Time moves exceedingly slowly, or ceases to move at all. This temporal perceptual anomaly may shed light on Van Kaam's (1965) suggestion that there is a sense for the addicted person that now is all there is, each moment seems to take on the weight of eternity.

> Example: I felt frozen, yea, very trapped, very trapped . . . like time had ceased to exist . . . so to get beyond this I've got to realize I'm not here forever . . . the illusion is I'm stuck, it's like we don't recognize that it's going to go away . . . I found out that things do pass.

The inadequacy of words and the lack of sense of movement of time leaves the alcoholic in the grip of feelings for which there may be no modulation or relief.

The management of feeling states is essential for the development of adequate self-regulation and sense of self-efficacy (Khan, 1983). Another element which characterizes the alcoholic experience is a disturbance in the capacity for self-regulation and the regulation of feelings.

> Example: I was scared, deep, deep fear like I couldn't die . . . it was horrifying . . . it was very sad . . . I had a tremendous amount of feeling going on . . . the focus was on losing my feelings . . . I was sad, so lonely, so isolated. I remember feeling trapped in this moment of terror, dread, pain . . . this tremendous dread . . . for the most part my drug usage was around, I used to numb myself.

The lack of sense of agency goes beyond the regulation of feeling states and involves regulation of the self.

> Example: I like to play . . . I don't want to leave until it's getting dark . . . most people watch a movie . . . I want to watch 2 or 3 straight . . . I'm so into everything I do that I don't pay a lot of attention to everything around me. I was juggling full time school . . . I found myself into an all or nothing situation . . . I'm either full steam all the way or like right now. I was very passive . . . I didn't feel I could really take care of myself . . . I didn't choose anything . . . you just kinda do it even though you don't choose.

The lack of the capacity to reliably care for oneself and manage one's feeling states relate to the fourth area of difficulty for the alcoholic: intra/interpersonal relationships. The alcoholic reports experiencing a profound sense of alienation and disconnection from self and others.

> Example: I was alone and it was loneliness, it was intense. I think my only love in life has been drugs . . . I just felt so alone . . . I was sad, so lonely, so isolated, I wasn't me, but as far as having some friends, really being close to somebody, there wasn't anybody . . . I was unable to keep those connections.

Discussion

These findings indicate the addictive phenomena to be a manifestation of particular perceptual and experiential anomalies (Hopson, 1993). The addicted person experiences intense feelings for which there seems no possibility of participation, control, or titration. Language, as symbol, and as a mode of participation and management of feeling states, seems unavailable to the addicted person in the grip of these feelings. Out of this mode of experiencing emerges three phenomena: The addicted individual experiences a disruption in the temporal domain, there is a sense of being caught or frozen in time—time ceases to move. There is also a lack of the sense of agency and the capacity for self-regulation (self-governance, Mack, 1981) of feelings or behavior. Finally, there is a felt lack of connection to oneself and others, a sense of alienation.

External validation of the findings in this study are evident in psychological perspectives on the addictive experience. Khantzian (1981) views the alcoholic as suffering from a "range of ego impairments that affect their capacity to regulate their feeling life" (p. 166). Wilson et al. (1989) have also suggested defects in self-regulatory/self-soothing (ego) functions such as the inability to identify, verbalize, and modulate feelings. The capacity to identify affects and the signal function of affects is lost. Thus, feelings are experienced as unbearable, overwhelming and not transitory in time.

These findings provide empirical correspondences to the structure and function of AA. (See Table 6.1.) The perceptual and experiential anomalies detailed in these interviews indicate that the addictive experience is broader than the specific abuse of a substance. Rather, the addictive phenomenon is a particular manifestation of a way of being. This relates directly to the view of AA that "alcoholism is a mode of being and action in the world within which misuse of alcohol is only one component" (Flores, 1988, p. 78).

The addictive experience is characterized by the experience of intense affective states for which language is inadequate or unavailable. Alcoholism has been called a disease of feelings. These feelings may be positive or negative and are experienced with such intensity

TABLE 6.1   Psychological Function of AA

AA Structure/Practice	Psychological Function
Speaking about one's experience	Practice using language to represent present/ self; express feelings. Establishment of sense of self
Telling one's story My name is _____ and I'm an alcoholic.	Consolidation of sense of self
Sayings	
Don't Drink Now, Wait a Minute	Restoration of temporality
This Too Shall Pass, One Day at a Time	Tolerance of affect
Take It Easy/HALT Easy Does It	Modulation, regulation of feeling states
Meeting regularity	Restoration of sense of agency Self-regulation
12 Steps:	
Step 1 Powerlessness	Acknowledgment of loss of agency
Step 2 Higher Power	Compensation for lack of internal structure
Step 3 Decision to turn life and will over	Relief from effort to carry weight of strong feelings without assistance The presumption of agency
Emphasis upon fellowship	Restoration of sense of relatedness to others
Sponsor system	Self-acceptance, restored relationship with self and others
Unconditional acceptance	Overcoming alienation
"Keep Coming Back"	Restoration of sense of connection to others

that they threaten to overwhelm the individual. The inability to endure intense affective experiences results in a "short-circuit to the action system" (Wurmser, 1978), as a way of reducing the vague tension arising from these unarticulable feeling states.

The failure of the addicted person to endure suffering (intense negative feelings) has been understood as a refusal to live within the given limits of human existence (Flores, 1988). However, these findings indicate that rather than unwillingness to endure the normal vicissitudes of human existence, the addicted person experiences these vicissitudes with such intensity that he or she is incapable of enduring this angst without external assistance. In fact, Wurmser (1978) has referred to drug addiction as the use of a pharmaco-defense in face of the failure of the ego to provide adequate defense mechanisms against overwhelming affect.

The intense affective experiences are accompanied by a failure of language. Language functions as a symbol system which constitutes the self (Lacan, 1989) and has the potential to contain affective experiences, rendering these experiences at least partially articulable and therefore within the capacity of the individual to endure. The addicted person does not utilize language in this manner. Wurmser (1978) describes the addicted person as unable to adequately utilize "the verbal band out of the spectrum of symbolic processes" (p. 234), to modulate intense affective experiences. Thus is seen the impulsive problem, the determined search for relief from overwhelming feelings.

The structure of AA addresses this vulnerability to intense experiencing and the failure of language precisely by employing "the verbal band out of the spectrum of symbolic processes" as its fundamental tool. AA meetings offer a series of lessons in utilizing language to represent the self. The basic format of AA is that persons gather to speak of themselves. AA members listen to others speak about their experiences. New members often have the experience of 'hearing their story' in others who have spoken. This provides a powerful experience in modeling how to use language. Also, there is an expectation that members speak of their own experience, thereby practicing the use of language to express feelings. The AA literature maintains that AA provides experience, strength and hope through the telling of one's former life while drinking and the present life of sobriety (Alcoholics Anonymous, 1939).

The practice of speaking is supplemented by cognitive strategies which are taught to the AA member. Beck (1976) quotes Paul Dubois: "If we wish to change the sentiments it is necessary before all to modify the idea which has produced [them], and to recognize either that it is not correct in itself or that it does not touch our interests" (p. 213). This statement bears directly on the approach of AA. The AA member is taught certain phrases to utilize when experiencing uncomfortable feelings. The efficacy of self-talk in the relief of painful affective states has been elaborated by Beck (1976). These strategies serve to reduce the intensity of such experiences and the person is able to gain some objective distance from such overwhelming feelings. 'Take It Easy,' and 'Easy Does It' are such sayings which have developed in AA and provide cognitive strategies for dealing with potentially overwhelming emotion.

Martin Heidegger (1962) understands time to be inextricably linked to the experience of being, and being may only be understood through the temporal dimension. McInerney (1991) has elucidated Heidegger's main position in a manner that has direct relation to the addicted person's experience of time. "The world . . . has a time structure. Time is an essential parameter of that action-oriented system of meanings through which we encounter . . . other [beings), and ourselves . . . every moment of world time is understood with respect to some actual or potential action. Every "now" is experienced as the appropriate or inappropriate time to do something" (p. 123). The failure in the sense of the movement of time for the addicted person renders every "now" as the appropriate time to act. Inactivity threatens the sense of temporal flow and thus one's very existence. Thus we see impulsive behavior to acquire the drug, as the addicted person behaving in pseudo-courageous disregard for their own well-being. Indeed, the behavior of the addicted person may be understood as an instance of courage gone awry.

Excessive frustration may result in a disturbance of temporal perspective (Ingram, 1979). Rabin (1978) has empirically demonstrated that future time perspective and future orientation is linked to ego strength the capacity to bear frustration. Kohut (1971) links the precarious sense of continuity in time to the fear of fragmentation which must be warded off at any costs. The inability to experience the movement of time freezes the experience of the self in the present, and the person has trouble imagining that they will ever feel different than at the moment—especially, when they are emotionally upset. The result of this process is the often frantic search for relief which characterizes the addict in search of his/her drug of choice. No obstacle is too formidable as the addicted person seeks to reestablish the sense of being-in-time which has been threatened with the onset of strong emotion.

Several sayings have developed within AA which address the problem of time. "Don't Drink Now," "Wait a Minute," "This Too Shall Pass," and perhaps the most famous saying, "One Day at a Time," may be understood as cognitive strategies to intervene with the sense of disruption in the flow of time. "Don't Drink Now" and "Wait a Minute" intervene with the sense of urgency with which the impulse to drink is experienced and blocks the tendency to act impulsively. "This Too Shall Pass" restores the sense of the movement of time, particularly in those circumstances in which the person is experiencing stress or anxiety. It also orients the person to the future, in contrast to the predominant orientation to the past of persons with emotional problems (Smeltzer, 1969). "One Day at a Time" addresses the experience of the collapse of past and future into the present and the corresponding sense of overwhelm which accompanies the weight of eternity. The addict is encouraged to live only in the present, letting go of the past and leaving the future to itself.

The regularity of AA meetings also provides an important dimension of temporality. Members of AA are encouraged to establish a "home meeting" which they regularly attend. Members develop the expectation that others of their group be in attendance, thus the addicted person has the opportunity to practice a lifestyle of regularity and predictability rather than the erratic, unpredictable experience of the active phase of their addiction.

The failure of the capacity for self-regulation and the corresponding lack of sense of self-efficacy is the most obvious problem of the addictive experience. The often chaotic and irregular life of the addicted person reveals the lack of structure and the deficit in the capacity for self-management. This defect in self-care/management has been understood as a psychological problem which precedes development of the addiction (Mack, 1981), or as a consequence of the addictive process (Jellinek, 1960). Whichever etiological perspective one may subscribe to, the lack of structure and regularity is an important aspect of the addictive process.

AA assumes a paradoxical approach to the problem of self-efficacy and agency. The "first step" of the twelve steps of AA is to admit that the alcoholic is powerless over alcohol and that his/her life had become unmanageable. Step two insists that the alcoholic is in need of assistance from a greater power. Thus, the lack of agency and efficacy is established.

Kurtz (1982) has elaborated the function of these steps as a recognition, and indeed affirmation of the reality of human limitation. This analysis will extend Kurtz' application of existential philosophy to AA by including the reality of paradox as captured by the twelve steps. As the first two steps admit a loss of control, yet, the third step calls for the exercise of volition in the face of a loss of volition: "Made a decision to turn our will and our lives over . . . " AA acknowledges the alcoholic's inability to control the self, and paradoxically calls for the alcoholic to exercise the will to surrender control of the will to a beneficent higher power.

The reality of paradox as an essential element of the human condition is elaborated in much existential philosophy (e.g., Soren Kierkegaard). AA embraces this paradox by acknowledging the reality of volition in the midst of a loss of volition. The alcoholic is confronted with the seemingly insoluble human dilemma: relative freedom. In the midst of this dilemma, the alcoholic is encouraged to decide. Despite the sense of lack of efficacy, agency is assumed as the alcoholic is charged to act. However, this activity is not in keeping with the sense of loss of control and corresponding sense of alienation, but rather the action mandated assumes relationship with others and control by a power greater than the self. The second step of AA acknowledges the existence of a power greater than the self, thus intervening with the sense of demoralization, while the third step raises the possibility of relationship with this power, thereby addressing the sense of alienation.

The structure of AA answers the problem of freedom and aloneness as Keirkegaard (1980) would reply. Kierkegaard understands a key element in the experience of despair as the failure to relate oneself to oneself and others. The remediation of this situation is, for Kierkegaard, an exercise of the will in the face of the inevitable paradoxes of life. The decision to relate oneself to oneself and others, despite the reality of being alone, is the fundamental act of courage without which, one lives a shrunken, cowardly life.

AA was from the beginning a "fellowship." This emphasis upon relationship may be seen as an outgrowth of the fundamental experience of alienation and isolation experienced by persons who are addicted. Ramsey (1988) has discussed the link between alcoholism and the affective fraternal twins guilt and shame. Guilt and shame function to alienate one from others (Kaufman, 1985). The efficacy of AA in addressing this issue is derived from the explicit attention given the experience of alienation. The individual alcoholic is no longer alone, and even more importantly s/he is related to a powerful other. AA provides an immediate submerging of the member into an extensive interpersonal support system. "Upon entry into the program, members are available at once to provide unconditional acceptance and support to the newcomer and, together with a sponsor, bring about an end to the [member's] isolation" (Spiegel & Mulder, 1986, p. 38). The availability of others provides the interpersonal contact and opportunities for vulnerability which are essential in healing shame (Kurtz, 1982). Indeed, there are other structural elements of the AA program which also address this issue of alienation. The tradition in AA of securing a "sponsor," a confidante who is available at all times to provide support and guidance to the

AA member, is a powerful antidote to the isolation and alienation experienced by the addicted person.

The experience of alienation is not limited to the transcendent and interpersonal dimensions, there is also the experience of alienation from the self. Mack (1981) and Kohut (1984) have elaborated the "defects of the self" which they postulate are an element of the addictive problem. These self-deficits may be seen in the addicted person's failure in some areas of self care, as well as a lack of a cohesive sense of self. AA addresses this lack of sense of self in various ways.

The tradition in AA is that members begin each statement with the sentence: "My name is _____ and I'm an alcoholic." This sentence serves both to link the individual member to the community of alcoholics, as well as to reinforce one's sense of selfhood. The self is affirmed as the AA member names and identifies him/herself. Further, the members are encouraged to speak of their experiences. Schaffer (1992) has discussed the critical role of telling one's story in the consolidation of an "emotionally coherent account of [one's] life among people" (p. 34). As the members of AA tell their story, they experience a sense of relationship to others through recognition of the self in another's story, and develop an emotionally coherent account of their life.

Summary

In summary, the addictive experience was found to be characterized by intense emotions which are not amenable to (language as) symbolic representation. The wordless world of feelings gives rise to: (1) the loss of the movement of time and the related experience of flux or change; (2) a lack of sense of self-efficacy and the capacity for effective self-monitoring and self-regulation; and (3) a loss of relatedness to oneself and others. These categories reconcile divergent views of the addictive problem from biological to social and suggest an experiential paradigm for understanding addiction. The biopsychosocial aspects of the addictive problem may be reconciled by understanding addiction as a correlate of a particular mode of experiencing which is characterized by disturbances in the use of language, the perception of time and the experience of self and others. These findings also provide explanatory hypotheses for the effectiveness of AA and other self-help twelve step movements. The problematic dimensions of the addictive experience are addressed through the structure of the AA program. The effectiveness of AA may be accounted for by its thorough response to the addictive problem. AA provides cognitive strategies, compensatory psychological mechanisms, and intra/inter/transpersonal resources to assist the addicted person in successfully negotiating the vicissitudes of human living.

REFERENCES

Beck, A. T. (1976). *Cognitive Therapy and Emotional Disorders*. New York: International Universities Press.

Dapkus, M. (1985). A Thematic Analysis of the Experience of Time. *Journal of Personality and Social Psychology. Vol. 49 No. 2*, 408–419.

Donovan, D. M. & Marlatt, G. A. (Eds.). (1988). *Assessment of Addiction Behaviors*. New York: The Guilford Press.

Flores, Phillip. (1988). Alcoholics Anonymous: A Phenomenological and Existential Perspective. *Alcoholism Treatment Quarterly*, 5, (1/2), pp. 73–94.

Heidegger, M. (1962)[1927]. *Being and Time.* New York: Harper & Row.

Hopson, R. E. (1993). A Thematic Analysis of the Addictive Experience: Implications for Psychotherapy. *Psychotherapy 30 (*3), 481–494.

Husserl, E. (1970). *The Crisis of the European Sciences and Transcendental Phenomenology: An Introduction to Phenomenological Philosophy.* Tran. David Cut. Evanston: Northwestern University Press.

Ingram, D. H. (1979). Time and Timekeeping in Psychoanalysis and Psychotherapy. *The American Journal of Psychoanalysis, 39* (4), 319–328.

Jellinek, E. M. (1960). *The Disease Concept of Alcoholism.* Harland Park, MT: Hillhouse Press.

Kastenbaum, R. (1965). The Direction of Time Perspective: The Influence of Affective Set. *The Journal of General Psychology, 73,* 189–201.

Kaufman, G. (1985). *Shame, The Power of Caring.* Cambridge, MA: Schenkman Publishing Company.

Khan, M. (1983). *Hidden Selves.* New York: International Universities Press.

Khantzian, E. J. (1981). Some Treatment Implications of the Ego and Self Disturbances in Alcoholism. In Margaret Bean & Norman E. Zinberg (Eds.), *Dynamic Approaches to the Understanding and Treatment of Alcoholism.* New York: The Free Press.

Kierkegaard, S. (1849/1980). *The Sickness Unto Death.* Howard V. Hong, Edna H. Hong (Eds. and Trans.). Princeton, NJ: Princeton University Press.

Kohut. H. (1971). *The Analysis of the Self.* New York: Int'l. Universities Press.

Kohut, H. (1984). *How Does Analysis Cure?* Chicago: University of Chicago Press.

Kosten, T. and Rounsoville, B. J. (1986). Psychopathology in Opoid Addicts. *Substance Abuse, 9* (3).

Kurtz, E. (1982). Why AA works. The intellectual significance of Alcoholics Anonymous. *Journal of Studies on Alcohol, 40,* 230–239.

Labov, V., & Faneshel, D. (1977). *Therapeutic Discourse.* New York: Academic Press.

Lacan, J. (1968). *The Language of the Self.* Baltimore: Johns Hopkins Press.

Lorenz, K. (1950). The Comparative Method in Studying Inmate Behavior Patterns. In *Symposia of the Society for Experimental Biology.* Number IV Physiological Mechanisms in Animal Behavior (p. 221–268). Cambridge, England: Cambridge University Press.

Mack, J. (1981). Alcoholism, AA and the Governance of the Self. In Margaret Bean & Norman E. Zinberg (Eds.), *Dynamic Approaches to the Understanding and Treatment of Alcoholism.* New York: The Free Press.

McInerney, P. (1991). *Time and Experience.* Philadelphia: Temple University Press.

Merleau-Ponty, M. (1962). *Phenomenology of Perception.* (Collin Smith, trans). London: Routledge & Kegan Paul.

Messer, S. B., Sass, L. A. & Woolfolk, R. L. (1988). *Hermenevities and Psychological Theory: Interpretive Perspectives on Personality, Psychotherapy and Psychopathology.* New Brunswick: Rutgers University Press.

Polkinghorne, D. E., (1989). Phenomenological research methods. In Valle, R. S., & Halling, S. (Eds.) *Existential-Phenomenological Perspectives in Psychology 3.* New York: Plenum Press.

Rabin, A. I. (1978). Future Time Perspective and Ego Strength. In J. T. Fraser, N. Lawrence, & D. Park (Eds.), *The Study of Time III.* New York: Springer-Verlag.

Ramsey, E. (1988). From Guilt through Shame to AA: A Self-Reconciliation Process. *Alcoholism Treatment Quarterly,* 87–107.

Schafer, R. (1992). *Retelling a Life.* New York: Basic Books.

Shaffer, H. (1985). The Disease Controversy of Metaphors, Maps and Menus. *Journal of Psychoactive Drugs, 17* (2), 65–76.

Smeltzer, W. E. (1969). Time Orientation and Time Perspective in Psychotherapy. *Dissertation Abstracts International, 29,* 3922-B.

Spiegel, E., & Mulder, E. (1986). The Anonymous Program and Ego Functioning. *Issues in Ego Psychology, 9* (1), 34–42.

Sullivan, H. S. (1953). *The Interpersonal Theory of Psychiatry.* New York: W. W. Norton and Company.

Thompson, C. J., Locander, W. B., & Pollio, H. R. (1989). Putting Consumer Research: The Philosophy and Method of Existential-Phenomenology. *Journal of Consumer Research, 6,* 133–146.

Valle, R. S. & Halling, S. (1989). *Existential-Phenomenological Perspectives in Psychology.* New York: Plenum Press.

Van Kaam, A. (1965, Fall). The Addictive Personality. Insight. *Quarterly Review of Religion and Mental Health, 4* (2), 23–28.

Wallace, M. & Rabin, A. I. (1960). Temporal Experience. *Psychological Bulletin, 57* (3).

Wilson, A., Passick, S. A., Faud, J., Abrams, J., & Gordon, E. (1989). A Hierarchical Model of Opiate Addiction. Failures of Self-Regulation as a Central Aspect of Substance Abuse. *The Journal of Nervous and Mental Disease, 177* (6), 390–399.

Wurmser, L. (1978). *The Hidden Dimension Psychodynamics of Compulsive Drug Use.* New York: Jason Aronson.

SELECTION 19

The following selection, written by Stanton Peele, appeared in *The Sciences* (March–April, 1998), a publication of the New York Academy of Sciences. His article vigorously opposes the treatment assumptions of Alcoholics Anonymous, arguing that clinical data on twelve-step programs in general and Alcoholics Anonymous in particular are almost nonexistent. Stanton Peele is a social and clinical psychologist as well as an attorney. He has authored or coauthored several highly influential books on addiction, including *Love and Addiction* (1975), *The Meaning of Addiction* (1985), and *The Diseasing of America* (1989). He is currently a Fellow at the Drug Policy Alliance (formerly the Lindesmith Center–Drug Policy Foundation) and on the Board of Directors at the alcohol abuse treatment program, Moderation Management.

■ *All Wet*

The Gospel of Abstinence and Twelve-Step, Studies Show, Is Leading American Alcoholics Astray

STANTON PEELE

The week before Christmas 1996, as people dashed to the liquor store for reinforcements and clinked their glasses at holiday parties, the National Institute on Alcohol Abuse and Alcoholism (NIAAA) convened a press conference in Washington, D.C. The purpose was to herald the findings of Project MATCH, a government study devised to learn whether certain kinds of alcoholics respond best to specific forms of psychotherapeutic treatment. For example, twelve-step therapy and Alcoholics Anonymous (A.A.)—based in part on lifelong abstinence and personal surrender to a "higher power"—might work best for those seeking spiritual and religious meaning in their lives. Coping-skills therapy could help antisocial and emotionally disturbed alcoholics. And motivational therapy might best suit drinkers who show little desire for improvement, by spurring their desire to change.

Peele, Stanton (1998, March/April). All Wet: The gospel of abstinence and twelve-step, studies show, is leading American alcoholics astray. *The Sciences, 38,* 17–21. This article is reprinted with permission of *The Sciences* and is from the March/April 1998 issue.

Project MATCH had taken eight years to design and execute and had cost $27 million—the biggest and most expensive psychotherapy study ever mounted. It had encompassed thirty treatment sites and eighty therapists throughout the United States, along with dozens more of the country's most experienced investigators in alcoholism treatment, who had supervised and analyzed the study. The results of MATCH, much anticipated, promised to set firm guidelines for the therapy best suited to the particular needs of any given problem drinker.

Enoch Gordis, a physician and the director of NIAAA, stepped up to the microphone. "The good news is that treatment works," he announced. The therapies tested in Project MATCH all led to "excellent" overall results, he said.

But Project MATCH failed to find the links its organizers and most other alcoholism investigators had expected. The results showed virtually no differences in drinking reduction attributable to matching a patient's traits with a specific treatment. In fact, few clinical trials exist to show that the most popular American treatment for alcoholism, the twelve-step approach, is effective at all. Moreover, the results of both Project MATCH and a major 1996 NIAAA study showed that most people who had once struggled with alcohol abuse could later cut down on their drinking—a result that is anathema to the devotees of A.A., to the U.S. medical establishment and to the American way of temperance.

Last December the MATCH collaborators published a further analysis of their study in the British journal *Addiction,* which basically repeated their earlier conclusions. Thus the group's official position remains the same as a year ago: All is well with alcoholism treatment in America. In that view, whatever therapy people are pushed toward—which in the United States effectively means a twelve-step program with the aim of total abstinence—they will be fine. Such an outlook. Gordis's overoptimistic interpretation, notwithstanding, represents a public-relations triumph for the alcohol-treatment industry in America. But the blanket assurance that "treatment works" does precious little for most people who drink too much.

I'll call her Alice (not her real name). She is a woman I interviewed who tasted liquor for the first time in college and promptly went on party alert. She dropped out of school and drank heavily throughout her early twenties. Three to five times a week she got drunk, both alone and with a shifting cast of friends. During one nine-month binge and for several shorter stretches she drank virtually every night, polishing off nearly a pint of Scotch before she went to bed. Several times during her decade of drinking she was homeless.

Nevertheless, when she went home to visit her parents, sometimes for a couple of weeks, there was a major change in Alice's behavior. All she drank was wine over dinner with her father (her mother was a teetotaler). She did not want her parents to know how badly she was messing up her life: she controlled herself so she would not lose their love and support.

Alice had attended a few A.A. meetings, but she found the confessional atmosphere stultifying and oppressive. The ruining point for her came when, at age twenty-nine, she got a job as a receptionist in a dentist's office. The dentist reminded her of her father, a pharmacist; he was a new authority figure she wanted to please. She began spending her spare time with her coworkers—people who did not abuse alcohol. Alice realized she wanted to be like them: steady and productive. She took classes to become a dental hygienist, and she began drinking in moderation, wine with dinner only. In short, Alice's new job and new friends helped jump-start her desire for a stable life.

Alice is in her forties now, married with children, and still drinking moderately. Her case may sound unique: an alcoholic who recovered without treatment and who continues to drink. In fact, her story is typical of former alcoholics in the United States, according to NIAAA research. Indeed, Project MATCH, while finding no difference in results based on the kind of treatment received, did find that personal motivation and the drinking behavior of peers made a significant difference in a patient's success.

Alice and others like her demonstrate the need for a treatment focus besides A.A. and similar twelve-step programs. In the United States, unlike most other Western countries, alcoholism therapy clings to abstinence as the only acceptable goal. (In Britain and Australia, for instance, controlled drinking as a treatment goal is widely accepted.) According to a 1997 survey by the sociologists Paul M. Roman of the University of Georgia in Athens and Terry C. Blum of the Georgia Institute of Technology in Atlanta, nearly 99 percent of the treatment programs in the United States advocate abstinence.

That black-and-white view of alcoholism stems not from scientific evidence but from attitudes forged in the early nineteenth century, a topic I have discussed previously in this magazine [see "The New Prohibitionists," March/April 1984, and "Ain't Misbehavin'," July/August 1989]. Drinking in colonial America was widespread, accepted and over-whelmingly benign. But as the American frontier expanded, between 1790 and 1830, healthy social customs began to warp. Taverns, once places for entire families to gather, became male preserves in which the only women likely to be present were prostitutes. In such an atmosphere of male independence, alcoholism rates rose dramatically. In response, the Anti-Saloon League and similar temperance organizations flourished, culminating in Prohibition in 1919.

Prohibition collapsed in 1933. But it did not die—it simply moved off the streets and into the hospitals. In the eighteenth century the Philadelphia physician Benjamin Rush had propounded the idea that the chronic drinking of hard liquor causes a specific disease, one that makes it impossible for the drinker to imbibe moderately. Rush's idea took hold. By the latter half of the twentieth century, both A.A. and the American medical establishment had elaborated it into the theory that some people have an inbred susceptibility to alcoholism. The disease theory of alcoholism and its attendant focus on abstinence became orthodoxy in the United States.

The medicalization of alcohol abuse has spawned much interest in fine-tuning treatments for the problem. Project MATCH (which stands for Matching Alcoholism Treatments to Client Heterogeneity) was not the first effort to assess alcoholism therapies; a team led by the psychologist William R. Miller of the University of New Mexico in Albuquerque has been examining many smaller such studies for two decades. In 1995 Miller and his colleagues rated forty-three kinds of treatment by combining the results of 211 controlled trials that had compared the effectiveness of a treatment with either no treatment or with other alcoholism therapies. The treatment with by far the best overall score was "brief intervention"—followed by social-skills training and motivational enhancement.

Brief intervention shares elements with motivational enhancement, one of the treatments tested by Project MATCH, in that the patient and the therapist create a mutually agreed-upon goal. In brief intervention, the goal is usually reduced drinking: in motivational enhancement, it is either reduced drinking or total abstinence.

In a brief intervention session, the health-care worker simply sums up the goal: "So we agree you will reduce your drinking from forty-two drinks a week to twenty, no more than four on a given night." Motivational enhancement is a bit more subtle: the therapist nudges, though does not direct, the patient's own values and desire for change. The dialogue in a motivational-enhancement session might go like this:

THERAPIST: What is most important to you?

PATIENT: Getting ahead in life. Getting a mate.

T: What kind of job would you like? What training would that take?

P: [*Describes.*]

T: Describe the kind of mate you want. How would you have to act, where would you have to go, to meet and deal with a person like that?

P: [*Describes.*]

T: How are you doing at achieving this?

P: Not very well.

T: What leads to these problems?

P: When I drink, I can't concentrate on work. Drinking turns off the kind of person I want to go out with.

T: Can you think of any way to improve your chances of succeeding at work or with that kind of mate?

In both motivational enhancement and brief intervention, the discussion is nonjudgmental and the patient helps make the decision to drink less or to quit. Both processes are far less confrontational than the one used by most treatment professionals in the United States. The Miller report described the standard treatment in the United States as "a milieu advocating a spiritual twelve-step (A.A.) philosophy, typically augmented with group psychotherapy, educational lectures and films, and . . . general alcoholism counseling, often of a confrontational nature."

Yet those same therapies ranked at the bottom of the Miller team's list, with far less proof of their effectiveness than other treatments. The conclusion, then, is startling: The most frequently used therapies in American alcoholism treatment are those for which there is the least evidence of success.

The 1996 NIAAA study mentioned earlier was also surprising. That study stemmed from the National Longitudinal Alcohol Epidemiologic Survey (NLAES), conducted in 1992 by the U.S. Census Bureau. Census field workers did face-to-face interviews with nearly 43,000 respondents across America, a general sample of U.S. adults eighteen years of age and older. Each interview probed the use of alcohol and drugs over a person's entire life, with a focus on the preceding year.

Deborah A. Dawson, an NIAAA epidemiologist, then analyzed interviews with 4,585 NLAES subjects who had at some time in their lives been alcohol dependent (the most severe diagnosis of an alcohol problem). Only a quarter of the group Dawson studied had ever been treated for alcoholism; those people had had somewhat worse drinking problems initially than the ones who had gone untreated. In the year before the interviews, about a quarter of all the subjects still had mild to severe alcohol problems; a similar proportion had not touched a drop; and the rest had drunk without abuse.

Those who had received some kind of treatment were slightly *more* likely than their untreated counterparts to have had a drinking problem in the previous year. Dawson reported in the June 1996 issue of the journal *Alcoholism: Clinical and Experimental Research.* For those whose alcohol dependence had first appeared in the preceding five years and who had been treated, 70 percent had had a drinking problem in the past year. For those whose drinking problems had emerged twenty years or more before, twice as many of the treated alcoholics as the untreated ones were still abusing booze (20 percent versus 10 percent). Among the long-term group, fully 60 percent of the untreated subjects had reduced their drinking to the point where they had no diagnosable problem.

On the basis of a study such as Dawson's, in which the treated and untreated groups differed in the initial severity of their problems, it would not be fair to claim that therapy leads to worse results than no therapy. But the finding that so many treated alcoholics still had a drinking problem, while so many untreated alcoholics could moderate their drinking over time, certainly contradicts the impression created by the MATCH report, as well as popular American ideas about alcoholism.

Why does Miller's and Dawson's research indicate that current treatments are ineffective, whereas MATCH purportedly showed that treatment works so well? It is worth taking a closer look at Project MATCH, to discover just what it did and what it found.

The MATCH results were published directly after the NIAAA press conference, in a detailed report in the January 1997 issue of *Journal of Studies on Alcohol.* The complicated design of MATCH included two groups of patients: an outpatient group and an aftercare group, made up of outpatients who had recently received hospital treatment. The patients were not deliberately matched to a treatment at the outset. Rather, each patient was assigned randomly to a treatment, and the success of the match was measured afterward on the basis of how well that person fulfilled predictions of success for that treatment, according to his or her personal traits.

Twelve-step and coping-skills treatment were each scheduled in twelve weekly sessions; motivational-enhancement therapy involved four sessions spaced over the twelve-week period. The year of follow-up showed comparably good results for all treatments. Before treatment, the subjects imbibed, on average, on twenty-five days out of thirty; that number fell to six days of drinking a month by the end of follow-up. The amount consumed on drinking days also dropped markedly after treatment.

Going deeper into the MATCH methodology shows why its results could differ so dramatically from those of other research. Virtually all the subjects were alcohol dependent. But people simultaneously diagnosed with a drug problem were excluded from the study.

The implications of that exclusion are substantial. According to a survey of treatment admissions published last year by the Substance Abuse and Mental Health Services Administration in Rockville, Maryland, the combined abuse of alcohol and drugs is the most frequent problem for patients at the time of admission to treatment for substance abuse. On that ground alone, the statistical validity of extrapolating from the Project MATCH sample to the alcohol-abuser population as a whole is seriously compromised.

But much more than that was going on in the selection of subjects for MATCH. Initially, 4,481 potential subjects were identified; fewer than 1,800 of them were actually included. The MATCH participants were volunteers. Yet in real life, patients are increasingly being referred for treatment by the courts, by their employers or by social agencies. They are threatened with prison, loss of a job or loss of benefits if they do not get help. Furthermore, Project MATCH dropped potential subjects for reasons such as lack of a permanent home address and for legal or probation problems. Others declined to participate because of the "inconvenience" of treatment. Compared with the volunteers excluded from the study, those who participated in MATCH were motivated, stable and free of criminal or severe drug problems—all of which predict a greater likelihood of success.

Not only were the patients in MATCH atypical, but they did not receive typical alcoholism treatment. Counselors were carefully selected and trained. Each treatment session was videotaped, and the tapes were monitored by supervisors. The quality of the treatments in MATCH seems to be a far cry from that of standard treatment programs in the United States. In such programs the counselors are generally former alcoholics themselves, whose subsequent training has exposed them only to more of the therapy they received—namely, the twelve-step philosophy.

In *The Truth About Addiction and Recovery,* a book I cowrote in 1991 with Archie Brodsky, a senior investigator in the psychiatry department at Harvard Medical School, we noted that twelve-step treatment is typically delivered in an authoritarian, directive fashion. Patients are told their behavior is wrong and their lives are not working, and they are lectured to quit drinking. Such behavior on the part of the therapist does not jibe with effective therapy, which helps patients to "own" their problems and participate in the solutions. For that reason patients in alcoholism treatment are regularly tagged as being "in denial." In our experience, when their values and perceptions are respected, patients are more willing to identify and address their problems rather than fight the process of treatment.

Yet twelve-step therapy could be delivered in many ways. One wonders whether the success of that treatment in MATCH arose in part from a style of twelve-step therapy different from the one in standard treatment programs. Unlike A.A., the MATCH twelve-step treatment did not rely on group support; instead it concentrated on individual therapy sessions. The MATCH results, then, may point to the critical importance of the therapist's style of practice. Although MATCH did not find plug-in solutions, it did find that treatment success differed significantly depending on *where* the patients got help. That suggests that certain training programs, counselors and supervisors offer far better help than others, regardless of the kind of therapy they practice. Thus the research eye might do better to focus on how superior counselors deliver their therapy, whatever name that therapy goes by.

Other results of Project MATCH also challenge standard assumptions about alcoholism. The treatments that led to such excellent results required only about eight hours of outpatient therapy (the subjects, on average, attended only two-thirds of their scheduled twelve sessions). Yet the National Council on Alcoholism and Drug Dependence recommends hospital stays of several days for alcohol-dependent patients in the United States.

Although all the MATCH treatments led to equivalent results, not all were equal in effort and expense. The results of motivational enhancement were as good as those of the other therapies, but they required only a third as many sessions. And many studies show that even fewer sessions can be beneficial. Brief intervention is often restricted to a single session and follow-up. Although brief-intervention therapy has generally been reserved for nondependent alcohol abusers, several studies have looked at minimal treatments for people who are alcohol dependent. For example, in 1977 the psychiatrist Griffith Edwards and his colleagues at the Addiction Research Unit (now the National Addiction Center) of London's Maudsley Hospital compared a full hospital treatment program with a single advice session for an alcoholic population. No differences in outcome were found. Comparable studies conducted throughout the 1980s in Missouri, New Zealand and Canada confirmed that conclusion.

But perhaps the biggest heresy that MATCH supports—inadvertently so—is the value of reduced drinking as a goal in alcoholism treatment. The MATCH organizers chose to present their success in terms of the number of drinking days and the amount imbibed on those days. They did not trumpet the news of their subjects' abstinence rates. That figure was not particularly impressive: about 20 percent of the outpatient group and 35 percent of the aftercare group abstained throughout the follow-up period. Yet in the out-patient group, a third drank without bingeing.

The data from Project MATCH and other mainstream research conflict in many ways, but they make this much clear. Since the majority of alcoholics do not stop drinking, whether treated or untreated, whether measured in the general population or following a gold-standard set of treatments, the ironclad insistence on abstinence as the only goal of therapy is perverse indeed.

Those who treat alcoholics—and American society as a whole—need to recognize that the aim of reduced drinking may be the best and only achievable goal for many alcoholics. Clinicians must also develop alternatives to traditional therapies—treatments that could well be briefer and less expensive than the ones now in use. Above all, everyone must acknowledge that alcoholics are *not* powerless. With the right resources, more often than not they hold the keys to their own recovery.

Looking at Both Sides—The Debate Continues

The core arguments with regard to whether Alcoholics Anonymous is the best strategy for the treatment of alcoholism are aptly represented by the following excerpts from selections in this chapter:

> In summary, the addictive experience was found to be characterized by intense emotions which are not amenable to (language as) symbolic representation. The wordless world of feelings gives rise to: (1) the loss of the movement of time and the related experience of flux

or change; (2) a lack of sense of self-efficacy and the capacity for effective self-monitoring and self-regulation; and (3) a loss of relatedness to oneself and others. . . . The problematic dimensions of the addictive experience are addressed through the structure of the A.A. program. The effectiveness of A.A. may be accounted for by its thorough response to the addictive problem. A.A. provides cognitive strategies, compensatory psychological mechanisms, and intra/inter/transpersonal resources to assist the addicted person in successfully negotiating the vicissitudes of human living. (from Hopson and Beaird-Spiller's article, selection 18)

. . . (T)welve-step treatment is typically delivered in an authoritarian, directive fashion. Patients are told their behavior is wrong and their lives are not working, and they are lectured to quit drinking. Such behavior on the part of the therapist does not jibe with effective therapy, which helps patients to "own" their problems and participate in the solutions. For that reason patients in alcoholism treatment are regularly tagged as being "in denial." In our experience, when their values and perceptions are respected, patients are more willing to identify and address their problems rather than fight the process of treatment. (from Peele's article, selection 19)

Matters to Ponder

- If you had a drinking problem, which type of therapist do you think would be better suited to help you, a therapist represented in the Hopson and Beaird-Spiller article or a therapist represented in the Peele article? Explain your choice. Would the choice be different if the drug of abuse were cocaine or heroin?
- What is meant by the statement "the ironclad insistence on abstinence [among alcoholics] as the only goal in therapy is perverse indeed" in the Peele article? In what ways are the therapeutic goals in the Hopson and Beaird-Spiller article different from those in the Peele article?

Further Sources to Seek Out

Alcoholics Anonymous Worldwide, Inc. (1998). A newcomer asks. Pamphlet from the A. A. Grapevine, Inc., obtained through the web site: *www.alcoholics-anonymous.org.* A good introduction to the philosophy and process of A.A. treatment.

Kaskutas, Lee Ann (1996). A road less traveled: Choosing the "Women for Sobriety" program. *Journal of Drug Issues, 26* (1), 77–94. An examination of one of the alternatives to A.A. treatment, especially designed for women.

Levinthal, Charles F. (2002). *Drugs, behavior, and modern society* (3rd ed.). Boston: Allyn and Bacon, Chapters 9 and 10. A comprehensive survey of alcohol use as well as chronic alcohol abuse and alcoholism.

Maltzman, Irving (1996, January–March). Why alcoholism is a disease. *Journal of Psychoactive Drugs,* pp. 13–31. A defense of the disease concept of alcoholism.

Schmidt, Eric (1996). Rational recovery: Finding an alternative for addiction treatment. *Alcoholism Treatment Quarterly, 14* (4), 47–57. An examination of one of the alternatives to A.A. treatment, in which no reference is made to a "higher Power."

Shute, Nancy (1997, September 8). Drinking dilemma: By calling abstinence the only cure, we ensure that the nation's $100 billion alcohol problem won't be solved. *U.S. News & World Report,* pp. 55–65. A look at the strategy of treating alcoholism through a moderation rather than an elimination of alcohol drinking.

Web Sites to Explore

www.alcoholics-anonymous.org
The web site for Alcoholics Anonymous Worldwide, with a variety of publications and references to the A.A. approach in alcoholism treatment.

www.peele.net
The web site for the writings of Stanton Peele, opposing the zero-tolerance approach of A.A. with respect to alcohol drinking in cases of alcohol dependence.

Question: Should Stimulant Drugs Be Used to Treat Attention Deficit Disorder (ADD) in Children?

In educational circles, it is frequently called "the Ritalin problem." This refers to the use of the psychostimulant medication methylphenidate (brand name: Ritalin) for children who have such a level of inattentiveness or hyperactivity problems that they are not meeting academic standards, despite having average or above-average intelligence. As with most issues that are being debated in education today, the problem is far from simple.

First of all, there is the problem of diagnosis and the question of its validity. According to the fourth edition of the *Diagnostic and Statistical Manual of Mental Disorders,* issued by the American Psychiatric Association in 1994, a condition called Attention Deficit Hyperactivity Disorder (ADHD) exists if either inattention or hyperactivity/impulsivity can be demonstrated. The criteria for demonstrating this condition are very specific and tied to behavioral observations of the individual, as opposed to any physiological (e.g., hyperthyroidism) or biochemical information (e.g., elevated blood sugar).

The criteria for inattention require that at least six of the following nine symptoms have persisted for at least six months to a degree that is maladaptive or inconsistent with one's developmental level of functioning:

- often fails to give close attention to details or makes careless mistakes in schoolwork, work, or other activities
- often has difficulty sustaining attention in tasks or play activities
- often does not seem to listen when spoken to directly
- often does not follow through on instructions and fails to finish schoolwork, chores, or duties in the workplace (not due to oppositional behavior or failure to understand instructions)
- often has difficulty organizing tasks or activities
- often avoids, dislikes, or is reluctant to engage in tasks that require sustained mental effort (such as schoolwork or homework)
- often loses things necessary for tasks or activities (e.g., toys, school assignments, pencils, books, or tools)
- is often easily distracted by extraneous stimuli
- is often forgetful in daily activities

The criteria for hyperactivity/impulsivity require at least four of the following nine symptoms:

- often fidgets with hands or feet or squirms in seat
- often leaves seat in classroom or in other situations in which remaining seated is expected
- often runs about or climbs excessively in situations in which it is inappropriate
- often has difficulty playing or engaging in leisure activities quietly
- is often "on the go" or often acts as if "driven by a motor"
- often talks excessively
- often blurts out answers before questions have been completed
- often has difficulty awaiting turn
- often interrupts or intrudes on others (e.g., butts into conversations or games)

Three final criteria must also be met for the diagnosis to be complete:

- Some inattentive or hyperactive-impulsive symptoms that caused impairment were present before age 7 years
- Some impairment from the symptoms is present in two or more settings (e.g., at school or work and at home)
- There must be clear evidence of clinically significant impairment in social, academic, or occupational functioning.[1]

Technically, this condition is referred to as ADHD (in order to include the possibility of either an attention deficit, hyperactivity, or both). We will simplify the designation by calling it Attention Deficit Disorder (ADD).

The issues are essentially twofold. First, there is the question of whether ADD is a valid medical condition. If it is, then there is the second question of whether psychostimulant medications, such as methylphenidate (Ritalin) or a combination of dextroamphetamine and amphetamine (brand name: Adderall), are valid options for treatment. Should a pharmacological approach through drugs that stimulate the central nervous system be preferred over a behavioral approach? What are we saying about personal responsibility when we choose to address learning problems through medical means?

There is no doubt that pharmacological treatment of inattention and hyperactivity of students in school has now a firm hold on educational practice in the United States. Psychostimulant medications have been used in the treatment of children with ADD for more than fifty years. Children, more than three times as many boys as girls, who take medication for ADD are of average intelligence to above average intelligence but are underperforming academically. About 70 percent of the approximately one million children in the United States who take psychostimulants (chiefly Ritalin or Adderall) for ADD each year

---

[1]Reprinted with permission from the *Diagnostic and Statistical Manual of Mental Disorders, Fourth Edition, Text Revision.* © 2000 American Psychiatric Association, Washington, DC.

respond successfully to the treatment. In 1999, a major study examining the effects of medication over a fourteen-month period found that medication was more effective in reducing ADD symptoms than behavioral treatment and nearly as effective as a combination approach of medication and behavioral treatment. Interestingly, a 1999 study found that boys with ADD who are treated with psychostimulants are much less likely to abuse drugs or alcohol later in life than boys with ADD who either receive no treatment or a nonpharmacological treatment for the disorder.

Why psychostimulants would reduce inattention and hyperactivity, rather than introduce problems of their own, has been a great mystery among professionals in this field, and several theories have been advanced in an attempt to explain the beneficial effects. One prominent explanation holds that the primary advantage of psychostimulants in treating ADD is that they bolster the brain's ability to allocate attention during complex problem solving. For those children who have difficulty in maintaining attention in the classroom, a psychostimulant may allow them to perform better and reduce the frustration and agitation that stem from their failures.

Those opposed to the practice of psychostimulant medication treatment for ADD, as represented in the first selection by Mary Eberstadt, argue that there is too high a risk of drug misuse for circumstances unrelated to ADD and that there is the present danger of an overprescription of psychostimulant medications so that children who may not have ADD symptoms are nonetheless being medicated. Are these drugs "crutches" for an inadequate and outmoded educational system? Are children better off changing their behavior on their own rather than responding to a change in their nervous systems? The following two selections, originally published in medical journals, argue that ADD is a genuine medical syndrome and that there are genuine benefits to be gained from a biomedical approach.

REFERENCES

American Psychiatric Association (1994). *Diagnostic and statistical manual of mental disorders* (4th edition). Washington, DC: American Psychiatric Association.

Colgan, Craig (2001, February). Don't get rattled over Ritalin. *The Education Digest,* pp. 60–63.

Levinthal, Charles F. (2002). *Drugs, behavior, and modern society* (3rd ed.). Boston: Allyn and Bacon.

Study: Use of Ritalin for ADHD reduces substance abuse risk (1999, August 9). *Alcoholism and Drug Abuse Week,* p. 6.

SELECTION 20

The following selection is a portion of an essay written by Mary Eberstadt for the Heritage Foundation journal *Policy Review* (April–May, 1999). In this essay, Eberstadt assails the recent dramatic increase in Ritalin treatment among children and examines the circumstances that have encouraged such an increase. Eberstadt is a Contributing Editor of *Policy Review.*

■ *Why Ritalin Rules*

MARY EBERSTADT

There are stories that are mere signs of the times, and then there are stories so emblematic of a particular time and place that they demand to be designated cultural landmarks. Such a story was the *New York Times'* front-page report on January 18 appearing under the tame, even soporific headline, "For School Nurses, More Than Tending the Sick."

"Ritalin, Ritalin, seizure drugs, Ritalin," in the words of its sing-song opening. "So goes the rhythm of noontime" for a typical school nurse in East Boston "as she trots her tray of brown plastic vials and paper water cups from class to class, dispensing pills into out-stretched young palms." For this nurse, as for her counterparts in middle- and upper-middle class schools across the country, the day's routine is now driven by what the *Times* dubs "a ticklish question," to wit: "With the number of children across the country taking Ritalin estimated at well over three million, more than double the 1990 figure, who should be giving out the pills?"

"With nurses often serving more than one school at a time," the story goes on to explain, "the whole middle of the day can be taken up in a school-to-school scurry to dole out drugs." Massachusetts, for its part, has taken to having the nurse deputize "anyone from a principal to a secretary" to share the burden. In Florida, where the ratio of school nurses to students is particularly low, "many schools have clerical workers hand out the pills." So many pills, and so few professionals to go around. What else are the authorities to do?

Behold the uniquely American psychotropic universe, pediatrics zone—a place where "psychiatric medications in general have become more common in schools" and where, in particular, "Ritalin dominates." There are by now millions of stories in orbit here, and the particular one chosen by the *Times*—of how the drug has induced a professional labor shortage—is no doubt an estimable entry. But for the reader struck by some of the facts the *Times* mentions only in passing—for example, that Ritalin use more than doubled in the first half of the decade alone, that production has increased 700 percent since 1990, or that the number of schoolchildren taking the drug may now, by some estimates, be approaching the *4 million* mark—mere anecdote will only explain so much.

Fortunately, at least for the curious reader, there is a great deal of other material now on offer, for the explosion in Ritalin consumption has been very nearly matched by a publishing boom dedicated to that same phenomenon. Its harbingers include, for example, Barbara Ingersoll's now-classic 1988 *Your Hyperactive Child,* among the first works to popularize a drug regimen for what we now call Attention Deficit Disorder (ADD, called ADHD when it includes hyperactivity). Five years later; with ADD diagnoses and Ritalin prescriptions already rising steeply in the better-off neighborhoods and schools, Peter D. Kramer helped fuel the boom with his bestselling *Listening to Prozac*—a book that put the phrase "cosmetic pharmacology" into the vernacular and thereby inadvertently broke new conceptual ground for the advocates of Ritalin. In 1994, most important, psychiatrists

Eberstadt, Mary (1999, April/May). Why Ritalin rules. *Policy Review.* Washington, DC: Heritage Foundation, pp. 24–40. Shortened version reprinted with permission.

Edward M. Hallowell and John J. Ratey published their own bestselling *Driven to Distraction: Recognizing and Coping with Attention Deficit Disorder from Childhood to Adulthood,* a book that was perhaps the single most powerful force in the subsequent proliferation of ADD diagnoses; as its opening sentence accurately prophesied, "Once you catch on to what this syndrome is all about, you'll see it everywhere."

Not everyone received these soundings from the psychotropic beyond with the same enthusiasm. One noteworthy dissent came in 1995 with Thomas Armstrong's *The Myth of the ADD Child,* which attacked both the scientific claims made on behalf of ADD and what Armstrong decried as the "pathologizing" of normal children. Dissent also took the form of wary public pronouncements by the National Education Association (NEA), one of several groups to harbor the fear that ADD would be used to stigmatize minority children. Meanwhile, scare stories on the abuse and side effects of Ritalin popped out here and there in the mass media, and a national controversy was born. From the middle to the late 1990s, other interested parties from all over—the Drug Enforcement Administration (DEA), the Food and Drug Administration (FDA), the medical journals, the National Institutes of Health (NIH), and especially the extremely active advocacy group CHADD (Children and Adults with Attention Deficit Disorder)—further stoked the debate through countless reports, conferences, pamphlets, and exchanges on the Internet.

To this outpouring of information and opinion two new books, both on the critical side of the ledger, have just been added: Richard DeGrandpre's iconoclastic *Ritalin Nation: Rapid-Fire Culture and the Transformation of Human Consciousness* (Simon and Schuster, 1999), and physician Lawrence H. Diller's superbly analytical *Running on Ritalin: A Physician Reflects on Children, Society and Performance in a Pill* (Bantam Books, 1998). Their appearance marks an unusually opportune moment in which to sift through some ten years' worth of information on Ritalin and ADD and to ask what, if anything, we have learned from the national experiment that has made both terms into household words.

Let's put the question bluntly: How has it come to pass that in *fin-de-siècle* America, where every child from preschool onward can recite the "antidrug" catechism by heart, millions of middle- and upper-middle class children are being legally drugged with a substance so similar to cocaine that, as one journalist accurately summarized the science, "it takes a chemist to tell the difference"?

What Is Methylphenidate?

The first thing that has made the Ritalin explosion possible is that methylphenidate, to use the generic term, is perhaps the most widely misunderstood drug in America today. Despite the fact that it is, as Lawrence Diller observes in *Running on Ritalin,* "the most intensively studied drug in pediatrics," most laymen remain under a misimpression both about the nature of the drug itself and about its pharmacological effects on children.

What most people believe about this drug is the same erroneous characterization that appeared elsewhere in the *Times* piece quoted earlier—that it is "a mild stimulant of the central nervous system that, for reasons not fully understood, often helps children who are chronically distractible, impulsive and hyperactive settle down and concentrate." The word "stimulant" here is at least medically accurate. "Mild," a more ambiguous judgment, depends partly on the dosage, and partly on whether the reader can imagine describing as "mild" *any* dosage of the drugs to which methylphenidate is closely related. These include dextroamphetamine (street name: "dexies"), methamphetamine (street name: "crystal meth"), and, of course, cocaine. But the chief substance of the *Times'* formulation here—that the reasons *why* Ritalin does what it does to children remain a medical mystery—is, as informed writers from all over the debate have long acknowledged, an enduring public myth.

"Methylphenidate," in the words of a 1995 DEA background paper on the drug, "is a central nervous system (CNS) stimulant and shares many of the pharmacological effects of amphetamine, methamphetamine, and cocaine." Further, it "produces behavioral, psychological, subjective, and reinforcing effects similar to those of d-amphetamine including increases in rating of euphoria, drug liking and activity, and decreases in sedation." For comparative purposes, that same DEA report includes a table listing the potential adverse physiological effects of both methylphenidate and dextroamphetamine; they are, as the table shows, nearly identical (see Table 7.1). To put the point conversely, as Richard DeGrandpre does in *Ritalin Nation* by quoting a 1995 report in the *Archives of General Psychiatry,* "Cocaine, which is one of the most reinforcing and addicting of the abused drugs, has pharmacological actions that are very similar to those of methylphenidate, which is now the most commonly prescribed psychotropic medicine for children in the U.S."

Such pharmacological similarities have been explored over the years in numerous studies. DeGrandpre reports that "lab animals given the choice to self-administer comparative doses of cocaine and Ritalin do not favor one over another" and that "a similar study showed monkeys would work in the same fashion for Ritalin as they would for cocaine." The DEA reports another finding—that methylphenidate is actually "chosen *over* cocaine in preference studies" of non-human primates (emphasis added). In *Driven to Distraction,* pro-Ritalin psychiatrists Hallowell and Ratey underline the interchangeable nature of methylphenidate and cocaine when they observe that "people with ADD feel focused when they take cocaine, *just as they do when they take Ritalin* [emphasis added]." Moreover, methylphenidate (like other stimulants) appears to increase tolerance for related drugs. Recent evidence indicates, for example, that when people accustomed to prescribed Ritalin turn to cocaine, they seek higher doses of it than do others. To summarize, again from the DEA report, "it is clear that methylphenidate substitutes for cocaine and d-amphetamine in a number of behavioral paradigms."

All of which is to say that Ritalin "works" on children in the same way that related stimulants work on adults—sharpening the short-term attention span when the drug kicks in and producing equally predictable valleys ("coming down," in the old street parlance; "rebounding," in Ritalinese) when the effect wears off. Just as predictably, children are subject to the same adverse effects as adults imbibing such drugs, with the two most common—appetite suppression and insomnia—being of particular concern. That is why, for example, handbooks on ADD will counsel parents to see their doctor if they feel their child is losing too much weight, and why some children who take methylphenidate are also prescribed sedatives to help them sleep. It is also why one of the more Orwellian phrases in the psychotropic universe, "drug holidays"—meaning scheduled times, typically on weekends or school vacations, when the dosage of methylphenidate is lowered or the drug temporarily withdrawn in order to keep its adverse effects in check—is now so common in the literature that it no longer even appears in quotations. . . .

TABLE 7.1   **Crystal Lite? Potential Adverse Effects of Ritalin and Dexies**

Effects	Methylphenidate	Dextroamphetamine
Cardiovascular	Palpitation Tachycardia Increased blood pressure	Palpitation Tachycardia Increased blood pressure

Central Nervous System	Excessive CNS stimulation
	Psychosis
	Dizziness
	Headache
	Insomnia
	Nervousness
	Irritability
	Attacks of Gilles de la
	    Tourette or other tic
	    syndromes
		Excessive CNS stimulation
		Psychosis
		Dizziness
		Headache
		Insomnia
		Nervousness
		Irritability
		Attacks of Gilles de la
		    Tourette or other tic
		    syndromes

Gastrointestinal	Anorexia Nausea Vomiting Stomach pain Dry mouth	Anorexia Nausea Vomiting Stomach pain Dry mouth
Endocrine/metabolic	Weight loss Growth suppression	Weight loss Growth suppression
Other	Leukopenia Hypersensitivity reaction Anemia Blurred vision	Skin rash or hives Blurred vision

Source: U.S. Department of Justice, Drug Enforcement Administration

A third myth about methylphenidate is that it, alone among drugs of its kind, is immune to being abused. To the contrary: Abuse statistics have flourished alongside the boom in Ritalin prescription-writing. Though it is quite true that elementary schoolchildren are unlikely to ingest extra doses of the drug, which is presumably kept away from little hands, a very different pattern has emerged among teenagers and adults who have the manual dexterity to open prescription bottles and the wherewithal to chop up and snort their contents (a method that puts the drug into the bloodstream far faster than oral ingestion). For this group, statistics on the proliferating abuse of methylphenidate in schoolyards and on the street are dramatic.

According to the DEA, for example, as early as 1994 Ritalin was the fastest-growing amphetamine being used "non-medically" by high school seniors in Texas. In 1991, reports DeGrandpre in *Ritalin Nation,* "children between the ages of 10 and 14 years old were involved in only about 25 emergency room visits connected with Ritalin abuse. In 1995, just four years later, that number had climbed to more than 400 visits, which for this group was about the same number of visits as for cocaine." Not surprisingly, given these and other measures of methylphenidate's recreational appeal, criminal entrepreneurs have responded with interest to the drug's increased circulation. From 1990 to 1995, the DEA reports, there were about 2,000 thefts of methylphenidate, most of them night break-ins at pharmacies— meaning that the drug "ranks in the top 10 most frequently reported pharmaceutical drugs diverted from licensed handlers."

Because so many teenagers and college students have access to it, methylphenidate is par-ticularly likely to be abused on school grounds. "The prescription drug Ritalin," reported *Newsweek* in 1995, "is now a popular high on campus—with some serious side effects." DeGrandpre notes that at his own college in Vermont, Ritalin was cited as the third-favorite drug to snort in a campus survey. He also runs, without comment, scores of indi-vidual abuse stories from newspapers across the country over several pages of his book. In *Running on Ritalin,* Diller cites several undercover narcotics agents who confirm that "Ritalin is cheaper and easier to purchase at playgrounds than on the street." He further reports one particularly hazardous fact about Ritalin abuse, namely that teenagers, espe-cially, do not consider the drug to be anywhere near as dangerous as heroin or cocaine. To the contrary: "they think that since their younger brother takes it under a doctor's pre-scription, it must be safe."

In short, methylphenidate looks like an amphetamine, acts like an amphetamine, and is abused like an amphetamine. Perhaps not surprisingly, those who value its medicinal effects tend to explain the drug differently. To some, Ritalin is to children what Prozac and other psychotropic "mood brightening" drugs are to adults—a short-term fix for enhancing personality and performance. But the analogy is misleading. Prozac and its sisters are not stimulants with stimulant side effects; there is, ipso facto, no black market for drugs like these. Even more peculiar is the analogy favored by the advocates in CHADD: that "Just as a pair of glasses helps the nearsighted person focus," as Hallowell and Ratey explain, "so can medication help the person with ADD see the world more clearly." But there is no black market for eyeglasses, either—nor loss of appetite, insomnia, "dysphoria" (an unexplained feeling of sadness that sometimes accompanies pediatric Ritalin-taking), nor even the faintest risk of toxic psychosis, to cite one of Ritalin's rare but dramatically chilling possi-ble effects.

What is methylphenidate "really" like? Thomas Armstrong, writing in *The Myth of the ADD Child* four years ago, probably summarized the drug's appeal best. "Many middle and upper-middle class parents," he observed then, "see Ritalin and related drugs almost as 'cognitive steroids' that can be used to help their kids focus on their schoolwork better than the next kid." Put this way, the attraction to Ritalin makes considerable sense. In some ways, one can argue, that after-lunch hit of low-dose methylphenidate is much like the big cup from Starbucks that millions of adults swig to get them through the day—but only in some ways. There is no dramatic upswing in hospital emergency room visits and pharmacy break-ins due to caffeine abuse; the brain being jolted awake in one case is that of an adult, and in the other that of a developing child; and, of course, the substance doing the jolting on all those children is not legally available and ubiquitous caffeine, but a substance that the

DEA insists on calling a Schedule II drug, meaning that it is subject to the same controls, and for the same reasons of abuse potential, as related stimulants and other powerful drugs like morphine. . . .

In the field of higher education, where the first wave of Ritalin-taking students has recently landed, an ADD diagnosis can be parlayed into other sorts of special treatment. Diller reports that ADD-based requests for extra time on SATs, LSATs, and MCATs have risen sharply in the course of the 1990s. Yet the example of such high-profile tests is only one particularly measurable way of assessing ADD's impact on education; in many classrooms, including college classrooms, similar "accommodations" are made informally at a student's demand. A professor in the Ivy League tells me that students with an ADD diagnosis now come to him "waving doctor's letters and pills" and requesting extra time for routine assignments. To refuse "accommodation" is to risk a hornet's nest of liabilities, as a growing caseload shows. A 1996 article in *Forbes* cites the example of Whittler Law School, which was sued by an ADD-diagnosed student for giving only 20 extra minutes per hourlong exam instead of a full hour. The school, fearing an expensive legal battle, settled the suit. It further undertook a preventive measure: banning pop quizzes "because ADD students need separate rooms and extra time."

Concessions have also been won by advocates in the area of college athletics. The National College Athletic Association (NCAA) once prohibited Ritalin usage (as do the U.S. and International Olympic Committees today) because of what Diller calls its "possible acute performance-enhancing benefits." In 1993, citing legal jeopardy as a reason for changing course, the NCAA capitulated. Today a letter from the team physician will suffice to allow an athlete to ingest Ritalin, even though that same athlete would be disqualified from participating in the Olympics if he were to test positive for stimulants.

Nor are children and college students the only ones to claim benefits in the name of ADD. With adults now accounting for the fastest-growing subset of ADD diagnoses, services and accommodations are also proliferating in the workplace. The enabling regulations here are 1997 guidelines from the Equal Employment Opportunity Commission (EEOC) which linked traits like chronic lateness, poor judgment, and hostility to coworkers—in other words, the sorts of traits people get fired for—to "psychiatric impairments," meaning traits that are protected under the law. As one management analyst for the *Wall Street Journal* recently observed (and as CHADD regularly reminds its readers), these EEOC guidelines have already generated a list of accommodations for ADD-diagnosed employees, including special office furniture, special equipment such as tape recorders and laptops, and byzantine organizational schemes (color coding, buddy systems, alarm clocks, and other "reminders") designed to keep such employees on track. "Employers," this writer warned, "could find themselves facing civil suits and forced to restore the discharged people to their old positions, or even give them promotions as well as back pay or reasonable accommodation."

An ADD diagnosis can also be helpful in acquiring Supplemental Security Income (SSI) benefits. SSI takes income into account in providing benefits to the ADD diagnosed; in that, it is an exception to the trend. Most of the benefits now available, as even this brief review indicates, have come to be provided in principle, on account of the diagnosis per se.

Seen this way, and taking the class composition of the ADD-diagnosed into account, it is no wonder that more and more people, as Diller and many other doctors report, are now marching into medical offices demanding a letter, a diagnosis, and a prescription. The pharmacological charms of Ritalin quite apart, ADD can operate, in effect, as affirmative action for affluent white people. . . .

What Is Childhood?

The . . . most obvious reason millions of Americans, most of them children, are now taking Ritalin can be summarized in a single word that crops up everywhere in the dry-bones literature on ADD and its drug of choice: *compliance.* One day at a time, the drug continues to make children do what their parents and teachers either will not or cannot get them to do without it: Sit down, shut up, keep still, pay attention. That some children are born with or develop behavioral problems so severe that drugs like Ritalin are a godsend is true and sad. It is also irrelevant to the explosion in psychostimulant prescriptions. For most, the drug is serving a more nuanced purpose—that of "help[ing] your child to be more agreeable and less argumentative," as Barbara Ingersoll put it over a decade ago in *Your Hyperactive Child.*

There are, as was mentioned, millions of stories in the Ritalin universe, and the literature of advocates and critics alike all illustrates this point. There is no denying that millions of people benefit from having children take Ritalin—the many, many parents who will attest that the drug has improved their child's school performance, their home lives, often even their own marriages; the teachers who have been relieved by its effects in their classrooms, and have gone on to proselytize other parents of other unruly children (frequently, it is teachers who first suggest that a child be checked for the disorder); and the doctors who, when faced with all these grateful parents and teachers, find, as Diller finds, that "at times the pressure for me to medicate a child is intense."

Some other stories seep through the literature too, but only if one goes looking for them. These are the stories standing behind the clinical accounts of teenagers who lie and say they've taken the day's dose when they haven't, or of the children who cry in doctor's offices and "cheek" the pill (hide it rather than swallow, another linguistic innovation of Ritalinese) at home. These are the stories standing behind such statements as the following, culled from case studies throughout the literature: "It takes over of me [sic]; it takes control." "It numbed me." "Taking it meant I was dumb." "I feel rotten about taking pills; why me?" "It makes me feel like a baby." And, perhaps most evocative of all, "I don't know how to explain. I just don't want to take it any more."

But these quotes, as any reader will recognize, appeal only to sentiment; science, for its part, has long since declared its loyalties. In the end, what has made the Ritalin outbreak not only possible but inevitable is the ongoing blessing of the American medical establishment— and not only that establishment. In a particularly enthusiastic account of the drug in a recent issue of the *New Yorker,* writer Malcolm Gladwell exults in the idea that "we are now extending to the young cognitive aids of a kind that used to be reserved exclusively for the old" He further suggests that, given expert estimates of the prevalence of ADD (up to 10 percent of the population, depending on the expert), if anything "too few" children are taking the drug. Surely all these experts have a point. Surely this country can do more, much more, to reduce fidgeting, squirming, talking excessively, interrupting, losing things, ignoring adults, and all those other pathologies of what used to be called childhood.

SELECTION 21

The following selection is an article written by two pediatricians, Pasquale Accardo and Thomas A. Blondis, and published in the *Journal of Pediatrics* (January 2001). As the title suggests, their article is a response to critics of psychostimulant treatment for attention deficit/hyperactivity disorder. Accardo is Professor of Pediatrics at the New York Medical College, Westchester Institute for Human Development in Valhalla, New York. Blondis is Associate Professor of Clinical Pediatrics, University of Chicago, Pritzker School of Medicine in Chicago.

■ *What's All the Fuss about Ritalin?*

PASQUALE ACCARDO AND THOMAS A. BLONDIS

Recently, concerns about the possible overuse of psychostimulants in very young children have been disseminated in both the lay media and professional journals.[1] These derive from the following observations: (1) the perception of a dramatic increase in the use of psychostimulants over the past decade[2]; (2) marked regional, gender, and racial variations in the percentages both of children who are diagnosed with attention-deficit/hyperactivity disorder and of children who are treated with psychostimulants[3,4]; (3) an increase in the number of preschool-aged children who are both diagnosed with ADHD and treated with psychostimulants and other drugs[5,6]; and (4) a lack of knowledge about the long-term effects of psychostimulants on brain development.

Psychostimulant Increase

Although some studies have suggested the prevalence of ADHD at 16% to 17%,[7,8] communication disorders have been estimated to occur in 15% to 25% of children.[9] All these estimates are probably as far from determining the true occurrence of these conditions as those derived from counts of sometimes intermittent prescription use. As with an equation describing a chemical equilibrium reaction, the presence of an extremely effective treatment (or of readily available reimbursement for a treatment of unproven efficacy) will not unexpectedly contribute both to an increase in the use of that treatment and possibly to more accurate diagnosis. Although not every child who qualifies for a diagnosis of an attention disorder needs a trial of medication, the prescription rate would need to significantly exceed the 10% level before it can be interpreted as prima facie evidence of overuse. Several decades ago, there was an "epidemic" of learning disabilities, and more recently, there has been a "pandemic" of autistic spectrum disorders. For the most part, these increases do not reflect-faddish overdiagnosis but rather a recognition of cases that were previously misdiagnosed or just plain missed. Although Goldman et al[10] found little evidence of any "widespread overdiagnosis or misdiagnosis of ADHD or of widespread

Reproduced from Accardo, Pasquale, and Blondis, Thomas A. (2001, January). What's all the fuss about Ritalin? *Journal of Pediatrics, 138,* pp. 6–9 with permission from Mosby, Inc.

overprescription of methylphenidate," Angold et al[11] uncovered some confusing discrepancies between prescription practices and accurate diagnoses in a community setting. Commenting on the latter article, Jensen[12] interpreted this mismatch as not inconsistent with undertreatment as the primary phenomenon.

Variations in Use

African Americans apparently have decreased access (by a ratio of 2 to 1) to the benefits of medication.[3,4] This large difference with respect to race, possibly related to fiscal concerns, needs further investigation. Non-hyperactive girls with attentional disorders, remain a similarly underdiagnosed and undertreated group.

Preschool-Aged Children

Because ADHD is a life-span problem, the incidence of ADHD in preschoolers should not differ from that in older children. Differential diagnosis may be more challenging, but it is certainly not impossible in these younger children. It might be advisable to withhold a diagnosis of ADHD until the child's behavior can be observed in a group setting such as preschool, nursery school, or day care. In some states this recommendation is part of the formal policy of the state's Board of Pharmacy. Indeed, one of the major factors contributing to the increased identification of ADHD in preschool-aged children is the presence of more young children in out-of-home settings while their mothers work.

In view of the paucity of research on the diagnosis and treatment of ADHD in very young children, the pediatrician should proceed with caution. Such caution can be objectified in the collection of behavioral observations from multiple caregivers and in diverse settings, as well as by frequent follow-up visits. The level of caution exercised need, however, be no greater than that employed with the use of "orphan drugs." The force of analogy applied to developmental phenomena across contiguous age levels can be discussed with families. If the behavioral markers for ADHD can begin in utero, the diagnosis and treatment can certainly begin in the preschool years.

Clinical experience does suggest that psychostimulant medication is less effective in preschool-aged children, perhaps because of the greater ratio of liver to body mass and higher metabolic rate[13] or perhaps more simply because of the immaturity of the target organ. This should not preclude a trial. It is important that parents be advised of the lesser efficacy rate so that medication might be reconsidered in a timely fashion when the child is older.

Long-Term Effects

Little is known about the long-term effects of psychostimulants on the developing brain. Concern has been raised that both cocaine and methylphenidate target the dopamine transporter and have certain similarities in their action,[14] but their clinical effects have few similarities.[15] Stimulants have been used since the 1930s[16]; the only one to have exhibited any sort of unexpected long-term side effect was pemoline, and that involved the liver rather than the brain. Finally, stimulant use does not predispose to later substance abuse.[17]

Some Sources of Criticism

Progress in neuropsychopharmacology is revolutionizing the treatment of a wide variety of conditions previously resistant to behavioral interventions,[18,19] but not without criticism. Despite a long history,[20,21] such criticism seems unable to generate any novel arguments. Although the neuroscience of ADHD continues to progress with, for example, the identification of genetic linkages,[22] the same logical fallacies continue to reappear, sometimes under religious guises.[23-25] How can one make a diagnosis of a "disorder" that is composed of "normal" behaviors? *Because the "normal" behaviors appear at an inappropriate time and to an inordinate degree than expected for the child's developmental age.* Can not the setting of such arbitrary developmental expectations simply be modified by the school system? *Hadn't the school system lowered expectations enough already?* Why resort to drugs when behavioral alternatives would be less damaging? *Why choose anesthesia with the availability of meditation techniques?* Isn't this just a problem of parental incompetence and child laziness? *That's called "blaming the victim."* ADHD really does exist, and it can be distinguished from, as well as confused with, parent-child problems, maternal depression, inexperienced teachers, overcrowded classrooms, and a variety of other confounding conditions. *Is methylphenidate a type of cocaine?* Both chemicals target the dopamine transporter, but their clinical effects have little similarity.[15]

An important subtext in the debate over the use of stimulants in children derives from a discipline known as the sociology of medicine. One of the award-winning standard textbooks in this field describes to college students the horrendous social drama of the "medicalization of deviancy"—the ongoing relabeling of behavioral difference (a normal temperamental variant) as medical disorder in order to place the patient in the grip of a malevolent medical industrial complex.[26] In this scenario, drugs are interpreted as instruments of control. (Note the frequent references to a "chemical straight jacket.") Such a politicization of neuropsychopharmacology undercuts everything for which evidence-based medicine stands. It assumes that there is no objective truth and that anything can be modified simply by altering linguistic usage. The extremely deleterious impact such anticritical thinking can have on the advancement and application of science has been analyzed elsewhere,[27,28] but its insidious pervasiveness needs to be constantly kept in mind. It represents a quantum leap beyond mere disaffection with "the medical model."

This critique of psychostimulant use engenders two paradoxes: (1) at the very moment when new research is accumulating evidence to demonstrate that medication not only works but is much more effective than was previously thought, a recurring wave of anti-medication hysteria is unleashed; and (2) most parents are not rushing out to get prescriptions, and most physicians are not eager to write them. Indeed, the majority of both groups actually appear averse to medication use. Even when medication is demonstrated to be more effective than behavioral interventions, parents continue to strongly prefer the latter.[29]

This is not to suggest that all the key issues of neuropsychopharmacology have been resolved and only await the filling in of the blanks by current research programs.[30,31] The National Institutes of Health-funded Multimodal Treatment for ADHD study is demonstrating the superior impact of stimulant medication, but determination of the most appropriate balance between drugs and behavioral interventions requires further research.

Investigators in this multi-site project are currently applying for a 5-year longitudinal continuation to follow up subjects with ADHD through middle school.

Diagnosis and Treatment

With and without a complex multidisciplinary team assessment, ADHD is sometimes overdiagnosed but is possibly more often underdiagnosed. Although the magnitude of the error in both directions remains unknown, it is imperative to avoid both errors and not focus exclusively on the overdiagnosis.

As demonstrated by over a half century of clinical experience, psychostimulants exhibit an extremely low risk-to-benefit ratio.[32] Although psychostimulant medication is safe and effective,[33] it is also both overused and underused. Diagnostic errors and incomplete follow-up are the prime culprits here. Most side effects and other unwanted symptoms are related to dosage titration and can often be effectively managed without discontinuing an otherwise effective preparation. Often because of financial considerations, multimodal treatment components are significantly underused to support the positive impact of medication regimens. The use of psychostimulant medications by community physicians is not as effective as its use by subspecialists.

Recommendations

Pediatricians need to assume a proactive role in the screening, diagnosis, and treatment of ADHD: the screening, diagnosis, and treatment of ADHD should be the prerogative of the primary care pediatrician and not the purview of subspecialists and multidisciplinary teams. The majority of cases of ADHD can be managed in an efficient office setting.[34-36] The physician who does not believe in the existence of ADHD, except in the most severe cases, will not typically diagnose it. That reflects a disservice to the child and the family. The physician who accepts the diagnosis of ADHD but who is reluctant to recommend a trial of medication as one part of the treatment regimen is also guilty of a disservice. The physician who does not titrate the medication dosage to optimal effect performs a further disservice. Refusing to consider treatment of ADHD in preschool-aged children is one final disservice.

In the presence of all this negative press, parents need to be strongly reassured about both the accuracy of the diagnostic process and the efficacy of treatment regimens. Although it goes against the grain of many psychosocial theories and many alternative therapies, there is an overwhelming body of scientific evidence to support the following.

1. ADHD has objective existence as a neurodevelopmental syndrome.[37,38]
2. Psychostimulants (the "gold standard") are safe and effective components of a treatment regimen.[39]
3. With psychostimulants, as with all categories of drugs in pediatrics, there exists some degree of risk for overuse, underuse, and misuse (where the last refers to inappropriate dosage schedules).
4. Other behavioral supports (e.g., counseling, peer support groups, classroom accommodations, and 504 plans) remain important in the management of ADHD.
5. Comorbidities (in the form of learning disabilities, language disorders, psychiatric diagnoses, and socio-emotional difficulties) represent a significant area of both concern and potential confounding of treatment efficacy and long-term outcome.

6. The diagnosis and treatment of ADHD in preschool-aged children is challenging but not impossible.

7. ADHD in preschool-aged children represents a probable rather than standard indication for the use of psychostimulants.[13]

This is the state of the art in scientific medicine. All the rest is myth.

REFERENCES

1. Coyle J. T. Psychotropic drug use in very young children. *Journal of the American Medical Association* 2000; 283: 1059–60.
2. Safer D. J., Zito J. M., Fine E. M. Increased methylphenidate usage for attention deficit disorder in the 1990s. *Pediatrics* 1996; 98:1084–8.
3. LeFever G., Dawson K., Morrow A. The extent of drug therapy for attention deficit-hyperactivity disorder among children in public schools. *American Journal of Public Health* 1999; 89:1359–64.
4. Safer D. J., Malever M. Stimulant treatment in Maryland public schools. *Pediatrics* 2000; 106:533–9.
5. Zito J. M., Safer D. J., dos Reis S., Gardner J. F., Boles M., Lynch F. Trends in the prescribing of psychotropic medications to preschoolers. *Journal of the American Medical Association* 2000; 283:1025–30.
6. Rappley M. D., Mullan P. B., Alvarez A. J., Eneli I. U., Wang J., Gardiner J. C. Diagnosis of attention-deficit/hyperactivity disorder and the use of psychotropic medication in very young children. *Archives of Pediatric Adolescent Medicine* 1999; 153: 1039–45.
7. Baumgaertel A., Wolraich M. L., Dietrich M. Comparison of diagnostic criteria for attention deficit disorders in a German elementary school sample. *Journal of the American Academy of Child and Adolescent Psychiatry* 1995; 34:629–38.
8. Wolraich M. L., Hannah J. N., Baumgaertel A., Feurer I. D. Examination of DSM-IV criteria for attention deficit/hyperactivity disorder in a county-wide school sample. *Journal of Developmental Behavioral Pediatrics* 1998; 19:162–8.
9. Accardo P. J. (chair), Clinical Practice Guideline. Communication disorders: the guideline technical report. Albany: New York State Department of Health, Early Intervention Program; 1999. p. II–9. Publication 4220.
10. Goldman L. S., Genel M., Bezman R. J., Slanetz P. Diagnosis and treatment of attention-deficit/hyperactivity disorder in children and adolescents. *Journal of the American Medical Association* 1998; 279:1100–7.
11. Angold A., Erkanli A., Egger H. L., Costello E. J. Stimulant treatment for children: a community perspective, *Journal of the American Academy of Child and Adolescent Psychiatry* 2000; 39:975–84.
12. Jensen P. S. Commentary. *Journal of the American Academy of Child and Adolescent Psychiatry* 2000; 39: 984–7.
13. Dulcan M. Using psychostimulants to treat behavior disorders of children and adolescents. *Journal of Child and Adolescent Psychopharmacology* 1991; 1:7–20.
14. Volkow N. D., Ding Y-S., Fowler J. S., Wang G-J., Logan J., Galley J. S., et al. Is methylphenidate like cocaine? Studies on their pharmacokinetics and distribution in the human brain. *Archives of General Psychiatry* 1995; 52:456–63.
15. Ernst M., Earle A., Zametkin A. Brain imaging studies of the action of methylphenidate and cocaine in the human brain. In: Greenhill L. L., Osman B. B., editors. *Ritalin: theory and practice.* Larchmont (NY): Mary Ann Liebert; 2000. p. 375–84.
16. Bradley C. The behavior of children receiving Benzedrine. *American Journal of Psychiatry* 1937; 94:577–85.
17. Biederman J., Wilens T., Mick E., Spencer T., Faraone S. V. Pharmacotherapy of attention deficit/hyperactivity disorder reduces risk for substance use disorder. *Pediatrics* 1999; 104(2):e20.
18. Wender P. H., Klein D. F. *Mind, mood, and medicine: a guide to the new biopsychiatry.* New York: Farrar, Straus & Giroux; 1981.
19. Sacks O. *Awakenings.* New York: Doubleday; 1974.

20. Shrag P., Divoky D. *The myth of the hyperactive child and other means of child control.* New York: Random House; 1975.

21. DeGrandpre R. *Ritalin nation: Rapid-fire culture and the transformation of human consciousness.* New York: W. W Norton; 2000.

22. Doughtery D. D., Bonab A. A., Spencer J. J., Rauch S. L., Madras B. K., Fischman A. J. Dopamine transporter density in patients with attention deficit hyperactivity disorder. *Lancet* 1999; 354: 2132–3.

23. Psychiatry: education's ruin. Los Angeles: Citizen's Commission on Human Rights; 1995.

24. Wiseman B. *Psychiatry: the ultimate betrayal.* Los Angeles: Freedom Publications; 1995.

25. Narrett E. Progress and boy killing. *Culture Wars 2000;* 19:8–15.

26. Conrad P., Schneider J. W. *Deviance and medicalization: from badness to sickness.* Philadelphia: Temple University Press; 1992.

27. Gross P. R., Levitt N. *Higher superstition: the academic left and its quarrel with science.* Baltimore: Johns Hopkins University Press; 1998.

28. Gross P. R., Levitt N., Lewis M. W., editors. *The flight from science and reason.* New York: New York Academy of Science; 1996.

29. MTA Cooperative Group. 14-Month randomized clinical trial of treatment: strategies for ADHD. *Archives of General Psychiatry* 1999; 56:1073–86.

30. Valenstein E. S. *Blaming the brain: the truth about drugs and mental health.* New York: The Free Press; 1998.

31. Valenstein E. S., Charney D. Are we 'blaming' brain chemistry for mental illness? *Cerebrum* 2000; 2:87–114.

32. Zametkin A. J., Ernst M. Problems in the management of attention-deficit-hyperactivity disorder. *New England Journal of Medicine* 1999; 340:40–6.

33. Elia, J., Ambosini P. J., Rapaport J. L. Treatment of attention-deficit-hyperactivity disorder. *New England Journal of Medicine* 1999; 340:780–8.

34. Accardo P. J. A rational approach to the medical assessment of the child with attention deficit/hyperactivity disorder. *Pediatrics Clinic of North America* 1999; 46:845–56.

35. Committee on Quality Improvement, Subcommittee on Attention-Deficit/ Hyperactivity Disorder. Clinical practice guideline: diagnosis and evaluation of the child with attention-deficit/ hyperactivity disorder. *Pediatrics* 2000; 105:1156–70.

36. American Academy of Child and Adolescent Psychiatry. Practice parameter for the assessment and treatment of children, adolescents, and adults with attention-deficit/hyperactivity disorder. *Journal of the American Academy of Child and Adolescent Psychiatry* 1997; 36:85S-121S.

37. Accardo P. J., Blondis T. A., Whitman B. Y., Stein M., editors. *Attention deficits and hyperactivity in children and adults.* New York: Marcel Dekker, 2000.

38. NIH Consensus Development Program–110. Diagnosis and treatment of attention deficit hyperactivity disorder. Consensus development, conference statement. Bethesda (MD): National Institutes of Health; 1998.

39. Greenhill L. L., Osman B. B., editors. *Ritalin: theory and practice.* Larchmont (NY): Mary Ann Liebert; 2000.

SELECTION 22

The following selection is an article written by Eric Taylor and published in *Archives of General Psychiatry* (December 1999), in which he reviews the major findings and the implications of a major study comparing psychostimulant treatment and behavioral treatment for attention deficit/hyperactivity disorder in children. Taylor is affiliated with the Department of Child and Adolescent Psychiatry, Institute of Psychiatry—Kings College in London.

■ *Commentary: Development of Clinical Services for Attention-Deficit/Hyperactivity Disorder*

ERIC TAYLOR

The results of the Multimodal Treatment Study of Children with Attention-Deficit/ Hyperactivity Disorder (MTA) trial by the MTA Cooperative group[1,2] have been eagerly awaited internationally. It is a landmark in the evolution of children's mental health into an evidence-based discipline. It is particularly impressive that so detailed and intensive a treatment regimen was delivered consistently across sites for so many cases. For once, the number of subjects in a trial is enough for robust conclusions. The outcome measures do justice to the complexity of the disorder and include most of the major domains in which adverse outcomes are to be expected in untreated groups. The strong lesson is that ambitious trials are also feasible. Where there are the will and resources to test treatment practices, it can be done with sufficient rigor to command authority from statisticians, trial experts, and clinicians.

The questions asked will be highly relevant to current practice issues in North America. The main conclusion—that a carefully executed regimen of medication management is superior to alternative treatments and nearly as good as combined treatment—calls for services to make medication available for attention-deficit/hyperactivity disorder (ADHD). This simple lesson has clearly been learned already, for community care provided medication for most of the diagnosed children.

Practice, however, is different in North America than in much of the rest of the world. Pharmacoepidemiology does not yet give clear information, but commercial information about the quantities of medication used annually and the numbers of prescriptions suggest that stimulants are used between 10 and 30 times more frequently in the United States than in the United Kingdom. The rate in southern European countries, Scandinavia, eastern Europe, and south Asia is even lower than that for the United Kingdom. Of course, there is no question about the effectiveness of stimulant drugs. Previous trials have made it clear that stimulants are superior to placebo in the reduction of hyperactivity. The practice differences come from other questions that await solution: clinicians' lack of confidence in our knowledge of long-term effects, the power (or lack of power) of psychosocial interventions, and the boundaries of the disorder and who should be treated.[3]

Some of the trial results are relevant to the decisions confronting clinicians in different traditions of child mental health. This Commentary will attempt to draw them out, because the degree to which conclusions can be generalized is a complex issue. In one respect, much caution is needed: the treatments provided for the community care group are different from those in equivalent situations in most other countries, and simple comparisons between the experimental treatments and community care will not have the same impact in those countries as in the United States.

Taylor, Eric. (1999, December). Commentary: Development of clinical services for attention-deficit/hyperactivity disorder. *Archives of General Psychiatry, 11* (12), 1097–1099. Reprinted with permission.

The results have already been influential on the clinical scientific community. The grapevine has sometimes misinterpreted the results as indicating a lack of effect of intensive psychological intervention. These articles make it clear that this is not correct, and indeed that this was not one of the questions addressed. But the superiority of medication management to behavioral treatment looks robust, in spite of the possible objections considered below. Furthermore, it is plain that combined treatment adds a good deal to the outcome of those receiving it compared with those given behavioral treatment and that the extra benefits of combined treatment over medication management are surprisingly small.

In a low-medication culture, the direct comparison between medication management and behavioral treatment is only part of the information required to change practice. Let us accept that medication management is more effective than behavioral treatment. Clinicians may nevertheless not always wish to use the most powerful treatment available. For example, they may prefer a less-effective therapy if it carries lower hazard or lower cost. Reasoning such as this led to the recommendations of a European professional consensus development group[4] that medication is the first choice of treatment only in severe cases; in mild cases, home-based and school-based behavioral approaches should be the first-line therapy, followed by medication if these approaches are not sufficient. Such an approach is not overturned by this trial, although it could be by a more complete cost-benefit analysis or by a comparison of a regimen of medication management (with behavioral treatment added for those with suboptimal response) vs. behavioral treatment (with medication management added when required). There should in due course be relevant information forthcoming from this trial. Even with current knowledge, an important conclusion is that combined treatment offers greater power than behavioral treatment. Children with suboptimal responses to behavioral approaches should therefore be offered medication as well. This is quite often not done or done only after a long delay, perhaps years. The superiority of the combined treatment emphasizes that it is not normally acceptable for psychosocial interventions to be prolonged as the sole intervention in the face of lack of improvement. Medication is available as an effective supplement. It follows that one aspect of a clinical service that should be audited is its efficiency in progressing to medical management when indicated.

Are there any features of the trial that might not be generalizable to clinical practice? In particular, could the effects of behavioral treatment and combined treatment relative to medication management have been underestimated? Three design decisions need to be considered: (1) Psychological interventions were delivered in a fixed (high) dose, while the dose of medication was variable. This means that effects of behavioral approaches may be underestimated in the outcome measures of combined treatment. Improvements because of behavioral treatment may be reflected in a reduction in the dose of medication, while if two fixed-dose treatments had been compared, the outcome might have been better with combined treatment than with medication management. This is not special pleading: the same argument would apply the other way around. If medication had been given in a fixed dose while behavioral therapy varied in quantity, then (quite apart from the issue that the dose might have been suboptimal for some) some of the beneficial effects of medication would have been seen in a reduction of the amount of psychological treatment delivered rather than in a difference in final outcome. In fact, there was a considerably lower dose of medication for the combined treatment group than for the behavioral treatment group; this would be a clinically significant benefit in reducing the exposure of treated children to the hazards of medication. (2) Psychological interventions were tapered prior to outcome assessment, while medication was continued at full dosage. While superficially this may seem like an unfair comparison, it is faithful to the objectives of the different therapeutic approaches: to suppress symptoms for as long as necessary and to teach enduring coping strategies. Certainly it reflects differences in what would be done in conventional practice— but this is not a strong argument. In other respects, behavioral treatment does not reflect conventional behavioral therapy. It is an impressive bringing together of several different approaches and was evidently designed to give behavioral approaches the best opportunity to show their comparative value rather than to test normal practice. In spite of this, the decision to compare outcome after behavioral treatment but during medication management is reasonable and should not be taken as invalidating the results. (3) Psychological interventions were not based on fully validated approaches. A rationally based psychotherapy would seek to modify aspects of the psychological environment or the mental state of the child that were known to be associated with an adverse course. The aspects of parent–child relationships, peer relationships, and school performance that were the targets for intervention all make good clinical sense—but are not yet shown from longitudinal studies to be the key factors that determine the developmental course. For example, critical expressed emotion from parents was a predictor of long-term outcome in an untreated group of children with hyperactive behavior[5] but was not an explicit target for the intervention. It would be helpful to know the extent to which behavioral treatment had an impact on these and other key aspects of the process and the extent to which this impact is associated with a better or a worse outcome. It may be encouraging that combined treatment had a greater impact than medication management on some types of parental rating—it raises the possibility that it was effective for important aspects of the family environment.

In short, there is no reason to doubt the results of the trial, but application in different clinical contexts will call for careful judgment. Behavioral approaches should not be abandoned. It looks as though, in combination with medication, they are of particular importance in attaining excellent response. But services relying solely on them should change their practice.

Long-Term Effects

The long term has, of course, not yet arrived for the subjects of this trial. It is certainly helpful to know that in this, as in other evaluations of outcome over the course of a year or more, the benefits of treatment are sustained. However, the time elapsed is not yet long enough to be able to judge the full developmental impact. It is still possible that tachyphylaxis may appear in the medication-treated groups or that longer-term social learning or environmental modification will emerge as a benefit for the behaviorally treated groups. Follow-up will give some of the knowledge that is needed and should be supported.

Who Should Be Treated?

The study does not indicate that there is any subgroup of children with ADHD for whom the benefits of medication are particularly strong. However, the moderator and mediating variables selected do not yet provide a comprehensive answer. European practice is influenced by the notion that a subgroup with hyperkinetic disorder (i.e., a severely and pervasively affected group with evidence of impaired attention as well as hyperactive behavior) is particularly suitable for stimulant treatment, while the benefit for others is less well defined. This is neither supported nor disconfirmed by this report. However, some myths—for instance, the nonresponsiveness of girls—have been usefully dispelled.

Careful interpretation of the findings on moderators is needed. The design does not allow for a precise description of the moderators of drug action because of the lack of a placebo group. To be clear about whether anxiety moderates the action of stimulants, it would be necessary to test the influence of anxiety on the drug–placebo difference. This is because, in each treatment condition, there will be many influences on outcome in addition to the specified treatment. Anxiety might enhance compliance with medication or response to the nonspecific aspects of receiving and monitoring medication as well as the pharmacological action of the drug. There might be both harmful and beneficial influences. The lack of an influence of anxiety on the slope of behavior change during medication should not, therefore, be taken to contradict the earlier finding[6] (replicated by studies cited in the text) that high anxiety before treatment predicted an attenuation of the response to the pharmacological action of methylphenidate. Interestingly, the figure provided suggests that the main difference at outcome between those with and without anxiety is actually to be seen in the community care group, in which the outcome for those with anxiety is worse. What conclusion should be drawn?

Clinicians whose pattern of treatment is similar to that described herein—and that presumably includes most North American clinicians—should expect a less good outcome for children with anxiety if they give conventional treatment for ADHD and should vary their protocol in the direction either of more reliance on psychosocial interventions or of a much more carefully crafted medication design.

Planning

Treatments for ADHD are expensive and come as new burdens on underfunded services. Does the evidence help to plan how services should look?

There is scope for different policy decisions in different parts of the world. One particularly controversial question will be the extent to which the combination of therapies should be offered. It is current orthodoxy that multimodal interventions should be available and offered on an individually planned basis. This is perhaps the ideal rather than the usual reality. Commentators on the U.S. medical scene have often been troubled by the extent to which medication is provided as the single therapy, and commentators in Europe have been similarly concerned by a failure to include medication in treatment plans. Nevertheless, it is the aspiration. Is it now outdated? Proponents of a service built around medication might, after all, be tempted to argue that the benefits of adding psychological treatment (combined treatment vs. medication management) are rather small and do not justify their cost. This is probably false. As argued above, the added benefits of combined treatment are developmentally important. Furthermore, the situation of a child who is known to be a nonresponder to medication is clearly rather different from that of the general run of children with ADHD who were randomized to combined treatment. Where medication still leaves room for improvement, it will be necessary to offer psychological approaches. On this evidence, the addition of behavioral treatment can be expected either to reduce the amount of medication required or to improve outcome for those who continue to receive the same dose.

In addition, there may be particular benefits for outcomes (e.g., peer relationships) that are dominant in the individual case. The wishes of families are to be respected when possible, and it seems likely that many will continue to opt for nondrug treatments even when they are apprised of results such as these. Medication must clearly be provided by the services for children with ADHD. This is no doubt a banal conclusion in the United States, but it is still strongly debated in much of the rest of the world. Where there are doubts about the value of medication for aspects of child development other than reducing the "nuisance value" of noisy behavior to adults, they should be laid to rest. Furthermore, the superiority of medication management to community care argues that there is much to be done in the delivery of medication that can improve its value. Services will now need to review the way in which they monitor treatment and adjust dosage.

It is not clear exactly which aspect of medication management led to its superiority over medication in the community. Certainly it is a common finding that trial results are better than what can be achieved in routine practice. This time, however, the better results of the trial cannot be attributed to compliant and well-selected cases, because randomization led to comparable cases in the community care group. Intense and frequent monitoring of response—with clear guidelines about actions to be taken—is likely to be the key to improving results. This will be expensive, and it is not yet clear whether the best strategy will be to apply this careful crafting to all cases treated (which may carry the cost of fewer cases being treated) or to reserve it for those who have a suboptimal initial response to routine medication (which may not always be easy to determine). Treatment research in ordinary practice settings is now required.

It is more difficult to draw conclusions about the degree and type of psychological therapy that should be provided. The regimen in this trial was admirable, extensive, and, presumably, expensive. In the context of a publicly provided mental health service, it is unlikely to be affordable. The intensity may not, of course, be necessary for these effects, but practitioners will be reluctant to increase their input so drastically on the basis of the results achieved while remaining uncertain about which components of the package to emulate. The clearest conclusion is the challenge to improve the focus and methods of psychological therapies.

The authors have achieved an impressive evaluation of treatments; every clinic and practitioner in the field should study these lessons.

REFERENCES

1. The MTA Cooperative Group. A 14-month randomized clinical trial of treatment strategies for attention-deficit/hyperactivity disorder. *Archives of General Psychiatry.* 1999;56:1073–1086.
2. The MTA Cooperative Group. Moderators and mediators of treatment response for children with attention-deficit/hyperactivity disorder. *Archives of General Psychiatry.* 1999;56:1088–1096.
3. Overmeyer S, Taylor E. Principles of treatment for hyperkinetic disorder: practice approaches in the UK. *Journal of Child Psychology and Psychiatry.* In press.
4. Taylor E, Sergeant J, Doepfner M, Gunning B, Overmeyer S, Mobius HJ, Eisert HG. Clinical guidelines for hyperkinetic disorder. *European Child and Adolescent Psychiatry.* 1998;7:184–200
5. Rutter M, Maughan B, Meyer J, Pickles A, Sillberg J, Simonoff E, Taylor E. Heterogeneity of antisocial behavior: causes, continuities, and consequences. *Nebraska Symposium on Motivation* 1997; 44:45–118.
6. Taylor E, Schachar R, Thorley G, Wieselberg HM, Everitt B, Rutter M. Which boys respond to stimulant medication? A controlled trial of methylphenidate in boys with disruptive behaviour. *Psychological Medicine* 1987;17:121–143.

Looking at Both Sides—The Debate Continues

The core arguments with regard to whether stimulant drugs should be used to treat ADD in children are aptly represented by the following excerpts from selections in this chapter:

> In the end, what has made the Ritalin outbreak not only possible but inevitable is the ongoing blessing of the American medical establishment—and not only that establishment. In a particularly enthusiastic account of the drug in a recent issue of the *New Yorker,* writer Malcolm Gladwell exults in the idea that "we are now extending to the young cognitive aids of a kind that used to be reserved exclusively for the old." He further suggests that, given expert estimates of the prevalence of ADD (up to 10 percent of the population, depending on the expert), if anything "too few" children are taking the drug. Surely all these experts have a point. Surely this country can do more, much more, to reduce fidgeting, squirming, talking excessively, interrupting, losing things, ignoring adults, and all those other pathologies of what used to be called childhood. (from Eberstadt's article, selection 20)

> As demonstrated by over a half century of clinical experience, psychostimulants exhibit an extremely low risk-to-benefit ratio. Although psychostimulant medication is safe and effective, it is also both overused and underused. Diagnostic errors and incomplete follow-up are the prime culprits here. Most side effects and other unwanted symptoms are related to dosage titration [reduction] and can often be effectively managed without discontinuing an otherwise effective preparation. (from Accardo and Blondis's article, selection 21)

Matters to Ponder

- Do you think that ADD behavior is merely behavior of overexuberant childhood, or something different? Where do you think that you "cross the line" between behaviors that would not need medicational treatment and behaviors that would?
- If you know of someone who has been on Ritalin treatment for ADD (or perhaps yourself), what experiences can you relate that would argue either for or against psychostimulant therapy?

Further Sources to Seek Out

Challman, Thomas D., and Lipsky, James J. (2000, July). Methylphenidate: Its pharmacology and uses. *Mayo Clinic Proceedings,* pp. 711–721. A review of the current understanding of the mechanism of action and the effectiveness of Ritalin in a number of clinical conditions.

Greenhill, Lawrence L., and Osman, Betty B. (Eds.) (2000) *Ritalin: Theory and practice.* Larchmont, NY: MaryAnn Liebert. A comprehensive examination of all aspects of Ritalin treatment.

Magill-Lewis, Jillene (2000, July 3). Psychotropics and kids. *Drug Topics, 144* (13), 35–42. An analysis of the Ritalin controversy from the perspective of pharmacists and the pharmaceutical industry.

Web Sites to Explore

www.breggin.com/ritalin.html
The web site for the writings of Peter R. Breggin, an outspoken critic of Ritalin treatment as well as the general practice of treating psychological disorders with medications.

www.chadd.org
The web site for Children and Adults with Attention-Deficit/Hyperactivity Disorder (CHADD), an organization devoted to the promotion of understanding ADD as a medical disorder.

Question: Should Marijuana Be Legally Available as a Medicine?

One of the most intensely debated drug policy issues in recent years has concerned the question of medical marijuana. Critics opposing the introduction of marijuana as a medicinal option, which would revise its current status as a Schedule I drug "with no accepted medical use" (see Chapter 1), view the possibility of medical marijuana as a kind of "Trojan horse." In other words, permitting the use of marijuana as a medicine would be, from their perspective, a thinly veiled covert effort toward legalizing marijuana or, still worse, legalizing drugs in general. As we will see in the selections in this chapter, the issue of medical marijuana has been argued on political as well as medical grounds. Any change in the status of marijuana would be seen by many as a significant cultural shift in America's attitude toward psychoactive drugs, and significant segments of the American public are clearly unwilling to make any change for now.

The medicinal benefits of marijuana have been noted for thousands of years. The first direct reference to cannabis (the name for the hemp plant the leaves of which constitute marijuana) dates back to 2737 B.C. in the writings of the mythical Chinese emperor Shen Nung. The focus was on its powers as a medication for rheumatism, gout, malaria, and strangely enough, absent-mindedness. Mention was made of its intoxicating properties, but the medicinal possibilities evidently were considered more important. In 1964, a major step toward understanding the effects on the brain of marijuana and other cannabis products was the isolation and identification of THC (technically, delta-9-tetrahydrocannabinol) as the chief active ingredient that produces the intoxicating effects.

The psychoactive potencies of various forms of cannabis are tied to THC concentration, from marijuana having a THC concentration of 1–4 percent to hashish having a THC concentration of 8–14 percent. THC, however, is only one of about eighty separate chemical compounds (called cannabinoids) in the cannabis plant. Therefore, an important question that needs to be answered is whether medical benefits can be gained from ingesting THC alone without smoking marijuana itself or whether the benefits require smoking marijuana in its natural state, thus ingesting not only THC but all the other cannabinoids as well. Since 1985, two prescription drugs containing THC alone or a variation of it have been legally available in capsule form. Dronabinol (brand name: Marisol) is essentially THC in a sesame oil suspension. Nabilone (brand name: Cesamet) is a synthetic variation of THC. Those who promote medical marijuana argue that THC alone is not as effective from a medicinal point of view as marijuana, that somehow the combination of cannabinoids in the cannabis plant itself represent the essential therapeutic agent.

In the United States, antimarijuana sentiment, from the early 1930s to the late 1970s, made it difficult to conduct objective appraisals of the clinical applications of THC ingestion or marijuana smoking. In the last twenty years or so, however, this stance has softened, allowing for some medical research. There is fair agreement that three clinical areas are worth exploring: the treatment of glaucoma, the treatment of asthma, and the treatment of debilitating nausea.

In 1971, it was found that smoked marijuana significantly reduced intraocular (within the eye) pressure in normal human subjects. This discovery led to an important potential application for individuals suffering from glaucoma, a disease in which intraocular pressure rises so high as to damage the optic nerve and eventually produce blindness. Since then, experimental studies have examined the effectiveness of marijuana (either smoked or ingested orally) or in liquid eye drops in reducing glaucoma symptoms. These approaches have been shown to be effective, but the current medical consensus is that other nonmarijuana drugs are of equal or greater value.

Marijuana also produces changes in the bronchial passageways leading to the lungs. Initially, there is bronchodilation (a widening), followed by a subsequent bronchoconstriction. In the case of asthmatic conditions, in which the primary problem is a bronchoconstriction reducing the flow of air into and out of the lungs, it would appear that marijuana would not be advisable at all. However, it turns out that orally administered THC results in bronchodilation without the expected constriction later on. Consequently, THC has a positive effect on asthmatic symptoms. As in its application for the treatment of glaucoma, however, other forms of asthma treatment have been shown to be at least equally effective.

It is in the case of treating nausea that marijuana has shown the most promising effects. Chemotherapy in the course of cancer treatment produces an extreme and debilitating nausea, lack of appetite, and loss of body weight, symptoms that are clearly counterproductive in helping the individual contend with an ongoing fight against cancer. AIDS patients suffer from similar symptoms, as are those patients diagnosed with the gastrointestinal condition called Crohn's disease. During these circumstances, standard antiemetic (antivomiting) drugs are frequently ineffective. The beneficial effect of marijuana, specifically THC, as an antiemetic drug is an important application of marijuana as a medical treatment.

While Marisol and Cesamet are presently in use, U.S. federal authorities have refused to reclassify marijuana itself or any other cannabis product from a Schedule I category (defining drugs that are considered to have no medical application) to a less restrictive Schedule II category. Only a small handful of "compassionate-use" applications have ever been approved, and the entire procedure for reviewing new applications was canceled in 1992. Nonetheless, despite official opposition from federal authorities, advocacy for medical marijuana has grown considerably. In 1999, the Institute of Medicine, a branch of the National Academy of Sciences, issued a major report concluding that, while not recommending marijuana for long-term use, short-term use appeared to be suitable for treating certain physical conditions, particularly "debilitating symptoms," when patients failed to respond well to traditional medications. By 2000, eight U.S. states (Alaska, Arizona, California, Colorado, Hawaii, Maine, Nevada, Oregon, and Washington) had voted by public referenda to allow marijuana smoking for medical purposes, when prescribed by a physician. Importantly, the federal government has recently eased restrictions on the availability of high-grade marijuana for research studies on its effectiveness as a medical treatment. In the past, only low-grade marijuana had been available, a level of cannabis quality that has carried the derogatory designation "ditch weed." In 2001, Canada officially approved the medicinal use of marijuana. It is now legal for Canadian patients to grow and smoke marijuana if their symptoms have been certified by a physician as warranting this treatment. It is also permitted, under these circumstances, to request marijuana, free of charge, from government cannabis farms in Manitoba.

The three selections in this chapter explore this medical marijuana controversy. The first selection is a statement from the Drug Enforcement Administration (DEA), expressing the official federal position on this question and its arguments against any change in drug laws. The second selection by James R. McDonough, director of the Florida Office of Drug Control, covers a broader set of issues, chiefly from an anti-medical marijuana standpoint. The third selection by Lester Grinspoon offers a reasoned appraisal of where things stand now and where changes might be realistically expected to occur in the future.

REFERENCES

Goodman, Ellen (2001, August 5). Importing sense on pot. *Boston Globe,* p. D7.
Levinthal, Charles F. (2002). *Drugs, behavior, and modern society* (3rd ed.). Boston: Allyn and Bacon.
Schiff, Lisa (2001, October). Canada becomes the first to allow medical marijuana. *RN,* p. 10.

SELECTION 23

The following selection is taken from a set of publications issued by the Drug Enforcement Administration (DEA), in its effort to present counterarguments to those made in defense of medical marijuana. The article refers to two state initiatives passed in 1996, Proposition 215 in California and Proposition 200 in Arizona, in which regulations over marijuana treatment for various physical disorders were relaxed.

■ *Say It Straight: The Medical Myths of Marijuana*

Talking Points for Challenging the Medical Use of Marijuana Argument

DRUG ENFORCEMENT ADMINISTRATION

The Medical and Scientific Evidence

- ■ There are over 10,000 scientific studies that prove marijuana is a harmful addictive drug. There is not one reliable study that demonstrates marijuana has any medical value.

Press release (1995, June 20) from the Drug Enforcement Administration, U.S. Department of Justice, Washington, DC. Response to article in the *Journal of the American Medical Association,* "Marihuana as medicine."

■ Marijuana is an unstable mixture of more than 425 chemicals that convert to thousands when smoked. Many of these chemicals are toxic, psychoactive chemicals which are largely unstudied and appear in uncontrolled strengths.

■ The harmful consequences of smoking marijuana include, but are not limited to the following: premature cancer, addiction, coordination and perception impairment, a number of mental disorders including depression, hostility and increased aggressiveness, general apathy, memory loss, reproductive disabilities, and impairment to the immune system.

■ The Food and Drug Administration, the Drug Enforcement Administration and the U.S. Public Health Service have rejected smoking crude marijuana as a medicine.

■ Medical marijuana has been promoted for "compassionate use" to assist people with cancer, AIDS and glaucoma. Scientific studies show the opposite is true; marijuana is damaging to individuals with these illnesses. In fact, people suffering with AIDS and glaucoma are being used unfairly by groups whose real agenda is to legalize marijuana.

AIDS: Scientific studies indicate marijuana damages the immune system, causing further peril to already weakened immune systems. HIV-positive marijuana smokers progress to full-blown AIDS twice as fast as non-smokers and have an increased incidence of bacterial pneumonia.

Cancer: Marijuana contains many cancer-causing substances, many of which are present in higher concentrations in marijuana than in tobacco.

Glaucoma: Marijuana does not prevent blindness due to glaucoma.

■ Marijuana is currently up to 25 times more potent than it was in the 1960s, making the drug even more addictive.

■ Americans take their medicine in pills, solutions, sprays, shots, drops, creams, and sometimes in suppositories, but never by smoking. No medicine prescribed for us today is smoked.

■ The main psychoactive ingredient in marijuana, THC (tetrahydrocannabinol), is already legally available in pharmaceutical capsule form by prescription from medical doctors. This drug, Marinol, is less often prescribed because of the potential adverse effects, and there are more effective new medicines currently available.

■ While a biomedical or causal relationship between marijuana and the use of hard drugs has not been established, the statistical association is quite convincing. Twelve- to 17-year-olds who smoke marijuana are 85 times more likely to use cocaine than those who do not. Sixty percent of adolescents who use marijuana before age 15 will later use cocaine. These correlations are many times higher than the initial relationships found between smoking and lung cancer in the 1964 Surgeon General's report (nine to ten times higher).

■ Major medical and health organizations, as well as the vast majority of nationally recognized expert medical doctors, scientists and researchers, have concluded that smoking marijuana is not a safe and effective medicine. These organizations include: the American Medical Association, the American Cancer Society, National Sclerosis

Association, the American Glaucoma Association, American Academy of Opthal-mology, National Eye Institute, and the National Cancer Institute.

- In 1994, a U.S. Court of Appeals ruled that marijuana should remain a Schedule I drug: highly addictive with no medical usefulness. The court noted that the pro-marijuana physicians had relied on non-scientific evidence.

Political Issues: The California and Arizona Ballot Initiatives

California's Proposition 215, The Compassionate Use Act of 1996, states: *"Section 11357 (criminal penalties), relating to the possession of marijuana, and Section 11358 (criminal penalties), relating to the cultivation of marijuana, shall not apply to a patient, or to a patient's primary caregiver, who possesses or cultivates marijuana for the personal medical purposes of the patient upon the written or oral recommendation or approval of a physician."*

Arizona's Proposition 200, the Drug Medicalization, Prevention, and Control Act of 1996, states: *"We must toughen Arizona's laws against violent criminals on drugs. Any person who commits a violent crime while under the influence of illegal drugs should serve 100% of his or her sentence with absolutely no early release."* The proposition then goes on to say doctors may be permitted *"to prescribe Schedule I controlled substances to treat a disease, or to relieve the pain and suffering of seriously ill and terminally ill patients."*

Both of these ballot initiatives passed, with 56 percent support for Proposition 215 and 65 percent support for Proposition 200.

- The language in these ballot initiatives for California and Arizona are so loosely worded that they basically legalize marijuana for everyone, sick or well, adult or child. Physicians will be able to legally dispense marijuana for migraines, depression, or any other ailments.
- Legalizing marijuana through the political process bypasses the safeguards established by the Food and Drug Administration to protect the public from dangerous or ineffective drugs. Every other prescribed drug must be tested according to scientifically rigorous protocols to ensure that it is safe and effective before it can be sold.
- The California ballot initiative will make marijuana available without a written prescription, bypassing all established medical guidelines for dispensing drugs.
- The Arizona ballot initiative will legalize all Schedule I drugs for medical use. Schedule I drugs are drugs that have a high potential for abuse and have no currently accepted medical use in treatment. Examples of Schedule I drugs are marijuana, LSD, and heroin. Under Arizona's proposition all of these drugs would be essentially legalized for any so-called medical use.
- Both of these laws allow for the possession of marijuana for medicinal purposes; however, buying and selling marijuana will remain illegal.
- These ballot initiatives were passed through a major disinformation campaign financed by wealthy individuals from outside these states. The billionaire financier George Soros gave over half a million dollars to support these initiatives. Other significant contributors include George Zimmer, president and CEO of the Men's Wearhouse clothing store chain, Peter Lewis of The Progressive Corporation Insurance

company in Ohio, and John Sperling, CEO of the Apollo Group, a Phoenix holding company for numerous educational institutions.

■ The true agenda for Proposition 215 and 200 is revealed when you examine the backers of these initiatives. The National Organization to Reform Marijuana Laws (NORML), the Drug Policy Foundation and the Cannabis Buyers Club in San Francisco have spearheaded the passage of the propositions. The radical legalization agenda of these groups leaves little doubt about their broader goal to legalize marijuana and other drugs. As reported in *High Times* magazine, the director of NORML expressly stated that the medical use of marijuana is an integral part of the strategy to legalize marijuana. A former director of NORML told an Emory University audience that NORML would be using the issue of medicinal marijuana as a red herring to give marijuana a good name.

Social and Cultural Issues

■ The medical marijuana movement and its million dollar media campaign have helped contribute to the changing attitude among our youth that marijuana use is harmless. This softening in antidrug attitudes among teens has led to a 140 percent increase in marijuana use among high school seniors from 1994 to 1995.

■ The prolegalization organizations behind these ballot initiatives deny that there is a drug problem among our youth. As much as they seek to focus on people suffering with illnesses, we must keep the debate properly centered on the safety of our kids. In a time where drug use among kids has increased 78 percent in the last four years, this country cannot afford to undermine drug prevention efforts with these promarijuana ballot initiatives.

■ The strategy to link marijuana with current legal substances such as alcohol and tobacco is used regularly by the prolegalization groups. The response to this argument is to state that current use among teens is 50 percent for alcohol, 34 percent for tobacco and 19 percent for marijuana. If we want to see marijuana use among youth equal to alcohol and tobacco, then we should go ahead and legalize marijuana.

■ Legalizing marijuana would add a third drug that combines some of the most serious risks of alcohol and tobacco. Marijuana offers both the intoxicating effects of alcohol and the long-term lung damage of tobacco.

■ Tobacco companies similarly advertised cigarettes as medicinal until the Federal Trade Commission put a stop to it in 1955. Medicinal marijuana is the "Joe Camel" of the promarijuana lobby, since it is children, the first-time users, who are most impressed by these erroneous health claims.

SELECTION 24

The following selection is an article written by James R. McDonough and published in *Policy Review* (April/May 2000). It examines the medical marijuana initiatives in California, Arizona, and elsewhere in the later 1990s, principally from an antimarijuana perspective. McDonough is Director of the Florida Office of Drug Control.

■ *Marijuana on the Ballot*

JAMES R. MCDONOUGH

While it has long been clear that chemical compounds found in the marijuana plant offer potential for medical use, smoking the raw plant is a method of delivery supported neither by law nor recent scientific evidence. The Food and Drug Administration's approval process, which seeks to ensure the purity of chemical compounds in legitimate drugs, sets the standard for medical validation of prescription drugs as safe and effective. Diametrically opposed to this long-standing safeguard of medical science is the recent spate of state election ballots that have advocated the use of a smoked plant—the marijuana leaf—for "treating" an unspecified number of ailments. It is a tribute to the power of political activism that popular vote has displaced objective science in advancing what would be the only smoked drug in America under the guise of good medicine.

Two recent studies of the potential medical utility of marijuana advocate development of a non-smoked, rapid onset delivery system of the cannabis compounds. But state ballot initiatives that seek legalization of smoking marijuana as medicine threaten to circumvent credible research. Advocates for smoking marijuana appear to want to move ahead at all costs, irrespective of dangers to the user. They make a well-financed, emotional appeal to the voting public claiming that what they demand is humane, useful, and safe. Although they rely largely on anecdote to document their claims, they seize upon partial statements that purport to validate their assertions. At the same time, these partisans—described by Chris Wren, the highly respected journalist for the *New York Times,* as a small coalition of libertarians, liberals, humanitarians, and hedonists—reject the main conclusions of medical science: that there is little future in smoked marijuana as a medically approved medication.

A Dearth of Scientific Support

Compounds found in marijuana may have medical potential, but science does not support smoking the plant in its crude form as an appropriate delivery system. An exploration of two comprehensive inquiries into the medical potential of marijuana indicates the following:

- Science has identified only the *potential* medical benefit of chemical compounds, such as THC, found in marijuana. Ambitious research is necessary to understand fully how these substances affect the human body.
- Experts who have dealt with all available data *do not* recommend that the goal of research should be smoked marijuana for medical conditions. Rather, they support development of a smoke-free, rapid-onset delivery system for compounds found in the plant.

In 1997, the National Institutes of Health (NIH) met "to review the scientific data concerning the potential therapeutic uses of marijuana and the need for and feasibility of additional research." The collection of experts had experience in relevant studies and clinical

McDonough, James R. (2000, April–May). Marijuana on the ballot. *Policy Review.* Washington, DC: Heritage Foundation, pp. 51–61. Reprinted with permission.

research, but held no preconceived opinions about the medical use of marijuana. They were asked the following questions: What is the current state of scientific knowledge; what significant questions remain unanswered; what is the medical potential; what possible uses deserve further research; and what issues should be considered if clinical trials are conducted?

Shortly thereafter, the White House Office of National Drug Control Policy (ONDCP) asked the Institute of Medicine (IOM) to execute a similar task: to form a panel that would "conduct a review of the scientific evidence to assess the potential health benefits and risks of marijuana and its constituent cannabinoids." Selected reviewers were among the most accomplished in the disciplines of neuroscience, pharmacology, immunology, drug abuse, drug laws, oncology, infectious diseases, and ophthalmology. Their analysis focused on the effects of isolated cannabinoids, risks associated with medical use of marijuana, and the use of smoked marijuana. Their findings in the IOM study stated:

> Compared to most drugs, the accumulation of medical knowledge about marijuana has proceeded in reverse. Typically, during the course of drug development, a compound is first found to have some medical benefit. Following this, extensive tests are undertaken to determine the safety and proper dose of the drug for medical use. Marijuana, in contrast, has been widely used in the United State for decades. . . . The data on the adverse effects of marijuana are more extensive than the data on effectiveness. Clinical studies of marijuana are difficult to conduct.

Nevertheless, the IOM report concluded that cannabinoid drugs do have *potential* for therapeutic use. It specifically named pain, nausea and vomiting, and lack of appetite as symptoms for which cannabinoids may be of benefit, stating that cannabinoids are "moderately well suited" for AIDS wasting and nausea resulting from chemotherapy. The report found that cannabinoids "probably have a natural role in pain modulation, control of movement, and memory," but that this role "is likely to be multi-faceted and remains unclear."

In addressing the possible effects of smoked marijuana on pain, the NIH report explained that no clinical trials involving patients with "naturally occurring pain" have ever been conducted but that two credible studies of cancer pain indicated analgesic benefit. Addressing another possible benefit—the reduction of nausea related to chemotherapy— the NIH report described a study comparing oral administration of THC (via a drug called Dronabinol) and smoked marijuana. Of 20 patients, nine expressed no preference between the two, seven preferred the oral THC, and only four preferred smoked marijuana. In summary, the report states, "No scientific questions have been definitively answered about the efficacy of smoked marijuana in chemotherapy-related nausea and vomiting."

In the area of glaucoma, the effect of marijuana on intraocular pressure (the cause of optic nerve damage that typifies glaucoma) was explored, and smoked marijuana was found to reduce this pressure. However, the NIH report failed to find evidence that marijuana can "safely and effectively lower intraocular pressure enough to prevent optic nerve damage." The report concluded that the "mechanism of action" of smoked marijuana or THC in pill form on intraocular pressure is not known and calls for more research.

In addressing appetite stimulation and wasting related to AIDS, the NIH report recognized the potential benefit of marijuana. However, the report also noted the lack of pertinent data. The researchers pointed out that the evidence known to date, although plentiful, is anecdotal, and "no objective data relative to body composition alterations, HIV replication, or immunologic function in HIV patients are available."

Smoking marijuana as medicine was recommended by neither report. The IOM report called smoked marijuana a "crude THC delivery system" that is not recommended because it delivers harmful substances, pointing out that botanical products are susceptible to problems with consistency, contaminations, uncertain potencies, and instabilities. The NIH report reached the same conclusion and explained that eliminating the smoked aspect of marijuana would "remove an important obstacle" from research into the potential medical benefits of the plant.

These studies present a consistent theme: Cannabinoids in marijuana do show potential for symptom management of several conditions, but research is inadequate to explain definitively *how* cannabinoids operate to deliver these potential benefits. Nor did the studies attribute any curative effects to marijuana; at best, only the symptoms of particular medical conditions are affected. The finding most important to the debate is that the studies did not advocate smoked marijuana as medicine. To the contrary, the NIH report called for a non-smoked alternative as a focus of further research. The IOM report recommended smoking marijuana as medicine only in the most extreme circumstances *when all other medication has failed* and then only when administration of marijuana is under strict medical supervision.

These conclusions from two studies, based not on rhetorical conjecture but on credible scientific research, do not support the legalization of smoked marijuana as medicine.

The Scientific Community's Views

The conclusions of the NIH and IOM reports are supported by commentary published in the nation's medical journals. Much of this literature focuses on the problematic aspect of smoke as a delivery system when using cannabinoids for medical purposes. One physician-authored article describes smoking "crude plant material" as "troublesome" to many doctors and "unpleasant" to many patients. Dr. Eric Voth, chairman of the International Drug Strategy Institute, stated in a 1997 article published in the *Journal of the American Medical Association (JAMA)*: "To support research on smoked pot does not make sense. We're currently in a huge anti-tobacco thrust in this country, which is appropriate. So why should we waste money on drug delivery that is based on smoking?" Voth recommends non-smoked analogs to THC.

In September, 1998, the editor in chief of the *New England Journal of Medicine,* Dr. Jerome P. Kassirer, in a coauthored piece with Dr. Marcia Angell, wrote:

> Until the 20th century, most remedies were botanical, a few of which were found through trial and error to be helpful. All of that began to change in the 20th century as a result of rapid advances in medical science. In particular, the evolution of the randomized, controlled clinical trial enabled researchers to study with precision the safety, efficacy, and dose effects of proposed treatments and the indications for them. No longer do we have to rely on trial and error and anecdotes. We have learned to ask and expect statistically reliable evidence before accepting conclusions about remedies.

Dr. Robert DuPont of the Georgetown University Department of Psychiatry points out that those who aggressively advocate smoking marijuana as medicine "undermine" the potentially beneficial roles of the NIH and IOM studies. As does Dr. Voth, DuPont discusses the possibility of non-smoked delivery methods. He asserts that if the scientific community were to accept smoked marijuana as medicine, the public would likely perceive the decision as influenced by politics rather than science. Dupont concludes that if research is primarily concerned with the needs of the sick, it is unlikely that science will approve of smoked marijuana as medicine.

Even those who advocate smoking marijuana for medicine are occasionally driven to caution. Dr. Lester Grinspoon, a Harvard University professor and advocate of smoking marijuana, warned in a 1994 *JAMA* article: "The one area we have to be concerned about is pulmonary function. The lungs were not made to inhale anything but fresh air." Other experts have only disdain for the loose medical claims for smoked marijuana. Dr. Janet Lapey, executive director of Concerned Citizens for Drug Prevention, likened research on smoked marijuana to using opium pipes to test morphine. She advocates research on isolated active compounds rather than smoked marijuana.

The findings of the NIH and IOM reports, and other commentary by members of the scientific and medical communities, contradict the idea that plant smoking is an appropriate vehicle for delivering whatever compounds research may find to be of benefit.

Enter the FDA

The mission of the Food and Drug Administration's (FDA) Center for Drug Evaluation and Research is "to assure that safe and effective drugs are available to the American people." Circumvention of the FDA approval process would remove this essential safety mechanism intended to safeguard public health. The FDA approval process is not designed to keep drugs out of the hands of the sick but to offer a system to ensure that drugs prevent, cure, or treat a medical condition. FDA approval can involve testing of hundreds of compounds, which allows scientists to alter them for improved performance. The IOM report addresses this situation explicitly: "Medicines today are expected to be of known composition and quantity. Even in cases where marijuana can provide relief from symptoms, the crude plant mixture does not meet this modern expectation."

For a proposed drug to gain approval by the FDA, a potential manufacturer must produce a new drug application. The application must provide enough information for FDA reviewers to determine (among other criteria) "whether the drug is safe and effective for its proposed use(s), whether the benefits of the drug outweigh its risks [and] whether the methods used in manufacturing the drug and the controls used to maintain the drug's quality are adequate to preserve the drug's integrity, strength, quality, and purity."

On the "benefits" side, the Institute of Medicine found that the therapeutic effects of cannabinoids are "generally modest" and that for the majority of symptoms there are approved drugs that are more effective. For example, superior glaucoma and anti-nausea medications have already been developed. In addition, the new drug Zofran may provide more relief than THC for chemotherapy patients. Dronabinol, the synthetic THC, offers immunocompromised HIV patients a safe alternative to inhaling marijuana smoke, which contains carcinogens.

On the "risks" side, there is strong evidence that smoking marijuana has detrimental health effects. Unrefined marijuana contains approximately 400 chemicals that become combustible when smoked, producing in turn over 2,000 impure chemicals. These substances, many of which remain unidentified, include carcinogens. The IOM report states that, when used chronically, "marijuana smoking is associated with abnormalities of cells lining the human respiratory tract. Marijuana smoke, like tobacco smoke, is associated with increased risk of cancer, lung damage, and poor pregnancy outcomes." A subsequent study by Dr. Zuo-Feng Zhary of the Jonsson Cancer Center at UCLA determined that the carcinogens in marijuana are much stronger than those in tobacco.

Chronic bronchitis and increased incidence of pulmonary disease are associated with frequent use of smoked marijuana, as are reduced sperm motility and testosterone levels in males. Decreased immune system response, which is likely to increase vulnerability to infection and tumors, is also associated with frequent use. Even a slight decrease in immune response can have major public health ramifications. Because marijuana by-products remain in body fat for several weeks, interference with normal body functioning may continue beyond the time of use. Among the known effects of smoking marijuana is impaired lung function similar to the type caused by cigarette smoking.

In addressing the efficacy of cannabinoid drugs, the IOM report—after recognizing "potential therapeutic value"—added that smoked marijuana is "a crude THC delivery system that also delivers harmful substances." Purified cannabinoid compounds are preferable to plants in crude form, which contain inconsistent chemical composition. The "therapeutic window" between the desirable and adverse effects of marijuana and THC is narrow at best and may not exist at all, in many cases.

The scientific evidence that marijuana's potential therapeutic benefits are modest, that other approved drugs are generally more effective, and that smoking marijuana is unhealthy, indicates that smoked marijuana is not a viable candidate for FDA approval. Without such approval, smoked marijuana cannot achieve legitimate status as an approved drug that patients can readily use. This reality renders the advocacy of smoking marijuana as medicine both misguided and impractical.

Medicine by Ballot Initiative?

While ballot initiatives are an indispensable part of our democracy, they are imprudent in the context of advancing smoked marijuana as medicine because they confound our system of laws, create conflict between state and federal law, and fail to offer a proper substitute for science.

Ballot initiatives to legalize smoking marijuana as medicine have had a tumultuous history. In 1998 alone, initiatives were passed in five states, but any substantive benefits in the aftermath were lacking. For example, a Colorado proposal was ruled invalid before the election. An Ohio bill was passed but subsequently repealed. In the District of Colombia, Congress disallowed the counting of ballot results. Six other states permit patients to smoke marijuana as medicine but only by prescription, and doctors, dubious about the validity of a smoked medicine, wary of liability suits, and concerned about legal and professional risks are reluctant to prescribe it for their patients. Although voters passed Arizona's initiative, the state legislature originally blocked the measure. The version that eventually became Arizona law is problematic because it conflicts with federal statute.

Indeed, legalization at the state level creates a direct conflict between state and federal law in every case, placing patients, doctors, police, prosecutors, and public officials in a difficult position. The fundamental legal problem with prescription of marijuana is that federal law prohibits such use, rendering state law functionally ineffective.

To appreciate fully the legal ramifications of ballot initiatives, consider one specific example. California's is perhaps the most publicized, and illustrates the chaos that can result from such initiatives. Enacted in 1996, the California Compassionate Use Act (also known as Proposition 215) was a ballot initiative intended to afford legal protection to seriously ill patients who use marijuana therapeutically. The act explicitly states that marijuana used by patients must first be recommended by a physician, and refers to such use as a "right" of the people of California. According to the act, physicians and patients are not subject to prosecution if they are compliant with the terms of the legislation. The act names cancer, anorexia, AIDS, chronic pain, spasticity, glaucoma, arthritis, and migraine as conditions that may be appropriately treated by marijuana, but it also includes the proviso: "or any other illness for which marijuana provides relief."

Writing in December 1999, a California doctor, Ryan Thompson, summed up the medical problems with Proposition 215:

> As it stands, it creates vague, ill-defined guidelines that are obviously subject to abuse. The most glaring areas are as follows:
>
> ■ A patient does not necessarily need to be seen, evaluated or diagnosed as having any specific medical condition to qualify for the use of marijuana.
> ■ There is no requirement for a written prescription or even a written recommendation for its medical use.
> ■ Once "recommended," the patient never needs to be seen again to assess the effectiveness of the treatment and potentially could use that "recommendation" for the rest of his or her life.
> ■ There is no limitation to the conditions for which it can be used, it can be recommended for virtually any condition, even if it is not believed to be effective.

The doctor concludes by stating: "Certainly as a physician I have witnessed the detrimental effects of marijuana use on patients and their families. It is not a harmless substance."

Passage of Proposition 215 resulted in conflict between California and the federal government. In February 1997, the Executive Office of the President issued its response to the California Compassionate Use Act (as well as Arizona's Proposition 200). The notice stated:

> [The] Department of Justice's (D.O.J.) position is that a practitioner's practice of recommending or prescribing Schedule I controlled substances is not consistent with the public interest (as that phrase is used in the federal Controlled Substances Act) and will lead to administrative action by the Drug Enforcement Administration (DEA) to revoke the practitioner's registration.

The notice indicated that U.S. attorneys in California and Arizona would consider cases for prosecution using certain criteria. These included lack of a bona fide doctor–patient relationship, a "high volume" of prescriptions (or recommendations) for Schedule I drugs, "significant" profits derived from such prescriptions, prescriptions to minors, and "special circumstances" like impaired driving accidents involving serious injury.

The federal government's reasons for taking such a stance are solid. Dr. Donald Vereen of the Office of National Drug Control Policy explains that "research-based evidence" must be the focus when evaluating the risks and benefits of any drug, the only approach that provides a *rational* basis for making such a determination. He also explains that since testing by the Food and Drug Administration and other government agencies is designed to protect public health, circumvention of the process is unwise.

While the federal government supports FDA approved cannabinoid-based drugs, it maintains that ballot initiatives should not be allowed to remove marijuana evaluation from the realm of science and the drug approval process—a position based on a concern for public health. The Department of Health and Human Services has revised its regulations by making research-grade marijuana more available and intends to facilitate more research of cannabinoids. The department does not, however, intend to lower its standards of scientific proof.

Problems resulting from the California initiative are not isolated to conflict between the state and federal government. California courts themselves limited the distribution of medical marijuana. A 1997 California appellate decision held that the state's Compassionate Use Act only allowed purchase of medical marijuana from a patient's "primary caregiver," not from "drug dealers on street corners" or "sales centers such as the Cannabis Buyers' Club." This decision allowed courts to enjoin marijuana clubs.

The course of California's initiative and those of other states illustrate that such ballot-driven movements are not a legally effective or reliable way to supply the sick with whatever medical benefit the marijuana plant might hold. If the focus were shifted away from smoking the plant and toward a non-smoked alternative based on scientific research, much of this conflict could be avoided.

Filling "Prescriptions"

It is one thing to pass a ballot initiative defining a burning plant as medicine. It is yet another to make available such "medicine" if the plant itself remains—as it should—illegal. Recreational use, after all, cannot be equated with medicinal use, and none of the ballots passed were constructed to do so.

Nonetheless, cannabis buyers' clubs were quick to present the fiction that, for medical benefit, they were now in business to provided relief for the sick. In California, 13 such clubs rapidly went into operation, selling marijuana openly under the guise that doing so had been legitimized at the polls. The problem was that these organizations were selling to people under the flimsiest of facades. One club went so far as to proclaim: "All use of marijuana is medical. It makes you smarter. It touches the right brain and allows you to slow down, to smell the flowers."

Depending on the wording of the specific ballots, legal interpretation of what was allowed became problematic. The buyers' clubs became notorious for liberal interpretations of "prescription," "doctor's recommendation," and "medical." In California, Lucy Mae Tuck obtained a prescription for marijuana to treat hot flashes. Another citizen arrested for possession claimed he was medically entitled to his stash to treat a condition exacerbated by an ingrown toenail. Undercover police in several buyers' clubs reported blatant sales to minors and adults with little attention to claims of medical need or a doctor's direction. Eventually, 10 of the 13 clubs in California were closed.

Further exacerbating the confusion over smoked marijuana as medicine are doctors' concerns over medical liability. Without the Food and Drug Administration's approval, marijuana cannot become a pharmaceutical drug to be purchased at local drug stores. Nor can there be any degree of confidence that proper doses can be measured out and chemical impurities eliminated in the marijuana that is obtained. After all, we are talking about a leaf, and a burning one at that. In the meantime, the harmful effects of marijuana have been documented in greater scientific detail than any findings about the medical benefits of smoking the plant.

Given the serious illnesses (for example, cancer and AIDS) of some of those who are purported to be in need of smoked marijuana for medical relief and their vulnerability to impurities and other toxic substances present in the plant, doctors are loath to risk their patients' health and their own financial well-being by prescribing it. As Dr. Peter Byeff, an oncologist at a Connecticut cancer center, points out: "If there's no mechanism for dispensing it, that doesn't help many of my patients. They're not going to go out and grow it in their backyards." Recognizing the availability of effective prescription medications to control nausea and vomiting, Byeff adds: "There's no reason to prescribe or dispense marijuana."

Medical professionals recognize what marijuana-as-medicine advocates seek to obscure. The chemical makeup of any two marijuana plants can differ significantly due to minor variations in cultivation. For example, should one plant receive relative to another as little as four more hours of collective sunlight before cultivation, the two could turn out to be significantly different in chemical composition. Potency also varies according to climate and geographical origin; it can also be affected by the way in which the plant is harvested and stored. Differences can be so profound that under current medical standards, two marijuana plants could be considered completely different drugs. Prescribing unproven, unmeasured, impure burnt leaves to relieve symptoms of a wide range of ailments does not seem to be the high point of American medical practice.

Illegal Because Harmful

Cannabinoids found in the marijuana plant offer the potential for medical use. However, lighting the leaves of the plant on fire and smoking them amount to an impractical delivery system that involves health risks and deleterious legal consequences. There is a profound difference between an approval process that seeks to purify isolated compounds for safe and effective delivery, and legalization of smoking the raw plant material as medicine. To advocate the latter is to bypass the safety and efficacy built into America's medical system. Ballot initiatives for smoked marijuana comprise a dangerous, impractical shortcut that circumvents the drug-approval process. The resulting decriminalization of a dangerous and harmful drug turns out to be counterproductive—legally, politically, and scientifically.

Advocacy for smoked marijuana has been cast in terms of relief from suffering. The Hippocratic oath that doctors take specifies that they must "first, do no harm." Clearly some people supporting medical marijuana are genuinely concerned about the sick. But violating established medical procedure *does* do harm, and it confounds the political, medical, and legal processes that best serve American society. In the single-minded pursuit of an extreme position that harkens back to an era of home medicine and herbal remedies, advocates for smoked marijuana as medicinal therapy not only retard legitimate scientific progress but become easy prey for less noble-minded zealots who seek to promote the acceptance and use of marijuana, an essentially harmful—and, therefore, illegal—drug.

SELECTION 25

The following selection is an article written by Lester Grinspoon and published in *Contemporary Drug Problems* (Spring 2000). It surveys the history of marijuana as a medical treatment and evaluates the future of medical marijuana in the United States. Grinspoon's involvement in marijuana research spans a period of more than thirty years. Books he has authored or coauthored include *Marihuana Reconsidered* (1971) and a revised and expanded edition of *Marihuana, the Forbidden Medicine* (1997). Grinspoon is Associate Professor of Psychiatry at Harvard University.

■ *Whither Medical Marijuana?*

LESTER GRINSPOON

Given the very limited toxicity of cannabis and its increasingly acknowledged therapeutic value, it will undoubtedly find increasing application as a medicine in the coming years. But there is uncertainty about the forms in which it will be made available. Governments are unlikely to approve it because of concern about its use for nonmedical purposes and the difficulties of distributing as a medicine a substance that is already easily available. An alternative is the development of commercial cannabis pharmaceuticals that can be regulated and controlled, but pharmaceutical firms will be reluctant to invest the necessary money if they believe they cannot compete successfully with marijuana. Although some of these products may have advantages over whole smoked or ingested marijuana, most will not, and they will all be quite expensive. Ultimately, we can anticipate two medical distribution networks: a legal one for cannabinoid pharmaceuticals and an illegal one for street or homegrown marijuana.

Cannabis was first admitted to Western pharmacopoeias one and a half centuries ago. In 1839 W. B. O'Shaughnessy at the Medical College of Calcutta observed its use in the indigenous treatment of various disorders and found that tincture of hemp was an effective analgesic, anticonvulsant, and muscle relaxant.[1] Publication of O'Shaughnessy's paper created a stir within a medical establishment that at that time had access to only a few effective medicines. In the next several decades, many papers on cannabis appeared in the Western medical literature. It was widely used until the first decades of the 20th century, especially as an analgesic and a hypnotic. Symptoms and conditions for which it was found helpful included tetanus, neuralgia, labor pain, dysmenorrhea, convulsions, asthma, and rheumatism.[2]

Administering a medicine through smoking was unheard of until the late 19th century, when pharmaceutical houses prepared coca leaf cigars and cheroots were occasionally used in lieu of cocaine.[3] If physicians had realized that titration of the dose was easier and relief came faster when marijuana was inhaled, they might have preferred to administer it by smoking. However, in the 19th century it was prepared chiefly as a tincture (alcoholic

Grinspoon, Lester. (2000, Spring). Whither medical marijuana? *Contemporary Drug Problems*, 27, pp. 3–15. Reprinted with permission.

solution), generally referred to as tincture of hemp, tincture of cannabis, or Cannabis indica. The potency and bioavailability of oral cannabis varied widely, and there were no reliable bioassay techniques. Nevertheless physicians prescribed cannabis without much concern about overdoses or side effects because they knew how safe it was. But, understandably, they considered it less reliable as an analgesic than opium and opium derivatives. Furthermore, unlike opiates, it could not be used parenterally because it was not water-soluble. Then, at the turn of the century, the first synthetic analgesics and hypnotics (aspirin and barbiturates) became available. Physicians were immediately attracted to these drugs because their potencies were fixed and they were easily dispensed as pills.

Beginning in the 1920s, interest in cannabis as a recreational drug grew, along with a disinformation campaign calculated to discourage that use. In 1937 the first draconian federal legislation against marijuana, the Marijuana Tax Act, was passed. At that time the medical use of cannabis had already declined considerably; the act made prescription of marijuana so cumbersome that physicians abandoned it. Now physicians themselves became victims of the "Reefer Madness" madness. Beginning with an editorial published in the *Journal of the American Medical Association* in 1945, the medical establishment became one of the most effective agents of cannabis prohibition.[4]

The modern renaissance of medicinal cannabis began in the early 1970s, when several young patients who were being treated with the recently developed cancer chemotherapies discovered that marijuana was much more effective than conventional medicines for the relief of the intense and prolonged nausea and vomiting induced by some of these agents.[5] Word spread rapidly over the cancer treatment grapevine. By mid-decade the capacity of marijuana to lower intraocular pressure had been observed, and patients suffering from glaucoma began to experiment with it.[6] As the AIDS epidemic gathered momentum, many patients who suffered HIV-associated weight loss learned that marijuana was the most effective and least toxic treatment for this life-threatening symptom. These three new medical uses of cannabis have led to wider folk experimentation. The use of marijuana in the symptomatic treatment of convulsive disorders, migraine, insomnia, and dysmenorrhea has been rediscovered.

We have now identified more than 30 symptoms and syndromes for which patients have found cannabis useful,[7] and others will undoubtedly be discovered. Many patients regard it as more effective than conventional medicines, with fewer or less-disturbing side effects. Consider the pain of osteoarthritis, which in the 19th century was often treated with tincture of cannabis. Aspirin, the first of the nonsteroidal anti-inflammatory drugs (NSAIDs), rapidly displaced cannabis as the treatment of choice for this and for many other kinds of mild to moderate pain. But NSAIDs now take more than 7,000 lives annually in the United States alone: cannabis, by contrast, has never killed anyone using it for the relief of pain or for any other purpose.[8] It is not surprising that many patients now treat their osteoarthritis with cannabis, asserting that it provides a better quality of pain relief than NSAIDs and also elevates their spirits.

The number of Americans who understand the medical uses of cannabis has grown greatly in the last few years. The passage in seven states of initiatives allowing some restricted legal use of cannabis as a medicine is the most striking political manifestation of this growing interest. The state laws have led to a battle with federal authorities who until recently proclaimed medical marijuana to be a hoax. Under public pressure to acknowledge the medical potential of marijuana, the director of the Office of National Drug Policy, Barry McCaffrey, authorized a review by the Institute of Medicine of the National Academy of Science, which was published in March 1999.[9]

The report acknowledged the medical value of marijuana, but grudgingly. One of its most important shortcomings was a failure to put into perspective the vast anecdotal evidence of marijuana's striking medicinal versatility and limited toxicity. The report states that smoking is too dangerous a form of delivery, but this conclusion is based on an exaggerated evaluation of the toxicity of the smoke. The report's Recommendation Six would allow patients with what it calls "debilitating symptoms (such as intractable pain or vomiting)" to use smoked marijuana for only six months, and then only after all other approved medicines have failed. The treatment would have to be monitored with "an oversight strategy comparable to an institutional review board process."[10] This would make legal use of medical cannabis impossible in practice. The Institute of Medicine would have patients who find cannabis helpful when taken by inhalation wait for years until a means of delivering smoke-free cannabinoids is developed. But there are already prototype devices that take advantage of the fact that cannabinoids vaporize at temperatures below the ignition point of dried cannabis plant material.

The authors of the Institute of Medicine report discuss marijuana as if it were a drug like thalidomide, with well-established serious toxicity (phocomelia) and limited clinical usefulness (leprosy). This is inappropriate for a drug with a long history, limited toxicity, unusual versatility, and easy availability. But at least the report confirms that even government officials no longer doubt that cannabis has medical uses. Inevitably cannabinoids will eventually be allowed to compete with other medicines in the treatment of a variety of symptoms and conditions; the only uncertainty involves the form in which they will be delivered.

When I first considered this issue in the early 1970s, I assumed that cannabis as medicine would be identical to the marijuana that is used for other purposes (the dried flowering tops of female *Cannabis indica* plants); its toxicity is minimal, its dosage is easily titrated, and, once freed of the prohibition tariff, it will be inexpensive. I thought the main problem was its classification in Schedule I of the Comprehensive Drug Abuse and Control Act of 1970, which describes it as having a high potential for abuse, no accepted medical use in the United States, and lack of accepted safety for use under medical supervision. At that time I naively believed that transferring it to Schedule II would overcome a major obstacle to its legal availability as a medicine. I had already come to believe that the greatest harm in recreational use of marijuana came not from the drug itself, but from the effects of prohibition. But I saw that as a separate issue: I believed that, like opiates and cocaine, cannabis could be used medically while remaining outlawed for other purposes. I thought that once it was transferred to Schedule II, clinical research on marijuana would be pursued eagerly. A quarter of a century later, I have begun to doubt this. It would be highly desirable if marijuana could be approved as a legitimate medicine within the present federal regulatory system, but that now seems to me unlikely.

Today, transferring marijuana to Schedule II (high potential for abuse, limited medical use) would not be enough to make it available as a prescription drug. Such drugs must undergo rigorous, expensive, time-consuming tests before they are approved by the FDA. This system is designed to regulate the commercial distribution of drug company products and protect the public against false or misleading claims about their efficacy and safety. The drug is generally a single synthetic chemical that a pharmaceutical company has developed and patented. The company submits an application to the FDA and tests it first for safety in animals and then for clinical safety and efficacy. The company must present evidence from double-blind controlled studies showing that the drug is more effective than a placebo and as effective as available drugs. Case reports, expert opinion, and clinical experience are not considered sufficient. The cost of this evaluation exceeds $200 million per drug.

It is unlikely that whole smoked marijuana should or will ever be developed as an officially recognized medicine via this route. Thousands of years of use have demonstrated its medical value; the extensive government-supported effort of the last three decades to establish a sufficient level of toxicity to justify the harsh prohibition has instead provided a record of safety that is more compelling than that of most approved medicines. The modern FDA protocol is not necessary to establish a risk-benefit estimate for a drug with such a history. To impose this protocol on cannabis would be like making the same demand of aspirin, which was accepted as a medicine more than 60 years before the advent of the double-blind controlled study. Many years of experience have shown us that aspirin has many uses and limited toxicity, yet today it could not be marshalled through the FDA approval process. The patent has long since expired, and with it the incentive to underwrite the enormous cost of this modern seal of approval. Cannabis too is unpatentable, so the only source of funding for a "start from scratch" approval would be the government, which, to put it mildly, is unlikely to be helpful. Other reasons for doubting that marijuana would ever be officially approved are today's antismoking climate and, most important, the widespread use of cannabis for purposes disapproved by the government.

To see the importance of this obstacle, consider the effects of granting marijuana legitimacy as a medicine while prohibiting it for any other use. How would the appropriate "labeled" uses be determined, and how would "off label" uses be proscribed? Then there is the question of who would provide the cannabis. The federal government currently provides marijuana from its farm in Mississippi to eight patients under a now discontinued Compassionate IND (Investigational New Drug) program. But surely the government could not or would not produce marijuana for many thousands of patients receiving prescriptions, any more than it does for other prescription drugs. If production were contracted out, would the farmers have to enclose their fields with security fences and protect them with security guards? How would the marijuana be distributed? If through pharmacies, how would they provide secure facilities capable of keeping fresh supplies? Would the price of pharmaceutical marijuana have to be controlled—not too high, lest patients be tempted to buy it on the street or grow their own; not too low, lest people with marginal or fictitious "medical" conditions besiege their doctors for prescriptions? What about the parallel problems with potency? When urine tests are demanded for workers, how would those who use marijuana legally as a medicine be distinguished from those who use it for other purposes?

To realize the full potential of cannabis as a medicine in the setting of the present prohibition system, we would have to address all these problems and more. A delivery system that successfully navigated this minefield would be cumbersome, inefficient, and bureaucratically top-heavy. Government and medical licensing boards would insist on tight restrictions, challenging physicians as though cannabis is a dangerous drug every time it was used for any new patient or purpose. There would be constant conflict, with one of two outcomes: patients would not get all the benefits they should, or they would get the benefits by abandoning the legal system for the black market or their own gardens and closets.

A solution now being proposed, notably in the Institute of Medicine report, is what might be called the "pharmaceuticalization" of cannabis: prescription of isolated individual cannabinoids, synthetic cannabinoids, and cannabinoid analogs. The Institute of Medicine report states that "if there is any future for marijuana as a medicine, it lies in its isolated components, the cannabinoids, and their synthetic derivatives." It goes on: "Therefore, the purpose of clinical trials of smoked marijuana would not be to develop marijuana as a licensed drug, but such trials could be a first step towards the development of rapid-onset, non-smoked cannabinoid delivery systems."[11] Some cannabinoids and analogs may have advantages over whole smoked or ingested marijuana in limited circumstances. For example, cannabidiol may be more effective as an anti-anxiety medicine and an anticonvulsant when it is not taken along with THC, which sometimes generates anxiety. Other cannabinoids and analogs may occasionally prove more useful than marijuana because they can be administered intravenously. For example, 15%–20% of patients lose consciousness after suffering a thrombotic or embolic stroke, and some people who suffer brain syndrome after a severe blow to the head become unconscious. The new analog dexanabinol (HU-211) has been shown to protect brain cells from damage by glutamate excitotoxicity in these circumstances, and it will be possible to give it intravenously to an unconscious person.[12] Presumably other analogs may offer related advantages. Some of these commercial products may also lack the psychoactive effects that make marijuana useful to some for nonmedical purposes. Therefore they will not be defined as "abusable" drugs subject to the constraints of the Comprehensive Drug Abuse and Control Act. Nasal sprays, nebulizers, skin patches, pills, and suppositories can be used to avoid exposure of the lungs to the particulate matter in marijuana smoke.

The question is whether these developments will make marijuana itself medically obsolete. Surely many of these new products would be useful and safe enough for commercial development. It is uncertain, however, whether pharmaceutical companies will find them worth the enormous development costs. Some may be (for example, a cannabinoid inverse agonist that reduces appetite might be highly lucrative); but for most specific symptoms, analogs or combinations of analogs are unlikely to be more useful than natural cannabis. Nor are they likely to have a significantly wider spectrum of therapeutic uses, since the natural product contains the compounds (and synergistic combinations of compounds) from which they are derived. THC and cannabidiol, as well as dexanabinol, protect brain cells after a stroke or traumatic injury. Synthetic tetrahydrocannabinol (dronabinol or Marinol) has been available for years, but patients generally find whole smoked marijuana to be more effective.

The cannabinoids in whole marijuana can be separated from the burnt plant products by vaporization devices that will be inexpensive when manufactured in large numbers. Inhalation is a highly effective means of delivery, and faster means will not be available for analogs (except in a few situations, such as parenteral injection in a patient who is unconscious or suffering from pulmonary impairment). Furthermore any new analog will have to have an acceptable therapeutic ratio. The therapeutic ratio of marijuana is not known because it has never caused an overdose death, but it is estimated on the basis of extrapolation from animal data to be 20,000 to 40,000. The therapeutic ratio of a new analog is unlikely to be higher than that; in fact, new analogs may be less safe than smoked marijuana because it will be physically possible to ingest more of them. And there is the problem of classification under the Comprehensive Drug Abuse and Control Act for analogs with psychoactive effects. The more restrictive the classification of a drug. the less likely drug companies are to develop it and physicians to prescribe it. Recognizing this economic fact of life, Unimed, the manufacturer of Marinol, recently succeeded in getting it reclassified from Schedule II to Schedule III. Nevertheless many physicians will continue to avoid prescribing it for fear of the drug enforcement authorities.

A somewhat different approach to the pharmaceuticalization of cannabis is being taken by a British company, G. W. Pharmaceuticals. Recognizing the great usefulness of naturally occurring cannabinoids, this firm is developing a seed bank of cannabis strains with particular value in the treatment of various symptoms and disorders. It is also attempting to develop products and delivery systems that will skirt the two primary concerns about the use of marijuana as a medicine: the smoke and the psychoactive effects (the "high").

To avoid the need for smoking, G. W. Pharmaceuticals is exploring the possibility of delivering cannabis extracts sublingually or via nebulizers. The company expects its products to be effective therapeutically at doses too low to produce the psychoactive effects sought by recreational and other users. My clinical experience leads me to question whether this is possible in most or even many cases. Furthermore, the issue is complicated by tolerance. Recreational users soon discover that the more often they use marijuana, the less "high" they feel. A patient who smokes cannabis frequently for the relief of, say, chronic pain or elevated intraocular pressure will not experience a "high" at all. Furthermore, as a clinician who has considerable experience with medical cannabis use, I have to question whether the psychoactive effect is necessarily undesirable. Many patients suffering from serious chronic illnesses say that cannabis generally improves their spirits. If they note psychoactive effects at all, they speak of a slight mood elevation—certainly nothing unwanted or incapacitating.

In principle, administration of cannabis extracts via a nebulizer has the same advantages as smoked marijuana: rapid onset and easy titratability of the effect. But the design of the G. W. Pharmaceuticals nebulizer negates this advantage. The device has electronic controls that monitor the dose and halt delivery if the patient tries to take more than the physician or pharmacist has set it to deliver. The proposal to use this cumbersome and expensive device apparently reflects a fear that patients cannot accurately citrate the amount or a concern that they might take more than they need and experience some degree of "high" (always assuming, doubtfully, that the two can easily be separated, especially when cannabis is used infrequently). Because these products will be considerably more expensive than natural marijuana, they will succeed only if patients and physicians take the health risks of smoking very seriously and feel that it is necessary to avoid any hint of a psychoactive effect.

In the end, the commercial success of any cannabinoid product will depend on how vigorously the prohibition against marijuana is enforced. It is safe to predict that new analogs and extracts will cost much more than whole smoked or ingested marijuana even at the inflated prices imposed by the prohibition tariff. I doubt that pharmaceutical companies would be interested in developing cannabinoid products if they had to compete with natural marijuana on a level playing field. The most common reason for using Marinol is the illegality of marijuana, and many patients choose to ignore the law for reasons of efficacy and price. Although the number of arrests on marijuana charges has been steadily increasing and has now reached nearly 700,000 annually, patients continue to use smoked cannabis as a medicine. I wonder whether any level of enforcement would compel enough compliance with the law to embolden drug companies to commit the many millions of dollars it would take to develop new cannabinoid products. Unimed is able to profit from the exorbitantly priced dronabinol only because the United States government underwrote much of the cost of development. Pharmaceutical companies will undoubtedly develop useful cannabinoid products, some of which may not be subject to the constraints of the Comprehensive Drug Abuse and Control Act. But this pharmaceuticalization will never displace natural marijuana for most medical purposes.

Thus two powerful forces are now colliding: the growing acceptance of medical cannabis and the proscription against any use of marijuana, medical or nonmedical. There are no signs that we are moving away from absolute prohibition to a regulatory system that would allow responsible use of marijuana. As a result, we are going to have two distribution systems for medical cannabis: the conventional model of pharmacy-filled prescriptions for FDA-approved medicines, and a model closer to the distribution of alternative and herbal medicines. The only difference, an enormous one, will be the continued illegality of whole smoked or ingested cannabis. In any case, increasing medical use by either distribution pathway will inevitably make growing numbers of people familiar with cannabis and its derivatives. As they learn that its harmfulness has been greatly exaggerated and its usefulness underestimated, the pressure will increase for drastic change in the way we as a society deal with this drug.

NOTES

1. W. B. O'Shaughnessy. On the Preparations of the Indian Hemp, or Gunjah (*Cannabis indica*): The Effects on the Animal System in Health, and Their Utility in the Treatment of Tetanus and Other Convulsive Diseases. *Transactions of the Medical and Physical Society of Bengal* (1838–1840), p. 460.
2. L. Grinspoon. *Marihuana Reconsidered.* Cambridge. MA: Harvard University Press, 1971, pp. 218–230.
3. L. Grinspoon and J. B. Bakalar. *Cocaine: A Drug and Its Social Evolution,* revised edition. New York. Basic Books, 1985, p. 279.
4. Marihuana Problems. Editorial, *Journal of the American Medical Association,* Vol. 127 (1945), p. 1129.
5. L. Grinspoon and J. B. Bakalar. *Marihuana, the Forbidden Medicine,* revised and expanded edition. New Haven: Yale University Press, 1997, pp. 25–27.
6. R. S. Hepler and I. M. Frank. Marihuana Smoking and Intraocular Pressure. *Journal of the American Medical Association.* Vol. 217 (1971), p. 1392.
7. L. Grinspoon and J. B. Bakalar. *Marihuana, the Forbidden Medicine,* revised and expanded edition. New Haven: Yale University Press, 1997.
8. S. Girkipal, D. R. Ramey, D. Morfeld, G. Singh, H. T. Hatoum, and J. F. Fries. Gastrointestinal Tract Complications of Nonsteroidal Anti-inflammatory Drug Treatment in Rheumatoid Arthritis. *Archives of Internal Medicine,* Vol. 156 (July 22, 1996), pp. 1530–1536.
9. *Marijuana and Medicine: Assessing the Science Base.* J. E. Joy, S. J. Watson. Jr., and J. A. Benson, Jr., editors. Institute of Medicine. Washington. DC: National Academy Press (1999).
10. *Ibid.,* pp. 7–8.
11. *Ibid.,* p. 11.
12. R. R. Leker, E. Shohami, O. Abramsky, and H. Ovadia Dexanabinol: A Novel Neuroprotective Drug in Experimental Focal Cerebral Ischemia. *Journal of Neurological Science.* Vol. 162, No. 2 (January 15, 1999). pp. 114–119. E. Shohami, M. Novikov, and R. Bass. Long-term Effect of HU-211, a Novel Non-competitive NMDA Antagonist. on Motor and Memory Functions After Closed Head Injury in the Rat. *Brain Research.* Vol. 671. No. 1 (March 13, 1995), pp. 55–62.

Looking at Both Sides—The Debate Continues

The core arguments with regard to whether marijuana should be legally available as a medicine range from the adamantly opposed faction to those who see this option as a relatively risk-free expression of compassion and common sense. The following three excerpts give a flavor of the range of opinions regarding this issue. Two of them are taken from selections in this chapter:

> While it has long been clear that chemical compounds found in the marijuana plant offer potential for medical use, smoking the raw plant is a method of delivery supported neither by law or recent scientific evidence. . . . It is a tribute to the power of political activism that popular vote has displaced objective science in advancing what would be the only smoked drug in America under the guise of good medicine. (from McDonough's article, selection 24)

> When I considered this issue in the early 1970s, I assumed that cannabis as medicine would be identical to the marijuana that is used for other purposes . . . ; its toxicity is minimal, its dosage is easily titrated, and, once freed of the prohibition tariff, it will be inexpensive. . . . At that time I naively believed that transferring it to Schedule II would overcome a major obstacle. . . . I thought that, like opiates and cocaine, cannabis could be used medically while remaining outlawed for other purposes. I thought that once it was transferred to Schedule II, clinical research on marijuana would be pursued eagerly. A quarter of a century later, I have begun to doubt this. It would be highly desirable if marijuana could be approved as a legitimate medicine within the present federal regulatory system, but that now seems to me unlikely. (from Grinspoon's article, selection 25)

> The Canadian government has just increased the number of its people who can used marijuana as medicine. As of this month, the terminally ill and those with chronic diseases from cancer to AIDS to MS can turn their back yards into their medicine cabinets. With the approval of a doctor, they can either grow it or get it free from the government, which is paying a company to nurture plants in an abandoned copper mine in Flin Flon, Manitoba. . . . The Canadian system has its own critics: doctors who worry about being gatekeepers and marijuana activists who think there are still too many hurdles. But we [in the United States] are in a marijuana muddle. The feds aren't likely to crack down on the terminally ill, nor are law enforcers eager to rip joints out the hands of AIDS patients. Asa Hutchinson, the Bush pick to head the Drug Enforcement Administration, said prosecuting the medical marijuana dealers wasn't "a priority." But meanwhile, patients are using drug dealers as doctors. And a treatment for suffering is a crime. (from an op-ed article by Ellen Goodman in the *Boston Globe,* August 5, 2001).

Matters to Ponder

- What do you think about one of the arguments made against medical marijuana, that there is a risk of damage to the lungs during marijuana smoking? Regardless of whether this is true, what impact would this possibility have on your opinion?
- Proponents of medical marijuana cite the difficulty in waiting for rigorous test studies on marijuana before it is allowed to be used as a medical treatment, when older

drugs such as penicillin and aspirin were accepted a long time ago without such scrutiny. What do you think of this argument?

■ Opponents of medical marijuana express their concern that marijuana legalization would be encouraged if a shift in policy were to be made, while proponents argue that necessary distinctions among different types of drugs are not being made. In the words of one recent writer, "Compare this [situation] to morphine. We don't allow morphine on the street, but we permit it in the doctor's arsenal for the treatment of pain. Imagine the uproar if we made morphine illegal." What do you think about the connection between medical marijuana and legalized marijuana?

Further Sources to Seek Out

Frater, Elizabeth (2001, March 17). Medical marijuana: The smoldering debate. *National Journal,* pp. 808–9. An examination of the federal government's response to state initiatives promoting medical marijuana.

Guterman, Lila (2000, June 2). The dope on medical marijuana. *Chronicle of Higher Education,* pp. A21–A22. A close look at the political motives surrounding the U.S. government's reluctance to sponsor medical trials involving marijuana.

Levinthal, Charles F. (2002). *Drugs, behavior, and modern society* (3rd ed.). Boston: Allyn and Bacon, Chapter 7. A summary of the historical, biological, psychological, and sociological aspects of marijuana use in the United States.

Medical marijuana: Should doctors be able to prescribe the drugs? (1999, August 20). *CQ Researcher,* pp. 705–728. An entire issue of this periodical, published by Congressional Quarterly Inc., on the topic of medical marijuana.

Taylor, Stuart (2001, March 19). Medical marijuana and the folly of the drug war. *National Journal,* pp. 1467–68. An analysis of how the medical marijuana campaign fits within the larger effort to legalize drugs.

United States House of Representatives (1998, March 18). Sense of the House of Representatives with respect to marijuana for medicinal use. House Report 105–451, Part I. *Congressional Record.* A summary of the divergent views on medical marijuana from the congressional floor debates in 1998.

Web Sites to Explore

www.dea.org
The web site for the Drug Enforcement Administration, with publications and reports opposing changes in existing marijuana regulations.

www.norml.org
The web site for the National Organization for the Reform of Marijuana Laws (NORML), a leading advocate for the relaxation of existing marijuana regulations.

Question: Should the Government Act More Aggressively in Regulating Drugs and Drug Prices?

The next time you are in a pharmacy or drug store, take a minute to look around you. Besides the overwhelming variety of paper goods, cosmetics, shaving creams, toothpastes, deodorants, and all the other products that become part of our daily lives, three important categories of products are available for purchase as medications.

The first group of medicinal products, roughly 2,500 of them, placed mostly out of view and behind the pharmacist's counter, are prescription drugs. Their purchase and use, as we know, require the submission of a written prescription form with an appropriate signature (or a doctor's phone call) that certifies that you are taking one of these drugs for an approved medical condition. The amount of the drug that you are allowed to purchase at any one time is specified, and a limit on the number of prescription renewals offers some control over that drug's use. By law, only licensed physicians or dentists can issue prescriptions and only registered pharmacists are permitted to fill these prescriptions and dispense these drugs to the consumer.

The second group of products, roughly 300,000 of them, are over-the-counter (OTC) drugs. Headache remedies, stomach antacids, and cough-and-cold medicines are common examples. Unlike prescription drugs, OTC drugs are available to you directly. With OTC drugs, you are essentially your own physician. The guidelines are posted on the package, but no one will require that you stop using these drugs at any particular point and no one can make any guarantee that the drugs were appropriate to take in the first place.

In the United States, regulation of both prescription and OTC drugs is the responsibility of the U.S. Food and Drug Administration (FDA). The FDA determines whether an existing prescription drug should continue to be available and whether a newly developed compound passes an established set of standards for safety and effectiveness. Only if these standards are met can these compounds be marketed to the public.

In contrast to prescription drugs and OTC drugs, a third group of products, dietary supplements, are relatively new. Dietary supplements are generally available to the public in the form of vitamins or herbal preparations. While they are marketed like OTC drugs, there is a significant difference. As defined by the Dietary Supplement Health and Education Act in 1994, dietary supplement labels must contain the statement that the product has *not* been evaluated by the FDA and that the claims of benefit from using the product are limited only to helping certain common physical conditions associated with different stages of life (adolescence, pregnancy, menopause, and aging). Dietary supplement manufacturers are not allowed to claim benefits with respect to the diagnosis, treatment, cure, or prevention of more uncommon conditions or diseases.

Historically, there has been a kind of tug-of-war over the appropriate level of regulatory control regarding medicinal drugs. Some argue that the FDA is too strict in its procedures for approving new drugs, causing an undue delay in their availability to individuals who need them; others argue that the FDA is not strict enough in its procedures, causing new compounds to be available before there is sufficient evidence that they are safe.

In recent years, another important issue has come into play. The increasing costs of medications (particularly new medications) have resulted in a demand by some advocacy groups that price controls be put into effect. They argue that elderly populations who take a greater proportion of medications than the general population are in the worst financial position to purchase them. Stories in the media highlight indigent senior citizens who have faced the painful dilemma of deciding whether to pay for the medications that keep them alive or pay for food or housing. An upper limit on the cost of a medication, these groups contend, would help resolve these difficulties. Others have argued, however, that price controls would have a devastating effect on the quality of health care in the United States. Price controls, in their view, would destroy the competitiveness in the pharmaceutical industry that sustains the development of new drugs and new treatments. All of society would suffer as a result. In January 2002, the Bush administration formally proposed a new plan to endorse and regulate drug discounts for Medicare beneficiaries. Whether this concept will be approved by Congress and ruled constitutional by the courts remains to be seen.

The following three selections address the important issues of governmental regulatory policy with regard to the pharmaceutical industry. The first selection by John E. Calfee strenuously argues against pharmaceutical price controls and against additional regulations over the pharmaceutical industry by federal authorities. The second selection by Christopher F. Koller explores the need for Medicare coverage for medications used by the elderly, in light of the steep climb in pharmaceutical costs in recent years. In the third selection, Henry I. Miller and David Longtin make the argument for the increased regulation over dietary supplements, a category of medications that, at the present time, receives relatively little scrutiny by the FDA.

REFERENCES

Levinthal, Charles F. (2002). *Drugs, behavior, and modern society* (3rd ed.). Boston: Allyn and Bacon.
Pear, Robert (2001, November 25). Administration revising its drug discount proposal: New plan is response to court's objections. *New York Times*, p. A32.

SELECTION 26

The following selection, written by John E. Calfee and published in *Consumers' Research* (May, 2000), examines the controversy over the escalating prices of prescription medications. His argument is that patients and consumers are about to sustain better health, live longer lives with less pain and discomfort than ever before, and these benefits are due in large part to the advances in modern drug therapy. In his view, governmentally sponsored price controls would sound the death knell to innovation, research, and progress. Calfee is a former Federal Trade Commission economist and a resident scholar at the American Enterprise Institute in Washington, DC. He is the author of *Prices, Markets, and the Pharmaceutical Revolution* (2000).

■ *Drugs, Drug Prices and Your Health*

JOHN E. CALFEE

Pharmaceutical costs have aroused controversy for decades, but debate has intensified over the past year. Discussions have pursued several themes.

One is the rapid increase in expenditures for pharmaceuticals and the prices of some drugs. Another is the delineation and condemnation of price differences between the United States and other nations (especially Canada and Mexico) and among various domestic buyers, including the federal government, managed care organizations, and pharmacies that cater to individual consumers. Discussions also frequently target the promotion of pharmaceuticals (especially when directed at consumers), which is blamed for high prices, excessive expenditures, and inappropriate medication.

Price controls—to be achieved by design or by implication—have become a political issue. Numerous federal and state legislators have proposed reducing pharmaceutical prices by various methods such as extending Medicaid discounts to neighborhood pharmacies, cutting U.S. prices to match those charged in Canada and Mexico, and even implementing direct controls.

It is certainly true that pharmaceutical expenditures have been increasing rapidly. Outpatient expenditures on prescription drugs (with inflation taken into account) almost doubled between 1990 and 1998. The increases have been larger in recent years, with the largest (12.3%) in 1998. Pharmaceuticals are also claiming an increasing share of the U.S. health care budget. Some historical perspective is useful here. Prescription costs as a proportion of health care expenditures actually declined for many years after 1960, with the trend reversing in the early 1980s. Even today, the share of spending on pharmaceuticals is still far below the levels of the early 1960s, although it has climbed from 4.9% of health care costs in 1985 to 7.2% in 1997. Most forecasters see pharmaceutical expenditures continuing to increase at 10% or more annually.

Price increases are not, however, the main reason for increased drug expenditures. Since 1993, the prices of prescription drugs have been increasing at less than 4% annually, only slightly above the general inflation rate and far below the rate of increase in expenditures for prescription drugs. According to surveys, higher prices for existing drugs account for less than one-fourth of the increased expenditures. The remaining

Calfee, John E. (2000, May). Drugs, drug prices and your health. *Consumers' Research*, pp. 10–15. Reprinted with permission.

increases result from increased volume and particularly from a shift toward more expensive drugs, which are usually newer on the market. Even the modest role for price increases is exaggerated because measurements of pharmaceutical price changes are upwardly biased: pharmaceutical price indexes (like those for many other products) fail to adjust for the higher quality of new drugs and the increased benefits from new uses for old drugs.

The dominant role of new drugs in pharmaceutical spending is reflected in the disproportionate increases in expenditures in the more innovative therapeutic areas. The largest increases between 1997 and 1998 involved heart medications and antidepressants, propelled by the success of the statin class of cholesterol-reducing drugs and of improved antidepressants. The path-breaking painkillers Celebrex and Vioxx boosted total sales for arthritis treatments in 1999, even as sales for older analgesics declined.

Reduced expenditures on other forms of health care have partially offset the increased expenditures on drugs because drugs reduce many costly side effects and may prevent or simplify medical procedures. For example, H2 antagonists (Tagamet and other drugs that suppress stomach acid secretion) reduced the costs of surgery of gastrointestinal ulcers by more than half. The use of "clot-busters" in treating strokes has reduced health care costs by about four times as much as the cost of the drug (not to mention the benefits to patients and families).

Consumer Benefits of Treatment Advances

The ability of pharmaceuticals to reduce the total expenditures for health care, as well as business costs, is important but secondary—and even something of a distraction. For it is patients and consumers who are gaining the most from modern drug therapy through better health, longer life, reduced pain and discomfort, and other blessings. New drugs are treating conditions that had been undertreated or even underdiagnosed.

Such conditions include high blood pressure, elevated blood cholesterol, obesity, diabetes, depression and other mental illnesses, and osteoporosis. Many new treatments prevent sudden death and prolong life into old age. Almost certainly, the dramatic reduction in mortality from heart disease in the past 30 years, for example, is primarily due to improved medical treatments, including drug therapy.

One institutional innovation of recent years is a faster Food and Drug Administration. Since 1993, the percentage of new chemical entities approved in less than one year has increased from 20% to 50%, while the percentage approved after more than two years decreased from 45% to less than 5%, despite increases in the number of drugs submitted for approval. After decades of lagging behind the Europeans, the FDA now appears to match the speed of the evolving drug approval system of the European Union. However, demands for larger and more complex clinical trials have partly offset the greater regulatory speed. (See "Consumer Letters" *CR,* February 2000.)

Also important is a revamped clinical trials industry. Despite suspicions about the role of profits in drug testing, huge benefits have resulted. Efficiency has greatly increased. After being driven out by high costs, much of the drug testing has returned to the United States, where most new drugs are developed. More important, physicians who practice in the same environment in which most new drugs will be used now conduct the bulk of clinical testing and use subjects more representative of the general population than those in academic research centers.

The vast expansion in the enterprise of clinical testing provides more than just a faster way to get new drugs onto the market. It has also accelerated the rate at which new uses are found for existing drugs. New uses of drugs—including "off-label uses" that the FDA has not approved for inclusion in advertising or other promotional materials distributed by pharmaceutical firms—can be even more important than the original uses that led to FDA approval. Off-label applications have long dominated cancer therapy and pediatrics; new uses are also crucial for more standardized treatments such as the statin-class cholesterol-reducing drugs.

New medications for old problems are the most familiar results of recent pharmaceutical research. Medical journals and the popular press are full of accounts of new cures and palliatives. Examples include new treatments for adult-onset diabetes; manic depression and other mental illnesses; hypertension, elevated cholesterol, and other heart problems; and migraine headaches, osteoporosis, and diabetes.

A less obvious benefit of the pharmaceutical research revolution is quicker and more intense competition, including more competition in prices. Inderal, the first beta blocker for heart disease, was introduced in 1965; its first competitor, Lopressor, came 13 years later, in 1978. Tagamet, the first H2 antagonist (stomach acid suppressor) for ulcers, was introduced in 1977, followed by Zantac six years later. In the 1980s, breakthrough drugs included the ACE inhibitor Capoten for heart disease, the allergy-fighting antihistamine Seldane, the AIDS drug AZT, the first "statin" drug for high cholesterol (Mevacor), and the first SSRI for depression, Prozac. In each case, a competitor appeared within four years (five, in the case of Capoten).

Research moved even faster in the 1990s. Diflucan, a new antifungal, was approved in 1990 and met competition from Sporax in 1992. Recombinate, a new blood treatment for hemophiliacs, arrived in 1992 and faced competition the next year. The first protease inhibitor for HIV (Invirase) encountered a competitive market within a few months. The Cox-2 inhibitor Celebrex for arthritis pain enjoyed only a few months as the lone brand before it faced Vioxx in a battle over the arthritis pain market that quickly brought price cuts. Highly visible battles are raging among the statin class of cholesterol-reducing drugs as well as among the modern generation of antidepressants, including Prozac, Paxil, Zoloft, and Celexa. Before 1997, no useful treatments existed for early-onset diabetes, a devastating and extremely costly disease. Now two are competing in terms of their safety profiles as well as efficacy.

The notion of faster competition brings up an important related point about the prices of new and of older drugs. Some widely cited studies simply compare the prices of new drugs with those of the drugs that they replace, almost as if the new drugs did not provide a substantial therapeutic or other improvement. But from the standpoint of medical care and other relevant criteria such as ease of use, the new drugs are typically of higher quality—sometimes much higher. In the highly competitive markets for beta blockers, ACE inhibitors, and statin cholesterol-reducing drugs—all used to treat or prevent heart disease—the market pioneers have found their market share eroding, partly because of aggressive pricing from new entrants and partly because manufacturers of new drugs typically seek a market share by providing reduced side effects or greater ease of use.

The revolution in pharmaceutical research technology is also spawning entirely new areas of application, as is evident from the rapid advances in treating illnesses and conditions that had once proved more or less intractable. Examples include drugs that reverse obesity and thus provide a means for preventing or treating Type II diabetes; better treatments for depression, bipolar disorders, and other mental illnesses; and cholesterol-reducing drugs that offer an alternative to angioplasty for coronary heart disease.

The Benefits of Advertising

Sensibly, much pharmaceutical promotion focuses on closing the most consequential gaps in information between the research community and practitioners. The high cost of pharmaceutical promotion—about $6 billion during 1998, including media advertising, detailing, and other activities—reflects the cost of summarizing and delivering essential information where it can do the most good and repeating the information sufficiently for assimilation and use.

Consumer advertising of prescription drugs, like promotion directed at physicians, tends to provide essential information that would otherwise move far more slowly from the research community to patients and consumers. Again, many of the most-promoted drugs are for conditions for which the first line of therapy is not pharmaceuticals at all or for which generic or alternative brands may be acceptable.

The ability to promote a health benefit can provide an incentive to undertake research to document such a benefit. In 1989, a drug manufacturer wanting to compete more successfully with the market leader began clinical trials at a cost of nearly $50 million to demonstrate that its drug would prevent heart attacks in people who had not been regarded as at risk because they had only moderately elevated cholesterol levels and were otherwise healthy. After six years, the research demonstrated a 31% reduction in heart attacks, which led to FDA approval to market the drug for preventing heart attacks.

Most significant, this and other statin drug trials provided the first conclusive proof that reducing blood cholesterol could prevent heart attacks and save lives.

The Risks of Price Controls

The gains in pharmaceutical research technology make it almost impossible to predict the desired levels of spending on pharmaceuticals for more than a year or two. We cannot know what new drug therapies will become available, how well they will work, or what populations might benefit from new or existing therapies. The difficulty is apparent from the highly uneven nature of recent increases in drug expenditures. Some therapeutic categories increased by 20% or more within a single year while others remained stable or even declined. But the unevenness results not from shifting expenditures from one category to another, but from taking advantage of new opportunities as they appear: spending has escalated where new benefits from drug therapy have emerged.

If health care budgeting imposes strict limits on spending, rather than using a more flexible approach such as providing partial support for spending, it would prevent consumers from obtaining treatments that would be worth more than their cost.

The United States is perhaps the only large nation that does not impose government controls over drug prices in one way or another, although price controls are already in place in many other parts of the health care system.

Three factors make pharmaceuticals a perennial target for price controls. One is the peculiar cost structure of pharmaceutical development: high upfront research expenditures and low marginal costs of manufacturing and distribution. That structure ensures that new drugs will be sold at a price that far exceeds the costs of production, that is, at what appears to be a fat profit margin. The second factor is the lengthy time-lag between incurring costs and recouping them through sales. In turn, the lag guarantees that anyone in a position to control prices can easily ignore the true costs. The third factor is the unique nature of the product of pharmaceutical research. The real output from research is a piece of information. Once the information has been revealed, however, anyone can use it.

Such circumstances provide the government with an opportunity to give voters the appearance of receiving something for nothing. Capping drug prices would neither halt the supply of existing drugs nor destroy the supply of knowledge about their use. The real costs of controls would remain generally unseen or would at least be delayed until the deleterious impact of controls emerged.

Another factor that encourages price controls is the dominant role of third-party payments. In the United States, third-party reimbursement is encouraged because health insurance premiums paid by employers are exempt from taxation. Insurance firms, rather than consumers directly, have paid essentially the entire increase in nongovernmental pharmaceutical expenditures since 1990. (Thus the proportion of prescription drugs paid through insurance and other third-party mechanisms increased from 37% in 1990 to 75% in 1998.)

The impact of the peculiar cost structure of pharmaceuticals, combined with the motivation of third-party payers, is evident in other industrialized economies, where government or government-mandated organizations dominate health care. Those organizations have felt financial pressure from the advent of new and more valuable drugs. An astonishing variety of price controls has resulted. Some nations, especially smaller or poorer ones, have negotiated extremely low prices for drugs that were expensive to develop. Even wealthy nations, such as Canada and many European Union members, have demonstrated that they can often negotiate prices that are well below the long-run development costs but still high enough to yield a short-run profit for manufacturers.

Those arrangements may be less permanent than they appear, however. They can persist only if the nations with low prices can prevent the exportation of drugs to nations with uncontrolled prices or higher controlled prices. Maintaining a ban on pharmaceutical exports has been difficult in the European Union because of its lack of border control. The advent of Internet purchasing and other means for transborder shipments may soon end multitiered pricing. When that happens, nations that enjoy prices far below those set by a free market will be unable to maintain their advantage.

Numerous factors create uncertainty over the demand for new drugs. Of these, two stand out. First, many new drugs address conditions that had not been systematically treated. Data on the prevalence, health consequences, and social costs are sparse because conditions that are not treated tend not to be studied. Second, even if one does know the number of those suffering from a condition and the health consequences of that condition, we still may have only a vague idea of what people are willing to pay for the drugs that alleviate those conditions.

One danger from price controls is almost universally recognized: the likelihood that price controls would drastically reduce research. The market's reaction to the Clinton administration's 1993 health care proposal amply demonstrates the reality of that danger. The plan would have allowed the Department of Health and Human Services to set prices of new breakthrough drugs. The impact on research efforts was predictable. From 1981 through 1993, annual increases in the U.S. pharmaceutical industry R&D budget averaged 11% (in deflated dollars) and never dropped below 7% until 1994, when the industry faced President Clinton's health care plan.

Then the increase in R&D expenditures dropped to 3% in 1994 and 4% in 1995. In 1996, after Congress had decisively defeated the administration's health care plan, the spending increases for research and development resumed and have averaged about 11% since 1995. As other advanced nations have implemented pharmaceutical price controls, the locus of research has moved steadily to the United States, where firms produce eight of the top ten of the worldwide best-selling drugs.

Solving Tough Problems

There is no substitute for the profit motive for inducing and guiding research. The worst action would be to erect a ceiling on the rewards for solving the toughest problems in medical science: preventing Alzheimer's; curing schizophrenia; reversing heart disease; striking without error at cancer cells; reducing the estimated 350,000 deaths annually from obesity; preventing 10,000 amputations a year from poor circulation, nerve damage, and other consequences of diabetes; delineating the physiological foundations of neurological diseases like multiple sclerosis and Parkinson's; discovering new antibiotics for tuberculosis; finding AIDS cures that work in the long run; creating the next generation of antidepressants for the 60% of patients who cannot or do not use existing antidepressants; developing vaccines for AIDS, malaria, and other infections; and solving quality-of-life problems with cancer therapies that do not destroy ovaries, or insulin and biotech pills to replace injections.

The effects of controls on research incentives are apparent from worldwide trends. Because India and other underdeveloped nations have permitted domestic manufacturers to ignore international patents, pharmaceutical firms cannot protect their property rights to new drugs in those nations. The situation has encouraged low prices for modern antidepressants, heart medications, and other drugs developed for advanced economies but has completely forestalled the development of drugs specifically needed in India and other nations with unique sets of illnesses.*

Price controls on pharmaceuticals in Japan and, to a lesser extent, in France are designed to protect domestic pharmaceutical manufacturers. In both cases, these arrange-

---

*Malaria is an apposite example. The devastating illness, killing tens of millions annually, has been a forgotten stepchild in worldwide pharmaceutical research. A recent United Nations initiative in partnership with the pharmaceutical industry is motivated by the desire "to keep research in antimalarial drugs from ending because of the drugs' poor commercial potential." A medical advocacy group recently noted that of 1,223 new compounds developed during 1975–1997, only 11 were for tropical diseases.

ments work to the disadvantage of consumers, particularly in Japan, where many of the most effective drug therapies for cancer, heart disease, and other conditions are simply unavailable. Not only do manufacturers gain from controls but so do other parties, notably physicians in Japan and bureaucracies everywhere who carry out the crucial job of setting prices and otherwise administering controls.

Price control regimes for pharmaceuticals usually attempt to set higher prices for more innovative drugs (as in Canada, France, and elsewhere). That action requires price controllers to outguess the market in deciding which research areas are most promising and which new types of drugs would be most useful—an impossible task. Even the FDA has found it difficult to predict which new chemical entities the medical community will later regard as breakthrough treatments. For instance, the FDA did not consider the SSRI anti-depressants to be breakthrough drugs.

Even for drugs on the market, additional research can be expensive, yet extremely valuable. Nearly a century after its discovery and marketing, ordinary aspirin was shown to be an extraordinarily effective preventive and first-line treatment for heart attacks. Clinical trials and FDA approval for aspirin's new uses required two decades or more, however. The drug was off patent, and research incentives were undermined because any benefits uncovered through clinical trials could be promoted by any other aspirin manufacturer.

Such difficulties could combine to defeat the goals of advocates of price controls. Research would be curtailed or channeled into lines far less challenging than those that yielded the remarkable advances of the past two decades. Pharmaceuticals for the elderly would become a less lucrative pursuit: investments would shift to more profitable arenas. Prices would remain high, albeit not as high as for truly breakthrough products. Industry profits would be persistently comfortable as is typical for closely regulated industries. A disastrous equilibrium of high prices for inferior drugs and large expenditures with little innovation would result—roughly what has happened in the heavily controlled Japanese pharmaceutical market.

The greatest harm would be the absence of valuable therapies and treatments that would not be developed because of inadequate incentives or would not be imported because of controls over prices or difficulty in obtaining marketing approval. Those harms would be invisible to the public. The system would tend to persist, ensuring stability in prices and expenditures at a monumental cost to patients, who gain the most from new pharmaceuticals and must therefore lose the most when those drugs fail to appear.

SELECTION 27

The following selection, written by Christopher F. Koller and published in *Commonweal* (2001, June 15), considers the problems surrounding pharmaceutical insurance coverage for the elderly. His position is that a Medicare-based insurance program for medications "would represent an improvement over what is currently in place for the elderly." Koller is CEO of Neighborhood Health Plan of Rhode Island and his articles appear regularly in *Commonweal*.

■ *Prescription for Trouble*

Why Drug Prices Keep Exploding

CHRISTOPHER F. KOLLER

Consider Walter. At seventy, he has a history of high blood pressure, heart trouble, high cholesterol, stomach pains, and seasonal allergies. He used to smoke but gave it up a while back. He is only moderately overweight. For his various ailments, Walter has a variety of prescriptions from his doctor. His real problem, however—as for 26 percent of his fellow Americans, particularly the elderly, those most in need of medications—is that Walter has no insurance coverage for his medications. Medicare does not provide it.

Drug coverage makes a real difference in people's lives, for two reasons. Those who have it use prescriptions at a 50 percent higher rate than those without it, presumably to their benefit; and people without it spend on average $220 more per year for the few drugs they do get. Combine these facts and you have a recipe for not only moral but political outrage. Hence the increased attention being paid to a drug benefit for those on Medicare.

Yet there is something else at work here. Only eleven years ago, the percentage of Americans with no drug coverage was almost twice as high (48 percent) as it is today. By most measures of equity, then, things have gotten better: more people have coverage, and—for advocates of smaller government, something even more positive—this improvement has come about through private health insurance.

So why has drug coverage become a national issue? In 1999, $100 billion was spent on prescription drugs in the United States—8.3 percent of the total health-care ticket. By 2010, that figure is expected to rise to $366 billion (14 percent of total expenses). This works out to a predicted average annual growth rate of 11.3 percent for the next nine years—more than twice the growth rate of the country's economy as a whole. (Last year alone, spending for prescription drugs rose a stunning 18.8 percent.) The real problem we are facing, therefore, is providing not simply prescription-drug coverage but the total bill for such expenses. And this reality is finally registering with American consumers, previously shielded from the real costs of such services. Naturally, the first to feel it are uninsured, high utilizers—namely, the elderly.

Every drama needs its shadowy character, and in this story the pharmaceutical industry is ripe for the role. Under increasing scrutiny, "big pharma" is reaping what it has sown. Through the 1990s, it grew at an average of 12.5 percent per year—two and one-half times the rate of the economy as a whole, and posted profits between 15 and 20 percent, making it one of the most profitable businesses around. The industry achieved this growth by delivering new hope to people, by securing political protection for itself, and by exploiting the vulnerabilities of both patients and an insurance-based payment system that inured customers to price sensitivity.

How much can Americans afford to pay for their medications? Who benefits from the growth of the prescription-drug industry? Might consumers trade slower pharmaceutical

Koller, Christopher F. (2001, June 15). Prescription for trouble: Why drug prices keep exploding. *Commonweal*, pp. 12–15. © 2001 Commonweal Foundation, reprinted with permission. For subscriptions, call toll-free: 1-888-495-6755.

innovation for lower costs and broader coverage? To explore these issues, let's return to Walter, our chronically unwell subject.

Table 9.1 illustrates the range Walter might pay for his drug regime, depending on the drugs prescribed and his insurance coverage. The table also serves to illustrate the difficulties associated with resource allocation in health care, particularly how to balance social benefit and individual need.

The table is based on generally accessible and accurate (but hardly definitive) information on drug pricing estimates, as they relate to the theoretical treatment of Walter's particular symptoms. Depending on insurance coverage, Walter could end up paying as little as nothing, or as much as $911 for his ninety-day course of drugs. The "system costs" (that is, the revenues to the drug companies) could range from $239 to $911, based on what is prescribed and who pays. A look at the table also indicates that there are few other markets for goods and services where product pricing varies so significantly, and largely to the benefit of the seller. Nonuniversal, third-party coverage compounds this issue by exposing some people to full costs while insulating other consumers from any sort of price sensitivity.

There are six elements at play in the pharmaceutical industry which contribute not only to its growth but also to the pressures it puts on the financing and delivery of health care in general.

Product Development

The key to growth in the pharmaceutical industry is the introduction of new products. Drug companies are masters at creating such innovations. They spent $25 billion in 1999—a whopping 25 percent of sales—on research and development. Their production pipeline is full of future products targeted for widespread chronic conditions like Walter's—heart disease, depression, and arthritis—where utilization will be high and sustained. It is estimated

TABLE 9.1   Approximate Costs for 90-Day Supply

Symptoms/ Condition	Medicine	Private Insurance		Medicaid		Medicare
		Patient	Company	Patient	State	(all paid by patient)
Stomach Pains/	Prilosec	$10	$273	0	$201	$336
Heartburn	Ranitidine	$5	$119	0	$92	$141
Hypertension	Accupril	$10	$94	0	$67	$112
	Atenolol	$5	$6	0	$2	$4
High Cholesterol	Lescol	$10	$137	0	$99	$183
Allergic Rhinitis	Claritin	$10	$232	0	$168	$280
(runny nose)	Semprex	$10	$66	0	$46	$78
Maximum paid		$40	$736	0	$535	$911
Minimum paid		$30	$328	0	$239	$406

Source: Author's Research of Average Wholesale Price (AWP) and Standard industry Discounts and Copayments.

that 46 percent of the rate of increase in prescription-drug spending each year comes from the introduction of new products. Companies search for blockbuster drugs that will deliver new benefits to patients and that will sustain their research and development programs. Of the $21 billion increase in spending for prescription drugs from 1999 to 2000, one-half was due to increased sales of just twenty-three individual drugs.

Marketing

Once a drug is developed, it is marketed intensively to differentiate it from its competition. In 1999, pharmaceutical companies spent more than $10 billion on marketing activities. Over 80 percent of this outlay was directed at physicians, trying to get them to recognize when to prescribe, and then to recommend a particular brand of drug. Company "detailers" (sales people) aggressively court doctors with information and entertainment. And marketing works. Between 1993 and 1998, sales of the ten most heavily marketed drugs contributed to more than one-fifth of the total increase in drug expenditures.

Yet the benefits of these blockbuster drugs are often overstated. Four out of five of Walter's conditions can be treated with much cheaper regimens of generally similar efficacy. There is, however, little incentive in the health system for doctors not to prescribe the latest thing, once it is proven safe and effective. Furthermore, today's fastest-growing marketing effort is direct-to-consumer advertising—getting *patients* to ask a physician for Claritin for a runny nose because they saw Joan Lunden recommend it on television. First permitted on television four years ago, consumer advertising was a $2.5 billion ticket in the year 2000. Such advertising campaigns offer only partial information about the products to the consumer, yet he or she can exert effective pressure on a physician to write a particular prescription.

Differential Pricing and Cost Responsibility

In a typical market, price is based on the consumer's perceived value of a particular good or service. But in pharmaceuticals, the consumer is not the only purchaser. His or her insurance plan also plays a part, and this has had the unintended consequence of contributing significantly to price insensitivity for pharmaceuticals—all the while enhancing the industry's profits. As Walter's table indicates, third-party insurance coverage has created significant opportunities for differential pricing by the industry, again resulting in increased revenues. By law, Medicaid gets the lowest price, but uninsured individual consumers may end up paying a retail price typically almost twice that of Medicaid.

If the market can't arrive at a fair or consistent price, is there some other workable mechanism? Efforts at price controls, common in Canada and Europe, are anathema in the United States. Every other major developed country employs some form of aggressive price and utilization control in its pharmaceutical program—whether as the provider of national health insurance or as a matter of industrial policy. (These include individual or product-group price controls, profit caps, monitoring the prescribing patterns of doctors, establishing national formularies, and patient cost sharing). The results are significant: per capita spending for prescription drugs in other major developed countries is 70 percent of the U.S. total—and growing at a slower rate. No wonder stories abound about Americans making shopping trips to Canada to purchase cheaper medicines. The U.S. pharmaceutical industry maintains that price controls in other countries force U.S. consumers to shoulder a disproportionate share of future product and development costs. But the industry is silent when it comes to whether Americans pay a greater share of its profits. The global reach of the industry may present an occasion for a global trade and industry policy.

Patent Protections

After a blockbuster drug is invented, marketed, and priced, a company works hard to protect its privileged position. Patent law exists to encourage innovation by preserving exclusivity and its benefits to the innovator for some time. The profits which accrue to the pharmaceutical industry, however, are truly extraordinary. Through diligent legislative activity, the industry has been able to more than double the potential effective patent life of a new drug, from 8.1 years in 1984 to 18.4 years in 2000. While not all drugs enjoy 18 years of exclusivity, the benefits of even six months of additional protection are considerable for a manufacturer, for once generic competition arrives on the market, prices can drop from 75 to 90 percent.

Political Spending

The pharmaceutical industry spent some $74 million for lobbying activities in 1998. The result? In addition to the patent protections noted above, federal tax credits for research resulted in the industry's massive profits being taxed at only 15 percent, almost half of the average corporate tax rate. In the recent presidential election, the industry contributed more than $6 million to the Bush campaign, and coughed up another $1.7 million for Bush's inaugural. Perhaps it is no surprise that an industry executive was named director of the Office of Management and Budget, or that three industry representatives served on the Department of Health and Human Services transition team—important positions from which to preserve current advantages and ensure that, for instance, a Medicare prescription-drug benefit proposal would steer away from governmental price controls.

The Technological Imperative

The last piece at work is probably the most difficult to harness: our collective desire for science to make our lives easier and to save us from our fears. The most important things Walter can do to help himself is to eat correctly, stay away from cigarettes, and get plenty of exercise and sleep. But these habits are hard to build and maintain. Virtue often loses to the quick fix promised by a pill, especially when it is cleverly marketed and the user does not directly pay for its full cost. Ultimately, of course, even good habits are no match for disease, let alone death. On the other hand, the benefits of medication, while not permanent, are incontestable. Still, we are guilty of a collective deceit when we let our faith in technology supplant a healthy respect for our bodies, both their strengths and their limitations. This deceit cannot be treated with a pill, and its results may be just as corrosive to the human spirit as any disease.

None of this helps Walter directly when he is trying to figure out how to pay for Lescol so he can lower his cholesterol and reduce the risk of a heart attack. And though it may make sense for him to pay a share of his costs, few of us would be comfortable with the idea that access to an effective drug should be rationed based on the ability to pay, let alone proof of a person's exercise habits. How, then, do we get ourselves out of this mess?

The focus on prescription-drug coverage for the elderly is the best place to begin thinking about costs and coverage, for clearly the needs are real and, finally, it is federal policy that shapes the market for health care.

Currently, the only prescription-drug coverage options available for the elderly are retiree coverage for the lucky few; small state-based, sliding-scale programs; and Medicaid (for the impoverished). If actuarial estimates are correct, however, simply adding a full benefit for the elderly could raise program costs by 25 percent, an untenable prospect. How then do we close this gap between the real and growing needs of an aging population, and our ability to pay for those needs? Prescription drugs for the elderly thus become a more focused version of the larger dilemma raised by advocates of universal health insurance.

Current proposals break down less over the size of federal participation than over how allocation decisions get made; that is, the extent to which one believes the private market can and should work. The Bush administration's original "Immediate Helping Hand Program" called for an annual block grant of $12 billion to the states. This would provide for means-tested subsidies to the needy elderly for purchasing necessary drugs, augmenting what some states already have in place. After a period of denial over the need for any federal role, the pharmaceutical industry has embraced this approach as the least intrusive of potential evils. It is easily administrable and is philosophically compatible with a limited and preferably state-based governmental role. It also lets the private sector take care of health, starts to create a lower tier of care and financing for the elderly, and does nothing to address the fact that prescription-drug costs are driving the system as a whole.

For their part, advocates of a broader Medicare prescription-drug coverage have a hard time making the numbers work. Means testing for any Medicare benefit would reduce the cost burden, but is politically difficult, given Medicare is a universal entitlement. Some proposals call for a separate, privately administered prescription insurance program. Medicare enrollees could use a voucher to buy into different types of coverage in a newly created "market" of privately administered, government-certified drug benefit programs. These policy administrators would hammer out their best deals for enrollees with the manufacturers. But advocates for these private-sector purchasing techniques conveniently overlook the fact that it is the private health-insurance sector that has produced the 15–20 percent per year growth rates that now threaten the whole system.

Installing greater patient cost-sharing mechanisms to foster price sensitivity is one potential means of lowering medical expenditures. But such a program would have to be carefully administered, lest people forgo needed drugs because of the expense. Finally, reducing costs by limiting the extent of the benefit becomes dicey. Just imagine the reaction when the first elderly patient with the need for an excluded medicine shows up on the nightly news.

Reform of the present system, therefore, will require money and real political will. Still, almost anything would represent an improvement over what is currently in place for the elderly. Medicare prescription drug plans should follow some of the time-tested patterns already established by Medicare.

- First, coverage rules should apply to all. A safety-net type of program would represent a break from Medicare's commitment to equitable treatment. Medicare, along with Social Security, is the strongest example of social solidarity we have in the United States. It must be preserved.
- Second, we must get as comprehensive a benefit plan as we can afford. Half a loaf is better than none, but we have to make sure everyone gets it. Let those who can afford it buy a bigger loaf.

- Third, program operations must address the factors that have landed us in this fix. Federal purchasing or price controls for prescriptions should be instituted, as is already done for hospitals and physicians under the Medicare program. Admittedly, such price setting is ugly and inelegant, but it has worked for thirty-five years. For all their anti-market appearances, Medicare's physician and hospital fees are the standard reference metrics used throughout the private health-care industry. In addition, let Medicare recipients buy those drugs not covered under Medicare for the same price Medicaid pays. The industry will howl in protest, but it will adjust.
- Fourth, a Medicare prescription drug program should install effective and means-tested patient cost sharing at the point of consumption. This will encourage more price sensitivity. Patients need a limited incentive to weigh the costs and benefits of various treatments. For example, in Germany the first $20 of the cost of any prescription is covered by public insurance, but all costs above that are privately financed.
- Finally, we should acknowledge that pharmacy costs—the fastest-rising element in health care—are emblematic of our infatuation with the technological fix and unlimited choices. Proposals for prescription-drug coverage—and any other health-care coverage—must address a fundamental tectonic force at work: the proliferation of products and technologies that push costs upward. Particularly at a time when health-care utilization is likely to increase as the population ages and diagnostic technologies, often gene-based, improve, we should recognize that the industry has no need for the protections it has been afforded legislatively in the form of excessive patent protection and tax credits. Furthermore, no credible argument has been made that direct-to-consumer advertising for drugs does anything more than increase costs and create unrealistic and partially informed demands on physicians by patients.

In the end, health care is a supply-driven business: The more options our friend Walter has, the more he will use. The unchallenged assumption is that the more we use, the better off we are. That assumption must be questioned. But the prescription drug industry has embraced that paradigm and profited immensely from it. At the same time, the commercial insurance sector has failed to control prescription costs, assuming, as we all have, that the benefits provided are worth the expense. How much different would our lives be, however, if lower industry profits and fewer legislative protections meant less capital for research and slower product development cycles? Can the American public learn to love last year's antihistamine if it means that Walter can get most of his medication paid for?

SELECTION 28

The following selection was written by Henry I. Miller and David Longtin and published in *Consumers' Research* (October 2000). Their position is that consumers currently have little or no protection against unsafe and ineffective dietary supplement products, despite the enormous increase in their presence in our lives. The situation has gotten so bad that we might be on the verge of a national public-health catastrophe, unless some regulatory mechanism is put into place. Miller is a senior research fellow at the Hoover Institution and a former FDA official. He has authored *To America's Health: A Proposal to Reform the Food and Drug Administration* (2000). Longtin is a freelance writer.

■ *Time to Assure Safe Dietary Supplements*

Innovative Protection Needed

HENRY I. MILLER AND DAVID LONGTIN

In his new book, *Dr. Atkins' Age-Defying Diet Revolution,* best-selling author Robert Atkins urges readers to take various dietary supplements—vitamins, herbs, and minerals—that he says will prevent or alleviate a host of ailments. Most of these concoctions are harmless enough, even if their purported health benefits are unproven.

But he is reckless in encouraging the use of ginkgo biloba, advocating large doses and saying, in effect, that one can ingest any amount without negative consequences. He never warns about this herb's anticoagulant, or blood-thinning, properties, a matter of concern to people who might require emergency surgery or who are being treated with blood thinners.

Yet Atkins is not alone in promoting dietary supplements. They are advertised everywhere, for all manner of ailments, and about one-third of Americans buy herbal products like echinacea, ginseng, and St. John's wort. They spend more than $5 billion annually at retail outlets, and sales are rising about 18% a year. Thousands of products cram the shelves of health food stores, grocery markets, and pharmacies nationwide. They are also widely available through catalogs and the Internet. Even major pharmaceutical companies are adding dietary supplements to their lines. But what assurances do consumers have about exactly what they are getting, and about the safety of the products?

Regulation of dietary supplements varies considerably among developed countries, even among member states of the European Union, which has yet to adopt any transnational standards for these products. Under the most extensive legal framework, Germany has tested more than 300 herbal remedies since 1980, finding about two-thirds of these products to be safe and at least minimally effective (under a very liberal standard). It controls these substances as drugs. But consumers in other Western societies receive little protection.

Last year, Canada allotted $7 million (Canadian) to establish an Office of Natural Health Products over a three-year period. Although this new agency will govern the premarket assessment, labeling, licensing, and monitoring of herbal supplements, the precise scope of its mandate has yet to be determined. And in the meantime, these products are blooming and booming in a regulatory vacuum.

In Britain, the majority of herbal remedies are classified as food supplements and are thus unlicensed. Others, sold by herbalists, are specifically exempt from licensing under a 1968 law. Only a small number of herbs that are regulated as drugs by the Medicines Control Agency carry any real assurance that they are safe and effective. But few places in the industrialized world, if any, have a more permissive environment than the United States.

Miller, Henry I., and Longtin, David. (2000, October). Time to assure safe dietary supplements: Innovative protection needed. *Consumers' Research*, pp. 10–15. Reprinted with permission.

The U.S. Congress has virtually exempted herbal remedies from government oversight. When the Food and Drug Administration (FDA) considered regulating these products in the early 1990s, manufacturers and health-food stores orchestrated a massive lobbying and letter-writing campaign against stricter controls. The industry produced television commercials that depicted movie star Mel Gibson handcuffed by FDA agents for possessing vitamins. The result was the Dietary Supplement and Health Act of 1994. Pushed heavily by Senator Orrin Hatch of Utah, the home base of many supplements makers, and passed over the objections of the FDA, the law created a new product class, the dietary supplement, that was not subject to regulations applied to drugs. Now any substance that can be found in foods, regardless of amount or action and including chemicals that act as hormones or toxins, can be produced and sold without any premarket testing or approval.

Thousands of Medical Problems

The FDA can restrict the sale of an herbal product only if the agency receives well-documented reports of health problems with it. The FDA formed its Special Nutritionals Adverse Event Monitoring System in 1993 as an important component of its MEDWatch program, designed to track problems with the range of drugs and medical devices that the agency is charged with regulating. The Special Nutritionals monitoring system was established to record adverse reactions associated with the more than 3,000 dietary supplement products that were then on the market.

But sometime around September 1998, after logging 2,621 "adverse reactions," including 184 fatalities, associated with these products, the FDA quietly stopped monitoring most cases in which herbal remedies had been linked to illness or death. Top agency officials said that they cut the monitoring program because of budgetary constraints. Although the FDA insists that it still collects data on medical emergencies linked to dietary supplements, only three staff members are now assigned to evaluate adverse reactions caused by the industry's products, which are made by hundreds of private companies.

The agency and its herbal monitoring system have been criticized by the General Accounting Office (GAO). In July 1999, the GAO said that the FDA's adverse-reaction reports were incomplete, poorly documented, and inadequate to use as a basis to establish dosages for herbal supplements. The FDA requested an additional $2.5 million specifically to improve its dietary-supplements tracking program in its fiscal 2000 budget, but this was among several FDA requests eliminated by a Senate subcommittee.

The number of medical emergencies linked to dietary supplements has unquestionably been underreported. Unlike the monitoring system for regulated drugs, which requires manufacturers to report side effects and illnesses, the dietary-supplement system relies on voluntary reports of adverse reactions from the makers of herbal products. This is rather like the IRS asking taxpayers to provide information voluntarily on their own underreporting of income. Some manufacturers have failed to report thousands of medical problems linked to their brands. Depositions in a recent court case involving the death of a woman from Sacramento, California, allege that E'ola, a Utah multilevel marketing firm, received 3,500 customer complaints about its Amp II, a diet formula containing the herbal stimulant ephedra. Not one of those incidents was ever revealed to the FDA, according to *The San Francisco Chronicle*.

In a regulation that went into effect earlier this year, the FDA worsened an already dangerous situation by freeing supplement manufacturers to make all manner of dubious health claims—that their products treat conditions such as premenstrual syndrome and acne, for example, although there is little or no evidence to support these assertions.

With FDA authority limited by the 1994 law, the Federal Trade Commission (FTC), which monitors advertising, has taken a more vigorous role in regulating the makers of supplements. In 1999, the FTC took legal action against seven manufacturers that had violated regulations requiring advertising to be truthful and verifiable. The companies were selling cure-alls for conditions such as impotence, cancer, and obesity. The Commission also sent warnings to 1,200 Internet sites that it said had made "incredible claims" for drugs, devices, and supplements, including herbal remedies that would supposedly ward off AIDS. Late last year, the Commission also issued its first set of advertising guidelines aimed specifically at the supplements industry.

No Assurance of Safety or Effectiveness

Even with these measures, however, consumers have no real guarantee that dietary supplements are safe or effective, that the information about dosage on the label is correct, or even that the substance in the container is genuine. Only a few herbal supplements—saw palmetto for treating enlarged prostates and ginkgo for improving memory slightly in Alzheimer's patients—have been shown to be at all efficacious.

Moreover, because the demand for some herbal remedies exceeds the supply from natural sources, unscrupulous manufacturers occasionally have switched to cheaper look-alike substances that are pharmacologically different. In February of this year, researchers in Britain discovered that eight brands of herbal skin ointments sold as "natural" treatments for eczema illegally contained dexamethasone, a potent prescription steroid. The creams had such huge quantities of steroid that they could have permanently damaged delicate skin. The creams for children, whose skin is most vulnerable, contained five times more steroid than the adult products. At about the same time, the FDA ordered four California supplement distributors to recall herbal compounds that illegally contained glyburide or phenformin, prescription drugs that lower blood-sugar levels. The action came after a diabetic in California developed hypoglycemia after he took some of the products which the manufacturers said contained only natural Chinese herbs.

When ConsumerLab.com, a new private company, tested various herbal remedies, it said that many of the products did not deliver what the manufacturers promised. It found fault with 10 of 27 brands of saw palmetto studied, and discovered that, in one quarter of the 30 brands of ginkgo biloba, the levels of the active ingredient were less than indicated on the labels. Chemists at the Good Housekeeping Institute recently analyzed eight brands of SAMe, an herbal preparation advertised as a "natural Prozac" to relieve depression, and found that two had only half the promised levels of active ingredient, while another contained none at all. *Consumer Reports* also examined 10 brands of ginseng and concluded that several contained almost none of the active ingredient.

There is no shortage of information available to consumers about dietary supplements, but it is heavy on advocacy and light on scientific proof. Putting it another way, until there is evidence that rises to the standards of the medical and scientific communities that a preventive or therapeutic nostrum actually works, we do not know that it does work. (See "Alternative Medicine: Value and Risks," *CR,* January 1999.)

Worse yet, many of these products are already known to be toxic, carcinogenic, or otherwise hazardous, causing high blood pressure, deadly allergic reactions, cardiac arrhythmias, and kidney or liver failure. Some also can exacerbate autoimmune diseases like arthritis and lupus. This past February, the medical journal *The Lancet* identified life-threatening side effects of St. John's wort: interference with the protease inhibitor indinavir, which can lead to treatment failure in AIDS patients; and rejection of heart transplants by an interaction with the immunosuppressant cyclosporine.

In June, *The New England Journal of Medicine* reported that a Chinese herb that caused kidney failure in dozens of Belgian dieters in the early 1990s appears to have even deadlier long-term effects—cancer and precancerous lesions. The subjects in this study were an unlucky subset of some 10,000 Belgian dieters who, between 1990 and 1992, took a combination of Chinese herbs and conventional drugs prescribed by weight-loss clinics. After dozens of victims suffered kidney failure, investigators discovered that Belgian pharmacists had been using mislabeled Chinese herbs to produce the diet pills. Instead of using *Stephania tetrandra,* the druggists had filled the pills with derivatives of the herb *Aristolochia fangchi,* which has long been known to damage kidneys and to cause cancer in animals. At least 70 people experienced complete kidney failure, while another 50 suffered kidney damage serious enough to require treatment.

The first urinary tract cancers were found among these victims in 1994. To prevent the onset of the disease in others, doctors in Brussels advised patients whose kidneys and ureters had stopped functioning to have the organs surgically removed. Thirty-nine people chose to have the operation over the past several years. When researchers studied the excised tissue, they were shocked to discover that 18 of the patients had already developed cancer, while 19 others had precancerous lesions.

Belgium banned the importation of Aristolochia in 1992. In May of this year, the FDA distributed warnings to health professionals and the supplements industry about the dangers of Aristolochia, and it plans to block the herb's entry into the United States in the near future. For many critics of the present U.S. policies on dietary supplements, this action is long overdue, considering that Germany banned Aristolochia in 1981 and that the World Health Organization issued a warning about the herb in 1982.

Medical organizations also have advised people to stop using herbal remedies such as St. John's wort, ginkgo biloba, and ginseng at least two or three weeks before any scheduled surgery to avoid dangerous interactions with the anesthesia.

Marketing to Kids

To the growing alarm of medical experts, dietary supplements companies have begun marketing their products aggressively to children and their parents. They peddle a variety of potent concoctions that supposedly will help kids gain strength or lose weight, or will treat illnesses ranging from colds and flu to depression and even attention deficit disorder. As a result, increasing numbers of children are gulping supplements, often at the insistence of parents in search of "natural" remedies or "healthful" alternatives for youngsters who eat too much junk food. In 1999, a study conducted by National Public Radio, the Kaiser Foundation, and the Kennedy School of Government found that 18% of parents were giving their children dietary supplements other than vitamins or minerals.

In Vancouver, Washington, Nutrition Now Inc., for example, uses a cute rhinoceros cartoon character to promote its line of dietary supplements for kids, including Rhino Pops, an echinacea-based cold remedy. From Saco, Maine, Fresh Samantha Inc. ships to grocery stores nationwide "body zoomers" and fruit smoothies that carry cartoon pictures of children to catch the eye. Their drinks contain ginseng, guarana, and spirulina (a green alga). The resemblance to hawking tobacco products to youngsters is unmistakable.

Although many supplements companies advise youngsters under 18 not to take the stimulant ephedra, many products contain this toxic ingredient, and a few industry representatives still recommend it for kids with attention deficit disorder. In a report earlier this year, the FDA documented 134 cases linking ephedra to serious reactions, including insomnia, nervousness, seizure, hypertension, stroke, and death, over a 33-month period ending in March 1999. Ten of the reports involved children younger than 18. But the manufacturers' position remains ambiguous. The industry opposes a proposed New York ordinance that would prohibit ephedra sales to minors, claiming that "it would be more effective as a labeling issue," says Wes Siegner, counsel to the ephedra committee of the American Herbal Products Association. "You don't want to cause trouble for salesclerks." Despite the warning labels, however, ephedra still enjoys considerable popularity among teenagers trying to lose weight.

Supporters of herbal supplements who scoff at reports of adverse reactions retort that, with tens of millions of people consuming them in this country alone, there would be a significant body count if the products were genuinely dangerous. There are several answers to such an assertion. Even with profound underreporting of problems, reports of serious adverse effects *are* mounting. In the absence of compelling evidence of benefit from the use of the vast majority of herbal supplements, severe—even life-threatening—side effects are particularly worrisome (some would say unacceptable). Finally, problems are likely to increase with some large retailers now selling new higher-potency formulations and consumers taking large doses for long periods of time.

Herbal supplements defenders often attempt to compare them to prescription drugs, citing the known side-effects—sometimes serious and even life-threatening—of these products. They ignore, however, that drugs are not approved by federal regulators unless they are judged both safe and effective, meaning that the benefits are greater than the risk. Such risk balancing cannot be performed in a meaningful way if, as is the case for most herbal supplements, no benefit can be demonstrated. Putting this another way, who would condone the sale of products that can cause high blood pressure or liver failure, or exacerbate autoimmune diseases, in the absence of significant benefits?

Safety Regulation Necessary

The supplements industry is moving voluntarily toward standards for "good manufacturing practices," a concept borrowed from drug makers that includes "adequately equipped manufacturing facilities, adequately trained personnel, stringent control over the manufacturing processes, reliable and secure computerized operations, and appropriate finished product examination and testing." But these measures address only the identity, purity and potency of the products, neglecting the fundamental question of whether the active ingredients themselves are safe and effective, and they offer no independent verification that the standards have been met.

At present, regulation of the herbal supplements industry is so lax, and some of the products so dangerous, that a public health catastrophe seems inevitable—and with it, demands for more stringent regulatory oversight. Consider that a mislabeled or contaminated product could cause numerous cases of organ failure or death. After such a major incident, Congress would probably reclassify herbal supplements as drugs—which are stringently regulated by the FDA—requiring a demonstration of safety and efficacy before they can be marketed. By this approach, every product would have to gain approval from the FDA, a process that involves time-consuming studies and clinical trials and extensive cost. Under the current regulatory regime, this wouldn't bode well for the supplement market. Typically, the drug approval process takes 12 years and more. Few of the herbal remedies now in stores could meet the criteria required for drug approval, and consumers would thus be denied access to many of them.

Some have suggested that herbal supplements might be provided a regulatory shortcut, in the form of a requirement for certification only of safety. But this proposal presents difficulties. For one thing, the safety of a drug (or herbal supplement) in normal clinical use is difficult to judge in a vacuum; safety and efficacy together are often necessarily a "global" judgment. The level of risk—side effects, or adverse reactions—that is acceptable varies widely and depends on the product's particular use, or "indication." For example, severe and frequent side effects that might be tolerable in a drug offering a definitive cure for AIDS or pancreatic cancer would be unacceptable if the product were intended to treat baldness or hay fever symptoms.

The current unregulated commerce in dietary supplements may pose a real threat to public health, and even those who believe that the new drug approval process is too stringent would not argue for the complete absence of oversight. Before a calamity occurs, the worldwide industry should find better ways to police itself.

Devising a Better Approach

Presently, the FDA and its monopoly over new product approvals represent government's standard approach to regulatory oversight. At the opposite pole from this government monopoly is laissez-faire, a self-regulating system in which government has no role at all and decisions about testing and marketing are made unilaterally by manufacturers. This is the system that currently exists for dietary supplements.

The extremes of monopoly and laissez-faire fail to serve the public interest; abuse of power is too easy in both. Government monopolies can foster abuses by bureaucrats, notably in regulatory delay and expense; useful and desirable remedies are blocked from the market, with patients suffering while awaiting the new therapies. (See "Still Hazardous to Your Health," *CR*, January 1998.) Laissez-faire creates another set of temptations, with more obvious public risk. Proponents of laissez-faire maintain that, in the absence of government oversight, companies would be induced to protect the integrity of their products by good will, a desire to preserve their reputations, and the fear of civil litigation or, rarely, criminal prosecution. But while an acceptable level of safety might be achieved much of the time, inevitably some manufacturers would take dangerous shortcuts in production, testing, or surveillance. The public reaction to isolated incidents of poisonings that led Congress to pass the Biological Act of 1902—which instituted the first statute requiring the federal government's premarket approval of a class of drugs—and the Food, Drug, and Cosmetic Act of 1938 illustrates some of the pitfalls and undesirable outcomes of a laissez-faire system.

If the extremes are undesirable, what other models are available? Fortunately, between the two extremes, other institutional alternatives offer various configurations of government oversight and non-governmental mechanisms that could effectively assure the safety and efficacy of the nation's supply of dietary supplements (and other products, for that matter). These alternative organizational arrangements involve varying degrees of privatization and FDA control of the certification process. One possible arrangement would be to allow for an independent, private organization to review and certify new products for safety and efficacy, perhaps under the sanction of the FDA or some other federal agency. This approach could follow several models.

For example, companies could elect to contract voluntarily with a newly established foundation that could operate like Underwriters Laboratories (UL), the large, not-for-profit organization that tests and certifies more than 16,500 types of products. Many of these items, such as electrical appliances and equipment, automotive and mechanical parts, fire-resistant building materials, and bullet-resistant glass, present inherent potential hazards to life and property.

UL and other similar organizations—known collectively as "nationally recognized testing laboratories"—hold no monopoly on safety certification, and their endorsements are not equivalent to government approval. Many retailers, however, are reluctant to carry products that lack certification by UL or one of its competitors. Insurers also occasionally deny liability coverage for products without it. Companies, insurers, and the independent testing laboratories all have incentives to maintain high standards both for consumer products and for manufacturers.

Another model for voluntary self-regulation that functions routinely and efficiently in the United States is the certification of plant seeds sold to agricultural producers or growers, in order to assure consistent seed quality. In California, for example, oversight is performed by the non-profit California Crop Improvement Association (CCIA), which provides a voluntary quality assurance program for the maintenance and increase of crop seed. Each variety that enters this program is evaluated for its unique characteristics such as pest resistance, adaptability, uniformity, quality, and yield. Seed production is closely monitored by CCIA to prevent out-crossing, weed, other crop, and disease contamination that may negatively affect seed quality. Seed movement is monitored from field harvest, through the conditioning plant, and into the bag. Samples can be rejected if "off-type" seeds are found at a percentage that is greater than standards permit, as is occasionally the case with beans, cereals, and sunflowers.

A third and perhaps the most apposite example is the regulation of the majority of medical devices in the European Union. This system relies heavily on various sets of product standards and normally does not involve government regulators directly in product oversight. For low-risk (so-called Class I) devices, such as tongue depressors and eyeglasses, manufacturers themselves are allowed to certify that their products meet the necessary standards. For higher-risk Class II devices, those that might inflict serious harm if they malfunction but that are unlikely to kill patients, manufacturers must obtain third-party review from private-sector, profit-making "notified bodies," which test products, inspect manufacturing systems, and ultimately verify that EU standards have been met. Following this certification, the products can be marketed. Since 1995, most Class II devices, such as

X-ray machines, dentists' drills, heartbeat monitors, and hip implants, have undergone this sort of nongovernmental third-party examination within the EU.

Because these "notified bodies" vie with each other for business, they have reason to be expeditious but thorough in their inspections. As a result, approval of new medical devices in Europe takes approximately half as long as it does in the United States, shortening the overall development process by roughly two years—and without compromising safety. The more favorable regulatory climate within the EU has allowed many companies to establish a positive cash flow by introducing new products in Europe before marketing them in the United States. A British consultancy firm, The Wilkerson Group, has compiled a list of 100 medical devices that are already available to patients in other developed nations, but not in the United States. This trend is most evident in the fast-moving areas of medicine, such as imaging and cardiology.

Voluntary mechanisms of self-regulation such as UL and CCIA could be adapted by the manufacturers of dietary supplements for effective oversight of their products with little or no involvement of federal regulators. UL and similar organizations are sanctioned by the Occupational Safety and Health Administration (OSHA), an agency of the U.S. Department of Labor. Such a government mandate arguably would not be necessary, however, as long as manufacturers of dietary supplements maintained an arm's-length relationship from the regulator. In other words, the overseer should be a certifier, not a collaborator.

Under any model of nongovernmental regulation that certifies herbal supplements on a voluntary basis, manufacturers that choose to participate would gain a measure of protection from liability should a mishap occur, and also support for claims that they make a premium product. Most important, consumers would be assured that the products bearing the UL-like seal of approval had met certain criteria for safety, potency, and quality. They would have access to the widest selection of herbal therapies, as well as the freedom to choose certified or non-certified brands.

Perhaps paradoxically, such an evolution to greater regulation—albeit voluntary and extragovernmental—would move us closer to a truly free market: consumers exercising independent and informed choice among a broad spectrum of competing products.

Looking at Both Sides—The Debate Continues

The range of issues and opinions regarding the question of whether the government should act more aggressively in regulating drugs and drug prices can be seen in the following excerpts from selections in this chapter. The first excerpt argues against governmental price controls on pharmaceutical products; the second argues in favor of increased regulatory involvement in Medicare coverage for prescriptions; the third argues in favor of regulation over dietary supplements.

> There is no substitute for the profit motive for inducing and guiding research. The worst action would be to erect a ceiling on the rewards for solving the toughest problems in medical science: preventing Alzheimer's; curing schizophrenia; reversing heart disease; striking

without error at cancer cells; reducing the estimated 350,000 deaths annual from obesity; preventing 10,000 amputations a year from poor circulation, nerve damage. . . . The greatest harm would be the absence of valuable therapies and treatments that would not be developed because of inadequate incentives or would not be imported because of controls over prices or difficulty in obtaining marketing approval. (from Calfee's article, selection 26)

The focus on prescription-drug coverage for the elderly is the best place to begin thinking about costs and coverage, for clearly the needs are real and, finally, it is federal policy that shapes the market for health care. . . . Reform of the present system, therefore, will require money and real political will. Still, almost anything would represent an improvement over what is currently in place for the elderly. Medicare prescription drug plans should follow some of the time-tested patterns already established by Medicare. . . . (W)e should acknowledge that pharmacy costs—the fastest-rising element in health care—are emblematic of our infatuation with the technological fix and unlimited choices. (from Koller's article, selection 27).

At present, regulation of the herbal supplements industry is so lax, and some of the products so dangerous, that a public health catastrophe seems inevitable—and with it, demands for more stringent regulatory oversight. . . . One possible arrangement would be to allow for an independent, private organization to review and certify new products for safety and efficacy, perhaps under the sanction of the FDA or some other federal agency. (from Miller and Longtin's article, selection 28)

Matters to Ponder

- How well do you think Calfee counters the position that price controls would help the elderly when drug prices escalate out of their financial reach? Evaluate Calfee's position in light of Koller's arguments.
- What do you think of the practicality of Miller and Longtin's proposal that herbal supplements be regulated either by an agency outside the FDA or by voluntary regulation within the herbal supplement industry?

Further Sources to Seek Out

Adams, Chris. (2001, March 28). FDA to review policy allowing drug ads on TV. *Wall Street Journal*, p. B1. A commentary on the 2001 FDA review of prescription drug advertising policies.

Levinthal, Charles F. (2002). *Drugs, behavior, and modern society* (3rd ed.). Boston: Allyn and Bacon, Chapter 14. A comprehensive look at prescription drugs, OTC drugs, and dietary supplements.

Marks, Alexandria. (2001, April 11). A harder look at prescription-drug ads: Critics say the commercials prompt consumers to spend too much. *Christian Science Monitor*, p. 1. A commentary on the increasing levels of public advertising for prescription medications.

Postel, Virginia I. (1996, November). The other drug war: The struggle over the FDA is our latest culture war. *Reason Online, Reason Magazine. www.reason.com/9611/ edit.vip.html* An argument against FDA regulation over the prescription drug industry.

Web Sites to Explore

www.consumeralert.org
The web site for Consumer Alert, an organization devoted to opposing the excessive growth of governmental regulations, including those regulations concerning food and drugs.

www.fda.gov
The web site for the Food and Drug Administration, where a variety of publications and reports on regulatory efforts can be found.